Happy Birthday
Bruce
    March 11, 1984

Love,

Keltie

Richard

Connor

Evan

Automobiles as an Investment

Automobiles as

RICHARD H. RUSH

AN INVESTMENT

MACMILLAN PUBLISHING CO., INC.

New York

Dedicated to those who love fine automobiles and own them (or would like to own one or more as an investment) and to spouses who enthusiastically support and encourage this interest—especially my wife, Julie.

Copyright © 1982 by Richard H. Rush

Macmillan Publishing Co., Inc.
866 Third Avenue, New York, N.Y. 10022
Collier Macmillan Canada, Inc.

Library of Congress Cataloging in Publication Data

Rush, Richard H.
    Automobiles as an investment.

    Includes index.
    1. Automobiles—Collectors and collecting.
I. Title.
TL7.A1R87   629.2'222'075   81-19316
ISBN 0-02-606210-0   AACR2

10   9   8   7   6   5   4   3   2
Printed in the United States of America

Contents

Introduction

COLLECTOR (OR INVESTMENT) CARS can be roughly classified into five categories: Postwar American Classics, such as the Ford Thunderbird and the Shelby Cobra; Postwar Foreign Classics, such as the Ferrari Daytona; Prewar American Classics, such as the Duesenberg; Prewar Foreign Classics, such as the Mercedes-Benz S series and 500-540K series; and Antiques, which vary all the way from the Mercer Raceabout to the Model T Ford. For market study and price determination, cars can be grouped into the above five categories.

Within certain broad limits there is a market price for many, if not most, collector (or investment) automobiles. There is also an index of prices that can be worked out for each of the five categories of car. Within each individual category prices tend to move more or less together, certainly in the same general direction.

The year 1970 can, in a very real sense, be designated Year One; for 1970 is the base year from which collector car prices rose. No previous decade saw such growth in collector car prices. In that ten-year period the price of collector cars—averaged for all cars in all of the five categories—rose almost seven times. The car that sold for $1,000 in 1970 rose to $7,000 in 1980. The $10,000 car rose to $70,000.

Individually, of course, the rise in price differed. The Mercedes-Benz 300S cabriolet that was offered in Washington, D.C., for $1,900 in 1970 would have sold for at least $35,000 in

1980—it rose over eighteen times in the decade. The antique curved-dash Olds of 1903 rose from perhaps $3,000 to $10,000.

A number of things changed between 1970 and 1980. In buying a car in 1970 one could afford to make mistakes as repairs were not expensive. My own 300S Mercedes was bought a few years before 1970, and I paid $800 for the car. To put it in absolutely mint condition cost only $4,000, and in the process of restoration I found many things wrong that I didn't know were wrong when I purchased the car. Also, labor charges at the Mercedes-Benz repair shops in my area ran from $6 an hour to $8 an hour in 1970. In 1980, $40–$45 an hour was not an unusual charge. A restoration that I completed in 1980, a far less extensive restoration, on a Rolls-Royce cost over $16,000— not $4,000. In addition to the rise in labor costs, the price of parts rose to ridiculous levels—a windshield for a Maserati Ghibli running to $980 and a water pump to $850.

As the decade from 1970 to 1980 progressed, prices did not falter, except very temporarily in the recession of the mid-decade. As the decade wore on prices in most cases accelerated. By 1980 the early Cadillac V-16, the Chrysler Imperial eight, and the Duesenberg J and SJ passed $100,000 and often passed $200,000. Important classics such as the prewar supercharged Mercedes-Benz cars sometimes topped $300,000.

Interest on the part of collectors has shifted, partly because the prices of some cars became very high—high on any basis. The year 1981 seemed to be the Year of the Ferrari. It also seemed to be the Year of the Ford Mustang.

By mid-1981 many collectibles—Old Master paintings, Oriental carpets, gold coins, stamps—were showing weakness in the market. But collector cars, overall, did not show any weakness. Where prices and demand will go is anybody's guess, but it is far from clear that the collector car boom has ended or is ending, at least for any extended period of time.

The year 1970 was Year One for most collector cars, but certainly not for all. In 1962, Duesenberg J models were selling for $10,000 and more. In 1965, I visited the "automobile artist," Peter Helck and looked at his great old-time racing car, Locomobile 16. At that time I valued this car at $50,000. What it would bring today is anyone's guess.

My price research on automobiles, such as it was, started

long ago in Hartford, Connecticut, in 1929. I combed the newspaper for "exotic cars for sale," and I visited the many dealers in Hartford and on Automobile Row in East Hartford. I visited dealers at least three afternoons a week after school, to see what they were offering and at what price.

On and off after my family left Hartford in 1930, I followed the "cars for sale" section of the *New York Times*, and as I got ready to leave college in the late 1930s I read these columns more closely. One of them finally hooked me on my first real collector car, the Mercedes-Benz supercharged S convertible, in 1938. (Ever since, I have been reading "cars for sale" advertisements and visiting people who had cars for sale, both in the United States and England.) I thus gained some idea of what was offered when, in what condition, and at what price, and I was able to develop price trends.

The result of this so-called market research is that I have been hooked many times on cars that I could not resist buying. In all, I have owned eighty-eight cars. Of these, fifty-four are considered collector cars today—investment automobiles. Fewer than fifty-four, but still a large number, are real classics. I have listed these fifty-four cars in the chapter, Price Trends of Investment Automobiles, with the car and model I bought, the date I bought it, what I paid for it, and what the car would be worth on today's market.

After years of interest, I have reached several conclusions about automobiles as an investment:

1. They have turned out to be very good investments in many cases: where they were bought at the right time for not too high a price in relation to the market, where they could be restored, if necessary, at reasonable cost, where they were held long enough for appreciation to take place, and where they were sold using a fair amount of merchandising sense.

Along the way, I developed at least a little merchandising sense. In the 1950s the motor show was the thing—or the international motor show—for pioneering new cars like the V-12 Ferraris, the Pegassos, the factory specials like the Packard Pan Americans, and the privately owned specials—unique cars of style, mechanical innovation, and perfection. Prizes were awarded for these cars, and particular attention was paid to paint, chrome, leather, and appearance under the hood. These shows were held in major auditoriums in New York, Philadelphia, Cleveland, Indianapolis, and many other cities.

My cars often took first prize, or at least second or third. The result of winning was that people came around looking to buy my car, and at elevated prices. That was the time to sell, and I sometimes did. In this era, my cars took over a dozen awards.

2. Cars are really not naturals as investments. They require storage, insurance, licensing, often the payment of special fees and personal property taxes. They frequently require repairs and constant refurbishing and restoration. Thus they are not like coins, stamps, and many other collectibles.

3. To invest intelligently in an automobile, you should know a good deal about automobiles; if you don't already, you should learn about them.

4. The ownership of a painting entails little trouble aside from insuring it and occasionally cleaning it. Cars can be a terrible headache, and the more cars the worse the headache.

5. When you buy a collector car, you often are buying a pig in a poke. Still, as time goes on, bad dealers and crooked auction houses are being weeded out, and the remaining dealers and auctions can be expected to serve the interests of the buyer better. There are, strange as it may seem, some dealers who will buy only the very best; they then fix up the best so that the car they offer the buying public is the very *very* best! Let's hope there will be more such dealers in the future.

6. If we could expect the decade of the 1970s to be repeated, we should all go out and invest fully in collector cars. There has never been a period of growth in values like the past decade, and there may never be again, but the market is still active and, in general, rising. The era of automobiles as an investment is far from over. In any event, I now own more collector cars and have far more invested in them than ever before. I have no intention of unloading—either to avoid any possible drop in the car market or to realize a capital gain. I feel the gain is yet to come!

Again, the price of collector cars—postwar classics, prewar classics, antique cars—has gone up almost seven times in the past decade, a record period. Maybe this rise will continue for another decade, and maybe not.

CHAPTER 1

What Makes an Automobile an Investment?

THERE ARE CERTAIN definite characteristics that make an automobile a good investment:

1. *The car should be exotic.* By exotic we do not necessarily mean foreign, the first meaning given in *Webster's*. Instead, we prefer to employ the second meaning: "strangely beautiful, enticing." Certain top investment cars make that definition more tangible at a single glance: Bugatti Royale, Mercedes-Benz SSK and 540K, Auburn boattail speedster, Duesenberg, Eldorado convertible, Maserati Ghibli, Ferrari, Rolls-Royce.

A mint condition 1973 Cadillac Eldorado convertible may be bought for $5,000. It may turn out to be a good investment. If used only occasionally, it will probably appreciate in value. This is because Eldorado convertibles stopped coming off the assembly line at the end of the 1976 season. In fact, there are virtually no convertibles coming off any assembly line in America today.

By comparison, a mint condition 1973 Cadillac Eldorado coupe may sell for $3,500. In average condition it may sell for $1,500. The 1973 Eldorado coupe is an excellent car and is highly thought of by every mechanic I have talked to about the

Eldorado. But it fails to make the grade as an investment. It is not exotic enough, at least not now.

2. *The car should be what critical opinion of the time thinks is exotic.* We didn't invent this standard. It came from the writings of the most prominent of all art historians—Bernard Berenson—who said, in effect: Great art is what the art intelligentsia of the time think is great art.

I once owned a Bentley coupe with Graber body, a unique automobile. I also owned a Mercedes-Benz 300S convertible, and I owned a Ferrari coupe with Buono body, a 250GT. About ten years ago, at least one person made the same comment about every one of these cars: "Boy, is that an old car!" Not, "that is a unique car," or "that is certainly a beautiful car." The emphasis was on old and out of date.

Now critical opinion has changed; so has the prevailing opinion of almost everybody else. These cars are treasures, sought after, worth a good deal of money.

Early in World War II one of the greatest Bugattis ever built came onto the market—the Bugatti Royale convertible. There were at most only seven of these cars made. I inquired of an expert on exotic cars about this make and model car, and I asked him whether it was advisable for me to buy it. He replied, "I would stay away from that car. It has shell bearings and is inclined to give a great deal of trouble."

I didn't buy the car. Today it would possibly sell for a thousand times the asking price back in the early 1940s!

Also at about that time, I inquired of the general manager of the Zumbach Mercedes dealership and repair shop in New York whether I should buy one of the big 770K Mercedes convertible sedans. This car was very much like the big Hitler parade cars. He replied, "The Grosser Mercedes? I would stay away from it. No parts came over from Germany with this model car, so repairs are too hard to make."

This make and model car appreciated perhaps one hundred times in the years between World War II and the present.

So critical opinion changes, sometimes unbelievably quickly.

3. *The car should be unique.* Here let's use as an example a very different type of car from the usual investment car: this is a new car, still being turned out by the company, in Modena,

Italy. It is the Lamborghini Countach. The new Countach is very much like previous ones; it is by no means a one-of-a-kind automobile. It sells in Italy for about $120,000.

What is unique about this car—tangibly unique? Everything! An article in the May 1980 issue of *Motor Trend* starts out: "Maybe you have heard of the Countach but have never seen one. Take a good look. This one is a rare, land-bound piece of aircraft that is more exotic, more coveted and more elusive than even the Ferrari 512 Boxer."

The Countach is about 41 inches high. It is angular and in that respect somewhat resembles a racing car; it may even have a spoiler at the back. It might have been designed for travel on the moon!

Almost every investor car has something tangibly unique about it. The Mustang is a beautifully designed sporty little car, especially the 1965–1966 model so much in demand today. (The later models were heavy and inferior in design.) The Eldorado convertible is a big, impressive luxury car. The Maserati Ghibli is probably the most beautiful sports coupe ever built. The Ferrari is mechanically superb, and most Ferraris are also good looking. It also has the Ferrari charisma.

4. *An investment automobile is something other collectors want.* Ultimately desirable automobiles include the Auburn boattail speedster, Bugatti Royale and probably every Bugatti ever built, every Ferrari America and a lot of other Ferrari models, and every supercharged Mercedes-Benz ever built. The greater the demand for the car in the face of limited supply, the higher the price and the future price potential.

There are all sorts of cars available between the hundred thousand or so Mustangs of 1965 and 1966 and the "no known cars available"—the Mercedes-Benz SSKL.

5. *Pioneering cars are very often investment cars.* The post-World War II Isotta Fraschini with rear engine was a pioneering car; so was the Tucker as well as the Italmeccanica. Today no Isotta Fraschini with rear engine is known to be in private hands, and no Tuckers ever seem to be offered for sale, although one collector seems to buy every Tucker he can lay his hands on. The one Italmeccanica seems to have disappeared.

6. *Mechanically good cars make better investments.* The Mas-

erati Ghibli is a sensational-looking car, but it is highly temperamental and the accessories are not as reliable as they might be.
The later Ghiblis (1972) have many of these bugs worked out,
and therefore the later cars are much more in demand than the
earlier cars (1967–1970), and they bring much higher prices.
Also, the engines of the later cars are larger and more powerful;
this is another factor in price: more powerful engines are
preferred.

Some later cars have distinct mechanical improvements and
are thus in greater demand. The 1957 Mercedes-Benz 300S convertible and cabriolet with the fuel-injection engine brings more
than the 1955 and earlier 300S without fuel injection. The later
car is considered a better car mechanically.

The Ferrari 275GTB has a twelve-cyclinder engine with one
overhead camshaft per bank of cylinders. The next model was
the 275GTB-4, and this engine has two overhead cams per bank
of cylinders. It brings twice the price of the earlier 275GTB.

7. *Big cars with big engines are most popular.*   The cars in greatest demand are the large-engined and, often, larger-bodied
cars, the "glamour machines." In antique cars in particular, the
little one- and two-cylinder jobs are not in as much demand as
the big ones, although the little cars too are rising in value. The
1903 Curved Dash Olds sells for under $10,000 today; fifteen
years ago, it brought about $3,500. There has been no dramatic
price rise paralleling that for the big, "important" cars.

8. *Historic Grand Prix cars (and all racing cars) are perpetually in
demand.*   Collectors want these cars even though many of them
cannot be driven much on highway or street, if they can be
driven at all. Their great speed and glamour more than out-
weigh practical driving considerations. Motor Classic Corporation of White Plains, New York, owns one of the six Gran
Turismo American Cobra coupes raced at LeMans in 1965. This
team car, driven by Dan Gurney, was the first American car to
win a FIA GT (Grand Touring) Championship. It was clocked
at LeMans at 186 miles per hour down the Mulsanne straight.

Even more exciting, a prewar Mercedes-Benz racing car
reached a top speed of 268.9 miles per hour. It could start up
after being passed by a car moving at 100 miles per hour and
pass that car within one mile! Such a car will probably never be

offered for sale; should it be, the price would likely rise over $500,000, even though it can never be driven on the highway.

9. *Prestige cars are usually investment cars.* The epitome of prestige-make cars is Rolls-Royce. It established this position in the 1920s, and except for a few decades when prestige and elegance were out of favor, such as during the Depression, it has remained the tops. Ten years ago, Rolls-Royce fell a bit from this position of prestige. Now it is back, and if one occasionally refers to his Rolls-Royce, he is a sure-fire candidate for an important office in his country club! Ferrari is certainly the runner-up in popularity among prestige cars, which also include Bugatti, Duesenberg, and Cobra and many other cars.

10. *Condition of the car is increasingly important.* Ten years ago, condition was not by any means as important as it is today. That's because it was not then tremendously difficult to overhaul an engine, transmission, and differential, to rechrome, to repaint in lacquer, and to upholster in leather, all for under $10,000. The Rolls-Royce expert in Westport, Connecticut, estimates that, today, to completely overhaul a Rolls-Royce Silver Ghost, where some parts are needed, might cost $100,000. Labor costs have nearly quadrupled in the last decade.

In 1980 a Lamborghini Miura was offered for sale in New York for $13,500. It was decidedly not in the best condition and certain parts had to be bought and installed. Some months earlier, a prime condition Miura was sold in Chicago for $60,000. Such is the premium paid for fine condition.

Low mileage cars are in tremendous demand. Motor Classic Corporation of White Plains, New York, has a Ferrari 275GTB-4 coupe for sale, one of the most-wanted Ferraris in the world. This car is perfect from paint to chrome to parts under the hood. In addition, the true mileage is a little over 5,000. The price of a good condition Ferrari 275GTB-4 in 1981 is $50,000, but the price of this car is over $65,000 due to the extremely low mileage.

11. *Authentic original condition is important.* The May/June 1980 issue of *Maserati Information Exchange* contains an article on installing a Chevrolet engine in a Maserati Ghibli. The Ghibli owner who put the Chevrolet engine in his car stated, "With only minor high performance equipment added to the 350

Chevy engine, the performance of the car seems unchanged, if not improved, with the added peace of mind that even with hard driving you can expect to get 100,000 miles."

Maybe so, but with a Chevrolet engine in place of the Maserati engine, the value of the car is cut at least in half, and such cars with replacement engines are often advertised for sale. They have some value, but they are hardly investment cars at all, and they will appreciate far less than the car with authentic parts.

Original condition is about as important in automobiles as in antique furniture, but it is easier to get a car back to original condition than an antique. Substitutions such as electronic ignition, fuel injection for carburetors, magnesium wheels substituted for the original wheels, a bargain rate exhaust system, or new instruments on the dashboard of a different make from the original all tend to make the car worth less.

12. *Top quality cars tend to appreciate the most.* This is the principle for investing in most art and antiques, and it holds true for investment cars as well. A $6,000 Mustang will almost certainly appreciate in value, but there are many good condition Mustangs available. Lesser-priced cars don't offer the investment potential of cars selling for larger sums. One has to invest perhaps $25,000 to buy a really fine car with a reasonable hope for a sizable capital gain. For $25,000 one can get a very good investment quality Rolls-Royce like a Silver Cloud I, II, or III, any number of Ferraris, possibly a Maserati Ghibli convertible, a Lamborghini Miura, a fine Packard prewar touring car, a Cord, a prime Mercedes-Benz 220 or 220S convertible, and many other cars that are strict investments, not simply old cars. For an investment of $60,000, one can secure a treasure of the classic car world: a prime Miura, a Ferrari 275GTB-4, a Ferrari Daytona coupe, or a Shelby Cobra in mint condition.

13. *It is probably better to buy one fine, more expensive investment car than several less expensive cars because of costs.* The more expensive the investment car, usually the better it is as an investment. A large car collection means greater annual costs for maintaining them: insurance, storage, licensing, and repairs.

Repairs are always part of the picture because, even if a car is not used at all, it deteriorates. The paint on a car deteriorates, and in ten years the car will certainly need a new paint job. The tires dry out and crack, as does the leather. Even the interior of the engine tends to rust. Engine wear on the cylinders takes place when the car is started only occasionally.

If one car is owned for an investment period of ten years, one paint job is required; if five cars are owned, five paint jobs are required, and the cost per car will be about the same whether one has a single car in his investment portfolio or five cars. If one owns ten cars, it is pretty safe to say that at all times during the year one car will be in the repair shop, and even at as low a labor rate as $25 an hour, the maintenance cost can be significant and cut into profits on resale. There is probably more chance for theft and vandalism the more cars one owns.

14. *Invest in a car with an up-price trend.*   It is far better to buy a car with an upward price movement than one which is doing nothing pricewise. The increase in the price of certain cars is common knowledge. Almost every Rolls-Royce has increased in price over the last ten years, and increased enormously. Almost every Ferrari has increased in price, with the Ferrari Super America probably at the top of price increase worldwide. The Ferrari GTB-4 has doubled in price over the past four years. This degree of rise holds true for the 275GTB-4 as well as the Ferrari Daytona GTB-4. The 365GTB-4 Daytona spyder has tripled in value in the past four years, and everybody seems in the market to buy this car.

The same great popularity exists for the Rolls-Royce Corniche convertible. Ten years ago a Rolls-Royce convertible of the latest model sat brand new for a long time in the Rolls-Royce showroom in Greenwich, Connecticut. It probably sold for under $35,000. Today this same car, used, probably will bring $50,000 in only average condition.

Price moves must be carefully studied and followed over time in the price reports and price guides. In the past five years, the price of the Ford Thunderbird of the mid-fifties has moved down from a level of $15,000 to $10,000–$12,000 as of 1981. The Mercedes-Benz 300 SEL 6.3 has moved down in the past three years (1978–1981) from about $12,000 to about $9,000, but it may now start rising again. This was at the time probably the highest performance sedan in the world. Now the body is considered somewhat out-of-date, and the performance may well have been exceeded by the recent 6.9 Mercedes—which sells, second-hand, at above $50,000.

CHAPTER **2**

Selecting an Investment Car

Flexibility in Buying

WHEN LOOKING FOR A CAR to buy, it is best to have some flexibility. You cannot always find exactly what you are looking for, at exactly the price you expected. Flexibility might mean a group of cars in which you have some interest: a 1965–1966 Mustang convertible, a Chevy Corvair, a Packard Caribbean convertible at the modest end of the price range. At the other extreme, you could consider a Stutz Bearcat, a Mercer Raceabout, or perhaps a comparable Simplex, if a Simplex can be found. Perhaps you are looking for the "best" in prewar classics, the Bugatti Royale. Maybe instead, a Mercedes-Benz SSK turns up. This too is a standout, and it might be bought instead of the Bugatti.

I used to look for a Maserati Ghibli spyder, a rather rare open car; but in the end I settled for a Ghibli coupe, a magnificent car and far more plentiful in supply than the spyder (convertible coupe, actually). A person might be looking for a Ferrari GTB but locate a GTB-4, a much more expensive car but one that might tempt him to pay more, since it is more desirable.

At one time I was looking for a Rolls-Royce. I knew what I wanted: a Silver Cloud III left drive sedan. In late 1979 I made a trip from Connecticut to New Orleans in response to an ad to look over a Cloud III. While I was still considering a Rolls, along came a Cloud II. Although not what I had wanted originally, this one had been gone over extensively from a mechanical point of view. It was a right-hand drive, but the price was well under market, so I bought it.

How Much Do You Want to Invest?

Deciding what amount to put into an investment car is a function of one's capital fund and also a function of the financial times. Ten years ago, in 1970, it was hard for a car investor to part with the $7,500 that was about market price for a Ferrari 275GTB. At the time, $7,500 was a high price for any used car, foreign or American, classic or not. Of course, there were some *very* high priced cars like the Mercer Raceabout and the Stutz Bearcat, but they were rare and sold to buyers with very specialized interests. A bid of under $50,000 would probably have bought one of these rarities then, but today the price might well be over $150,000.

Ten years ago it was not entirely clear that a car—any car—was or could be an investment. There was no clear indication that certain cars would go up in price to any appreciable degree. Today the history of price rise is there for the potential investor to see. It is easier to part with $25,000 if one can see it increasing as a car investment to $35,000 two years from now.

An investment car should not be compared with a used car from the point of view of price or the total costs of owning the car over a period of time. One car can provide everyday transportation; the other must be considered an investment like stocks, bonds, and Old Master paintings—except that the car may provide certain satisfactions that stocks and bonds do not, since it is a tangible object.

If you consider an investment car part of your investment portfolio, you might limit car investments to 10 percent or even less of the total, particularly if you're a novice car investor. Of course, if you are more or less an old pro at car investing, the percentage of your portfolio invested in cars can be higher; a car bug might even have 50 percent of his portfolio in investment cars. At one time during World War II, almost all of my own investment portfolio was in two automobiles: a Mercedes-Benz 500K convertible and a 540K sports coupe. These were not such bad investments in light of what has happened to prices since those years!

What Is Your Investment Car Supposed to Do for You?

You must ask yourself what you expect to get from an investment car besides a good investment that may appreciate in value.

Is the car going to be used for regular transportation? If the answer is yes, then your choice of cars is narrowed greatly. Antique cars and prewar classics are almost all ruled out. A few of the prewar cars might still be used as occasional, but not regular, transportation. These include the Ford V-8 models from 1932 up to the war, which often sell in prime condition for under $10,000, and sometimes in average condition for under $5,000. Replacement parts are not hard to find and are not expensive; repairs can be done competently in a number of shops. Then you can purchase a Chevrolet—from the six-cylinder car of 1929 on up to the 1942 models—for under $5,000 if the condition is average. These cars can be repaired fairly easily and parts are obtainable. Other choices could be Cadillacs of the late 1930s up to the war, some of which can be purchased for under $15,000; Buicks and Chryslers of the same era; Plymouths, Pontiacs, and Oldsmobiles from the mid-thirties to the war which often can be bought for under $5,000.

Almost all American postwar cars produced in large quantities can be used for transportation. Special edition cars like the Tucker 48 are impractical for use, and there is almost none on the market. In general, discontinued cars like the Kaiser and Frazer cannot be used for travel because parts are too hard to find. Unless one of these two makes is a convertible, the price is still low; $5,000 would be a high price.

Most real investment cars are cars that can be used only occasionally. Some exceptions are the Rolls-Royce postwar cars, as well as the Bentleys. Many of these are on the market, and parts can be obtained. In general, they are extremely reliable, particularly the six-cylinder cars from 1959 on back to the immediate postwar years.

Probably no Ferrari should be used for regular transportation. Repairs are too costly and take too much time. Occasionally one finds a mid-sixties Ferrari in fairly regular use. It is also fairly reliable, but repairs and parts do not come cheap. All Ferraris are investment cars today, and are likely to become more so in the future.

Many strict investment cars are simply too valuable to place on the highway or on the street.

Do you really need to use the car at all? One TV show of the 1960s, "The Avengers," was set in an important manor house in England. In the living room sat a one- or two-cylinder antique car, more or less as part of the furniture. This car was treated as an art object, and it fit in well with the antique furniture and Old Master paintings, but it obviously wasn't driven much. If you don't want a car in the living room, you can exhibit it in the garage, provided the garage is kept neat and in tune with the quality of the car. Even for a car that can be driven, there may be little or no need to drive it. When one considers the present cost of repairs and body and paint work, one tends to come to the conclusion that any investment car should probably be driven a maximum of 1,000 miles a year.

Choosing the Make and the Model

A two-cylinder Rolls-Royce can be a top investment. So can a Ferrari 275GTB-4. If you had the former for sale, you could sell it over the telephone for a sum in the high six figures. It is, however, entirely unlikely that such a car will ever be offered for sale anywhere. Of course it could not be used for transportation except possibly to go to meets—but even then it should be hauled on a truck. The Ferrari 275GTB-4 has a definite market and a definite market price. As this chapter was being written a mint 275GTB-4 was offered for sale at a price of $65,000. It could be driven anywhere at any time, but it would be inadvisable to drive such a car except on special occasions and perhaps on weekends.

At the other end of the price scale are Ford Mustangs of the years 1965 or 1966. You can drive such cars anywhere: they can be repaired almost anywhere and at minimum expense. Where you would get parts for a two-cylinder Rolls-Royce would be difficult to determine; every important part would almost certainly have to be made to order, and it would be hard indeed to locate shops that could make such parts with a degree of precision.

In between these extremes, there are all kinds of investment cars at all prices and with all degrees of usefulness or impracticality. For $12,000, you can get a four-passenger, fine-condition Ferrari 250GTE two-plus-two coupe with a high degree of reliability. For $25,000, you can get the same model Ferrari with a convertible body. For $1,500, you can buy a fine condition Cadillac Eldorado of the year 1967—a good-looking, usable car that has just started to appreciate. For double this sum, you might buy a Lincoln coupe of the same year, a car that looks completely up-to-date, can be used regularly for transportation, and is appreciating in value.

Can the Car Be Maintained?

There are essentially two types of cars from the point of view of condition: (1) completely restored cars, and (2) average and lesser condition cars. Of course there are all shades of these two types, but one either buys a car definitely in need of repairs and restoration, or a car in need of *few* repairs and restorations. You should always try to buy the latter unless you own your own repair shop, preferably one specializing in the type of car you are thinking of buying!

All investment cars will require some maintenance, even though they are driven rarely or not at all. For fifteen years I have owned a Mercedes-Benz 300S convertible. There have been four paint jobs on the car, and a fifth is required; yet the car has been driven only 3,000 miles in total in fifteen years. Maybe the fault was with the paint shops, but in fifteen years at least one competent new paint job would be required.

Some cars are fantastically expensive to maintain. One of these is the Maserati Ghibli. There are several temperamental features on this car: the water pump, the compressor for the air conditioner, the timing mechanism that tends to slip, the cooling system, and finally the engine which occasionally must be replaced. Fortunately, an organization has been established in the state of Washington—the Maserati Information Exchange —without which a number of us might well have to give up our Maseratis for good.

The Ferrari 250GT is also a complicated car, but it requires far fewer repairs, and adequate repairs at reasonable prices can be secured. The Ford Mustang requires very few repairs, even compared with brand-new cars sold today.

Parts can be extremely expensive and time-consuming to obtain. A Rolls-Royce Silver Cloud wheel cover (hubcap) costs $275 and is rising in price. A bumper guard costs $250. The radiator ornament (lady) can cost $450 second hand, if one can be found.

Where you live determines, to a degree, the car or cars in which you should invest. Buy an investment car that can be maintained in the area in which you live. If you live in a rural community or along the U.S./Canadian border, you probably should not invest in a Lamborghini Miura; there are too few specialists who know this car. The Maserati Ghibli is more temperamental. Even in Italy it has this reputation; the Florence industrialist, Count Giorgio Geddes da Filicaia, said, "A Ghibli can be maintained, but one must find the right mechanic." In Italy, however, these cars are much easier to maintain than in the U.S., just as it is much easier to maintain a Rolls-Royce in England than here.

Does the Car Supply Personal Satisfaction?

Many years ago an automobile journalist wrote, "If you buy a car that you are only lukewarm on, you will get to hate it." How right he was! A car is a personal thing, even if it is an investment car. The relationship between a man and his car is, odd as it may sound, an emotional relationship. Perhaps that's the reason a wife sometimes feels her husband's car is her rival for his affections. Personally, I don't like the inexpensive prewar Packards—the models 110, 115, and 120.

On the other hand, for about ten years I looked for a good Lamborghini Miura. When, in 1980, I finally found one I wanted, it cost at least twice what it might have when I first started to look for one. The satisfaction of owning that car is, to me, immense. It is an investment, but it will be very difficult for me to part with it.

Most men and many women are fond of cars—exotic, expensive cars. They know it is extravagant to go out and buy a new Rolls-Royce sedan for up to $120,000 or even a Mercedes-Benz 500SEL for $55,000. But it is not at all extravagant to buy a Mercer Raceabout for $125,000 (which is under market) or a Ferrari 275GTB-4 for $60,000. These are investments—strict investments priced on the low side when compared with the market. They will not go down in value, only up. A new Rolls or Mercedes most certainly will go down in value from the minute it is driven out of the showroom. So one might satisfy one's aesthetic taste, but still make a good investment.

Sleepers Due for a Rise in Price

You should be on the lookout for sleepers. For a number of years in the fine-art world, the eighteenth-century British portraitists were sleepers—Reynolds, Lawrence, Romney, and others. So was the American portraitist Gilbert Stuart. No one suspected the price potential in these painters' works. Then the paintings started going up in price and have continued to move upward. The same situation holds true for automobiles. The Aston Martin did not move in price for a long time; then, in 1975 it took off.

Today the Maserati Ghibli looks like a sleeper. For years the price of an early model Ghibli has remained around $12,000–$15,000; the late models (1971–1972) run up to $18,000. A number of Ghiblis are offered for sale fairly regularly. Critical opinion in the classic car field seems to be very much in favor of the Ghibli. It is a beauty: luxurious, with air conditioning, electric windows, power brakes, power steering, and fine leather upholstery. The car even comes with an automatic transmission. It is a top performer and is quite likely to move to much higher price levels even though it is a very complicated car.

Where Do You Find Price Information?

Before deciding where to look for your car, you must know the market. One of the best ways to learn the market is to read the *New York Times* every Sunday. Antique and classic cars and imported and sports cars are advertised for sale in the sports section. By reading this section month after month you begin to learn the price levels for various kinds of cars and, further, what the price trend is. I file these Sunday sections, so it is not hard to make comparisons by dates to see price trends.

Another must is the *Hemmings Motor News,* available from HMN Subscriptions, Box 100, Bennington, Vermont 05201. The subscription rate is $9.75 a year, and there are enough pages in each issue to provide constant study until the next issue comes out. If both of these publications are studied carefully and systematically, one might even set oneself up as an automobile market analyst—something like a securities analyst on Wall Street.

Buying a car is, of course, the reverse of selling a car; the chapter on selling collector cars lists the places to sell a car, together with their addresses, and describes them in some detail. The present chapter offers a summary of sources of cars. For more information, see chapter 11, Selling Investment Cars.

It is generally much easier to buy a car than to sell one. Both the *New York Times* and *Hemmings Motor News* can be used to locate cars to buy. Each issue of *Hemmings Motor News* must list close to 10,000 cars for sale. In a recent issue, one firm had four full pages of advertising, each page advertising a different car. All four cars were priced the same—$250,000 per car. In another recent issue, Ozark Classic Car farm advertised seventy-one cars for sale; eight were priced over $4,000, the rest under $4,000. So you can choose your cars and price ranges.

While reviewing these two publications regularly to get an idea of prices and what is being offered, you should also visit all the dealers in antique and classic cars in your area and discuss cars with the dealer.

Buy Opportunely—In the Right Place

Ordinary used cars can always be bought opportunely in one way or another. For example, go to the used car section of your city during the slow winter months, when the lots are covered with snow.

It is also possible to buy investment cars opportunely. I made one such good buy from an individual in February 1980 in New York City. The car was an advertised Lamborghini Miura; the time of the year was wrong for selling any car, investment or ordinary. The car still needed restoration, although much had been done by the owner over a period of a year. The owner had had all the headaches of restoration that he wanted, so he offered to sell at a bargain price if the buyer would take the car as is and undertake to complete the restoration himself.

In addition, this owner wanted cash. He had located another car that he had always wanted, at a very favorable price. The dealer in Georgia who had the car he wanted—a Ferrari 275GTB coupe—had offered to hold the car for him while he tried to sell his Miura. The deal we finally worked out was all cash; the seller agreed to pay for a certain number of the final restorations with the buyer (myself) paying for the rest, provided the seller saw to it that they were done.

One can buy opportunely in these ways:

- Buy from an overloaded dealer who needs cash.
- Buy in an area where cars are selling slowly.
- Buy from an individual who needs to move the car for some reason, such as an impending move to another part of the country or the need for quick cash.
- Buy a car that has some damage for which the owner has collected from the insurance company.

Many fine cars are offered for sale with damaged front end or interior burned in fire, etcetera. It does take something of an expert to buy intelligently in such cases, and estimates must be secured from specialist garages or body shops so that the restored car will not end up costing more than if one simply went out and bought a good car at market price. There are many such insurance jobs offered for sale and advertised in the newspapers and specialist car publications.

There are, of course, many other opportunities to make particularly advantageous buys in the area of specialist investment automobiles. One can look for possible arbitrage—there can be considerable price discrepancies between the American and European markets, for example. Two years ago in Italy, an excellent DeTomaso Pantera coupe was on sale for $6,500; the same model car sold in New York for double this figure. *If* the Italian car were equipped with emission controls so that it would be allowed to enter the U.S., it obviously would appreciate in worth as soon as it arrived. Around the same time, a Ghibli of 1967 vintage (one that required no emission controls to enter the U.S.) was offered for sale in Italy for $6,000. This car was worth at least $10,000 in the U.S. at the time, and there was enough leeway in price to pay the shipping, insurance, and import tax.

Arbitrage can operate within the U.S. as well. In 1977 a Ferrari 250GT convertible in good condition was offered for sale in California for $2,800. The same car in New York would bring $7,000 or even more. In addition, a California car is usually a car with no rust, while cars in the New York area often are badly rusted. Thus, in this case, buying in a different location had two advantages—price and better condition.

Buying the Car "Right"—At an Advantageous Price

It is sometimes said by sagacious people that you get what you pay for. I would say, "Always be sure you get the most for your money and get the thing you want at the lowest possible price." Nowhere does this advice apply better than to classic and antique cars. With investment cars there are no set and exact market prices. Many sales are made by private collectors who advertise in the newspapers to sell their cars. So the trick is to "buy right," which means buy under the market. If you buy at a favorable figure, then you can improve on your investment by repairing and restoring. If you buy enough under the

market, you will be able to restore and then sell the car again
—still under the market.

In June 1980 a McLean, Virginia, dealer offered a Bentley SIII
Continental coupe for $45,000. In Fairfield, Connecticut, at the
same time, an individual offered his Bentley SIII Continental
coupe for just $16,000. It would hardly be necessary to even
inspect the $16,000 Bentley before buying it, it is so far under
market. Another $10,000 investment would probably restore it
completely. The owner of the restored car would still have
spent a total sum under market value for such a restored car.

What Will the Final Investment Be?

To repeat: A fairly long-time owner of a Rolls-Royce Silver
Cloud II decided in 1978 that his car was in need of drastic
repairs. He spent $4,200 on those repairs. He then decided that
the car was too conspicuous, and so he offered it for sale. His
highest offer was $7,000, which he took, and that is how I got
my under-market Rolls.

I felt that there were still mechanical repairs required on the
Rolls, and I also decided to put it in excellent condition cosmetically. The paint was taken off and the body repaired where
needed; the car was repainted. New leather was installed in the
interior, and the bright parts were rechromed where necessary.
The cost of this work in total was $16,032.52, but the car was
now mint. Thus the cost of the restored car was $23,032.52, a
figure far above the original $7,000 bargain price.

Ten or fifteen years ago, repairs and restoration did not cost
nearly what they do today. At that time for this Rolls-Royce,
$1,000 would have secured a superb paint job, and the finest
leather couldn't have cost over $1,000, if that. The mechanical
repairs, after the original owner's $4,200 had been spent, could
not have cost as much as $1,000. Chrome work would have cost
about $500, so for $3,500 the car could have been put in near
mint condition in, say, 1965.

Buying a car in need of repairs is like buying a house in need
of repairs. Experts are needed to determine the condition of the
house: termite damage, drainage, rot in the wood, purity of

well water, condition of the roof, heating system and radiators, electric system and wiring, and so on. Similarly with a car, experts must be employed to determine the condition of the car: rust on the body, compression in the cylinders, transmission, differential, wiring, and the many other elements. Not even a long-time car buff can fully determine the condition of a car.

Building a Collection of Investment Cars

Building a collection of investment cars has certain advantages from an investment point of view. If you must sell, you can offer several cars simultaneously for sale, and see what sells. If you have just one car for sale, you may have to wait a long time to find a buyer in the collectible car market. If you offer three cars for sale you have tripled the chance of finding at least one buyer; therefore many for sale advertisements read, "Will sell one of these cars and keep the rest."

If you contemplate auctioning a car, you will get a much better reception from the auction firm, and possibly even a better commission arrangement, if four or five cars are offered for sale in the same auction, particularly if the cars are collector cars of quality. An auction house and a dealer sometimes court the possessor of a collection of cars just as they might a painting collector who has a dozen Old Masters that he might consider selling.

Yet keeping and maintaining a collection can be costly. As I wrote this chapter, I was in the process of placing three collectible or investment cars in my collection. One is the Rolls-Royce on which restorations costs came to $16,000. I am watching this car very carefully, mainly to determine whether or not the new paint job will crack up. It would not be the first collector car I have owned on which the "custom" paint job cracked after a few months.

I did not have any of these three cars fully checked out before purchase as to the required repairs, and one of them has required a solid eight months to work out the bugs, both mechanical and cosmetic. Additionally, none of the cars has yet been licensed. When each is licensed, a Connecticut sales tax of 7.5 percent of the purchase price must be paid, so I will pay a tax of

$1,575 on a $21,000 car. Then, insurance must be placed on every car, and on exotics this cost can be very high.

Garage space must be found for these three additional cars. In my case, I am getting bids on a new three-car garage, which may cost $25,000 to build. If a public garage is used, there is always danger of vandalism, and possible outright theft. The dead storage cost, if the car is not driven in and out regularly, may be $50 a month.

Times flies when cars are in dead storage: sometimes years fly by. When you go to start the cars up as you should do regularly in order to keep oil in the cylinders, you usually find that the battery is dead and one tire, at least, flat.

These all are collection costs. If the cars are strictly investment cars, the Internal Revenue Service *may* allow you to deduct these costs (or expenses) from your income before the income tax rate is applied, in which event your real collection costs may be only 60 percent or 50 percent of the actual dollar outlay, depending on your tax bracket.

Other collectibles can be used continually in the home; paintings can be hung, stamp and coin collections displayed or placed in safe deposit boxes. In any case, there is less worry with these than with collector cars. In addition, coins and stamps do not have to be rehabilitated or repainted from time to time, and insurance is not always necessary.

My first collector car was bought before World War II, the year I was graduated from college. This was not the era of car investment. It was the era of new cars and just plain second-hand cars that were, in general, worth very little—even Rolls-Royces, Duesenbergs, or Bugatti Royales. It was an era in which one could buy the finest car mechanically, the most beautiful car, for under $1,000.

Over the years the worst I did with my collector automobiles was to lose nothing on them in depreciation or to make just a little. I kept the cars running either through my own labor on weekends or by paying very little to repair shops.

As the years rolled on and I bought and sold these collector cars, expenses increased (repairs, storage, insurance), but so did prices. My cars showed a profit, not large, but at least a profit.

In the seventies everything changed, and despite the fact that repairs and other expenses skyrocketed, so did prices, including the prices of my own cars.

Was all of this buying of collector cars, fixing them up, and selling them worthwhile? Overall I did make a profit, and my transportation cost me little or nothing—simply the out-of-pocket for gas and oil. There was no overall depreciation in value.

But my return on these cars was far more than a profit. Over a period of four decades I had the joy of owning some of the great cars of all time—the Mercedes-Benz S, SS, 500K, 540K, the Rolls-Royce Phantom I, the great Phantom Corsair, the Offenhauser Cisitalia, the Ferrari, the Maserati Ghibli, and the Lamborghini Miura.

I had the joy of driving these cars thousands of miles and of knowing that even if I didn't want to drive a particular great car in my garage, I could get a great deal of satisfaction just looking at the car, just knowing that I owned it.

Right now I have an inconvenient number of automobiles—eight—and eight are too many for me to take care of. Still, why not keep them? They are all going up in value, at least 10 percent per year overall. As a pure investment they are worth it.

Assessing the Condition of a Car

Cars used to be bought after the prospective owner briefly inspected the car and drove it. Professional car buyers, mainly dealers, would look at the car and start it up. They generally would not bother to drive it, since what you could see cost the most money: body, paint, top, leather, chrome. Mechanical features, things they couldn't see, did not cost so much; not too long ago, a whole new Cadillac engine could be bought for $525.

Now, however, it is a different story. When, in 1977, I bought the Rolls-Royce Silver Cloud II, it sounded fairly good, and I could detect nothing seriously wrong. Then the work started, and the expenses started—and they continued. After the mechanical work, the body work, paint work, and refurbishing, the leather, carpets, and chrome all had to be done.

A car should be taken from repair shop to repair shop for several estimates on the costs of repair and rehabilitation. Each shop will prepare an estimate in the area of its specialty—carpets, chrome, paint, and body work, etcetera. The shop will prepare the estimate on its bill head and give you, the prospective buyer, a copy. *Usually* the shop will not charge for this estimate, but one must determine in advance whether there is a charge for the estimate, and, if so, what it is.

How much mechanical testing must be done depends on how expert the eye of the prospective buyer himself is. Experts or near-experts may make checks themselves. These are the areas, mechanically, on which to concentrate:

1. *The cylinders.* Each cylinder must be checked with a compression tester, and the compression of each cylinder recorded. The readings on the compression tester must be matched against the specifications for the engine. Above all, no cylinder should be down very much from the readings of the others. If one is, then the valves may need to be ground. Somewhere compression is being lost—either because of a leaking valve or because of worn piston rings. Where there are low readings, I myself forget about the car.

2. *The bearings and crankshaft.* The car must be thoroughly warmed up and driven, to see what happens on the oil pressure gauge. Recently I looked at a car with no oil pressure showing when the motor ran. I indicated to the seller that unless the trouble were simple and rectified—like a disconnected wire to the oil pressure gauge—I was not at all interested in buying the car. This is because I have owned cars that literally beat out the main bearings when the oil was not circulating properly. The engine had to be rebored and new bearings fitted, a job that today would cost in the thousands for the true exotics.

The crankshaft might be bent or scored—in which event the car should not be purchased.

3. *The differential.* This is commonly called the rear end. It should not whine, hum, or be noisy. If the car is an important exotic like the Mercedes-Benz 300S, a replacement differential is almost impossible to buy, and it is extremely difficult for even an expert to repair such a differential. But if the car is a Mustang

or other simple car turned out in volume, a new differential can be purchased, and for relatively little money.

4. *The transmission.* This should be tested by moving forward under acceleration at all speeds, as well as by moving backward. The brake should be applied when the car is standing still and the lever put in drive and then reverse—pushing the accelerator against the brake to see what happens when the pressure of the engine is applied to the transmission.

Manual transmissions should shift easily and noiselessly in all gears, and no noises should be heard from the transmission.

The clutch in manual transmission cars should be tested by pulling with the brake on—pressing down on the accelerator —to see if there is slippage, indicating a requirement for a new clutch. The car can also be accelerated in gear to see if there is slippage.

5. *The sound of the engine.* This test of what may be wrong with the engine is usually one of the first, and a seller will often start the engine up and say, "Doesn't that sound nice?"

An ear trained to detect troubles will then be able to hear noisy bearings, loose pistons, noisy valves and valve gear. Unless this ear test indicates a good engine (not necessarily a perfect engine), the car should be forgotten.

6. *The presence of cracks.* Among the important things to look for are cracks. A bright light should be shown on all parts of the engine: block under the hood; block and crank case with the car on a lift at a service station; heads, with the valve covers off. While the car is on the lift, the same light inspection should be conducted on axle housing, differential housing, and transmission housing.

The frame and front axle should be checked for cracks, for twists, and for repairs of actual breaks. Modern high performance cars often have flimsy frames, and a slight accident can break or twist—not just crack—the frame.

Serious mechanical faults plus serious areas of body rust are the major things that can doom a car, and a car with these serious faults should probably be bypassed by the prospective buyer. Somewhere between a car with such faults and a mint-condition car, you can find one which it will pay to acquire and put in condition.

How Well Can a Car's Condition Be Assessed?

The true condition of a car can be assessed only up to a point. There are unknowns that must remain unknown, even with the most thoroughgoing inspection and analysis. The condition of paint, chrome, leather, top, and carpets can all be assessed *fairly* accurately. It can be assumed that most will have to be replaced. But what is under the chrome is an unknown. Rust can show through the paint, but when all the paint is removed, there may be vastly more rust than anyone had imagined possible.

The fact is that one must buy sufficiently under the market to allow leeway for costs in restoration and repairs, and there should be plenty of leeway. This necessity for leeway is one reason dealers often say they can afford to pay only the seemingly low prices for the cars they buy. They need to make a markup, true, but they know they are in for at least some repairs and that these repairs can cost them. Labor costs a good deal more than it did a decade ago, but parts have gone through the roof.

The first place to get part prices is the dealer for the car you are contemplating buying. If you can shop around, getting substitutes and used parts, that is a plus for you and your restoration costs; but one should not count on such cut-rate parts. They may not be available when you want them in a hurry.

Actually, so far as condition goes, one should consider buying only three types of cars: (1) a mint condition car, (2) a very poor condition car that may be picked up at what seems a giveaway price, or (3) a car somewhere in between these two extremes, but one leaning toward the fine side, a good but not perfect car.

During the June 1980 Leake sale in Tulsa, not an offbeat but an important antique car was offered for sale: a 1904 Stevens Duryea, a milestone car in the development of the automobile in America. It was a two-cylinder car, one every automobile museum in America would be happy to have for its collection. Yet it brought the amazingly low price of $4,750 because it had no transmission!

In the same Leake sale, a 1904 Waverly electric roadster was sold for $15,000. This was not even a gasoline car like the Stevens Duryea, but it was intact.

Where could you get a replacement transmission for the Stevens Duryea? I don't know, and probably nobody else knows either. The only thing that might be done would be to locate plans for the transmission, but such plans might not be in existence. Perhaps a car museum or an owner would allow the transmission of a Stevens Duryea to be disassembled and copied piece by piece. On the other hand, how many of the cars are in existence to study, even in the unlikely event that an owner would allow his transmission to be disassembled? This car will probably end up with a fake transmission, one adapted from another car lock, stock and barrel, and the originality of the car and much of its value will have been destroyed.

So in buying investment cars, there must be a thoroughgoing inspection of the car in every respect, mechanically and cosmetically. A parts list must be prepared insofar as one can determine the parts that are needed, and the cost of these parts plus labor must be totaled. Then the total cost of the car can be estimated, and the cost (including repairs and restoration where needed) will almost certainly be far far underestimated.

CHAPTER 3

Rolls-Royce

ROLLS-ROYCE IS ONE OF THE BEST and at the same time one of the most conservative investments in the entire field of investment automobiles. There are many reasons. Rolls-Royce has been appreciating in value fairly steadily over the past decade. Just ten years ago, almost any classic Rolls-Royce of the years 1955 to 1965 up to the latest year was low in price on the used car market on almost any basis—in relation to its price new, in relation to other investment cars, in relation to the quality that the investment funds would buy. Since that time there has been definite and substantial appreciation for most of these cars. Sometimes the up-trend seemed to stick, but it was merely on a plateau, and prices after a period of months or even a year took off again, not wildly but steadily upward. Even so, prices of Rolls-Royce cars produced from the year 1955 through the 1970s are still not overhigh in relation to other investment cars.

The Rolls-Royce is the ultimate prestige car, and it is becoming more so all the time. If a person in search of prestige could afford just one car, it would certainly have to be a Rolls-Royce. Various tests to prove or disprove this prestige value of the Rolls have been conducted. One automotive magazine in California had editors drive three prestige cars—a Mercedes-Benz 450SL, an Aston Martin and a Rolls-Royce—around the city in which the magazine was located. The Rolls-Royce came out the decided winner in recognition value by other drivers. Another publication pointed out that you can park a Rolls-Royce anywhere. In particular, one can park it right in front of the door of the country club, where the sign says no parking—and get away with it! One Rolls-Royce owner regularly parks his Rolls-Royce Silver Cloud III long wheelbase at the front entrance of the Darien, Connecticut, Wee Burn Country Club. We know this is so because we lived just down the road, and whenever we saw this Rolls parked in front of the country club, we usually drove in to look it over. Maybe the Rolls-Royce added to the luster of the country club. In any event, apparently no one asked the owner to move the car to the parking lot.

The Rolls-Royce is an extremely well-made car, particularly the series that ended in the year 1965: the Silver Cloud series. In many ways the Silver Cloud III of the last year this series was made, 1965, was the ultimate car in quality: finest quality steel and wood, leather, paint, chrome, everything. The car was beautifully finished and thoroughly proven before delivery to the customer.

The Rolls-Royce has always been noted for its reliability. This reliability certainly extended up through the year 1965. Many Silver Clouds of the years 1955 through 1965 are advertised in the British newspapers. Very often mileage is included in the ads, and the mileage may be advertised as "only 102,000 miles," or "117,000 miles," as though this mileage is low. It probably is, for a Rolls-Royce.

The fact of the matter is that a Rolls-Royce is dependable. It usually starts when one turns the key and presses the starter. Once the engine starts, the car rarely breaks down. It gets you there and it gets you back. One cannot say quite the same thing about one of its competitors, the Mercedes-Benz 600, a fine and beautiful—and overcomplicated—car that tends to break down with fair regularity, often on the street or highway.

One could almost place the Rolls-Royce car of the postwar era in the class of a truck, it is so ruggedly built. It is the finest of quality cars, built to run and run and run, from the prewar

Silver Ghosts and Phantoms I and II to the postwar Silver Cloud Is, the last standard six-cylinder cars. The eight-cylinder Silver Cloud IIs and IIIs were very nearly as reliable as the Cloud Is. Most Rolls-Royce cars are beautiful and conservative. When the Silver Cloud I first came out in 1955, there were screams from many of the sports car purists that the Rolls-Royce was too big, too ungainly, two feet too high. The same Rolls-Royce today in mint condition is a beautiful thing, at least to many people. Many of us have apparently adjusted our spectacles and taken a new look at the Rolls-Royce.

A Rolls-Royce is not an overcomplicated or overstressed car. While it tends to run and run with relatively few repairs, some of the Italian super cars are definitely highly stressed and very complicated, with four overhead camshafts and six carburetors —among other things.

Many mechanics can be found who know how to repair a Rolls-Royce. Few mechanics can repair a Lamborghini Contach or Miura; very few can overhaul a Ferrari. Further, Rolls-Royce spare parts are available literally all over the place. If original factory parts cannot be located, then very good replacement parts made by other companies can be located, and many of the replacement parts are available in the United States.

In addition, second-hand parts can be purchased and at relatively reasonable prices. A windshield for a Silver Cloud I, II, and III can be bought in the U.S. for $250. Even fairly obscure parts can be located, like the radiator lady, Spirit of Ecstasy; and one Connecticut small-parts supplier has boxes full of small parts and emblems, plus wheel discs, bumper overriders, etcetera. I can order an entire exhaust system and get delivery in two days at most. I can get an oil pump, an antenna, or even an entire engine, transmission, or differential—but in the case of an engine, delivery might take longer than two days. Prices for obsolete parts are anything but high. On the other hand I got a quote on a water pump for a Maserati Ghibli—at $850!

Most Rolls-Royce cars are made for transportation. Almost all are standard sedans, but the relatively few convertibles seat at least three people in comfort, and the sedans seat five or seven people in comfort for one hundred miles or more. The same cannot be said of the DeTomaso Pantera, for instance.

There is a ready market for a Rolls-Royce of almost any description. It is very much of a standard commodity on the classic car market. If the market is slow the price can be reduced *a little* to move the car. The cars can often be bought and sold through newspaper advertisements in the local metropolitan newspaper. While Rolls-Royce cars are certainly in the antique category, at least the old ones dating to the early 1920s, there are very few fine antiques like the London-to-Edinburgh Rolls-Royce and the beautiful Alpine Rolls-Royce. Almost all of these antiques are in museums or very important collections, but if you should see the four-cylinder, the three-cylinder, or the two-cylinder Rolls-Royce, try to buy any one of these cars! It is difficult today, however, to buy even a very early six-cylinder Silver Ghost.

In a Rolls-Royce you have it both ways: an investment that has appreciated and that is appreciating, and also a transportation car. Almost any Rolls-Royce of the post-World War II era is a transportation car; we used one daily for three years, even going on 1,000-mile trips into areas with no Rolls-Royce shops or parts with confidence. In three years and about 40,000 miles, repairs came to well under $500 in total. In contrast, repairs in just one year on our Opel station wagon came to well over $2,500—more than the car cost us new. On our 300SE Mercedes-Benz sedan, the car made at least a dozen trips yearly to the Mercedes-Benz repair shop in Washington, D.C., for everything from a second transmission overhaul to an air-oil suspension that broke down every two or three months.

Not only are the Rolls Silver Cloud I, Silver Cloud II, Cloud III, and even earlier postwar Rolls-Royces (or the equivalent Bentleys made by Rolls-Royce) good transportation cars, but the Silver Shadows that were put out from 1966 to 1980 are also transportation cars. In fact they look more like transportation cars than the earlier big, impressive, luxurious cars of the Silver Cloud, Phantom, and Silver Ghost series. These Silver Shadows are appreciating in value steadily, if not spectacularly. They are not more reliable than the Silver Clouds and earlier cars and they are not such standouts, as they tend to have the overcomplicating features of most modern cars. The more so-called modern refinements on a car, the more trouble and the less reliable the car.

The Rolls-Royce Silver Clouds

The Silver Clouds were put out between 1955 and 1965, although only a few were sold in 1955; for the most part, they started appearing in 1956. A very few cars of the Silver Cloud series were sold as late as 1966.

The first of the Silver Cloud series, the Silver Cloud I, is a six-cylinder car, put out from 1955 through 1959. A few were made as late as 1960, and I owned one of these 1960 cars—a James Young bodied Silver Cloud I. It was the Geneva Show car of 1960.

In 1960 the Silver Cloud II, a V-8 with overhead valves, appeared. This car was refined after 1961 and discontinued in 1963; in appearance it was virtually indistinguishable from the Silver Cloud I unless one raised the hood and saw the V-8 engine.

In 1963 the Silver Cloud III appeared. This is a refined Cloud II with a lower hood line and four headlights instead of the usual two. It is probably a better and more reliable car than the Silver Cloud II, although there are those who prefer two headlights to four. This car was continued through 1965 when it gave way to the much smaller Silver Shadow which continued to 1980.

We consider these Silver Clouds to be the most standard investments of all Rolls-Royce cars. There are many of them on the market in England and the United States. They have a fairly definite market price; they are fairly easily bought and sold; they can be used as daily transportation. They can be repaired with a modicum of trouble, and parts are available. Very important, they are not sky-high in price.

As recently as 1970 the prices of Rolls-Royce (and the corresponding Bentley) cars were very low; from 1970 to 1973 the Silver Cloud series almost doubled in price and continued to move up sharply in 1974. We surveyed both the English and the American markets in some depth in 1973 and ended up by buying a Rolls-Royce ourselves.

Our survey of the London market in August 1973, and again in March 1974, included visiting a number of dealers, looking over private cars for sale and calling a number of private Rolls-Royce sellers on the telephone. These are the comparative price figures (translated to dollars):

London Prices, August 1973

Rolls-Royce	Bentley
Silver Cloud III—$7,000–$7,500	SIII—$4,300–$5,000
Silver Cloud II —$6,250–$6,850	SII —$3,000–$4,000
Silver Cloud I —$5,000	SI —$1,740–$2,200

At these levels, even though prices had risen from 1970, *relative* values were something like today's Cadillac Eldorados of the convertible model. In 1981 the early Eldorados brought about $2,000–$2,500. The last model Eldorado might sell at about the figure of the Silver Cloud III in August 1973, unless the Rolls was in mint condition. It seemed obvious that the only way for Rolls-Royce prices to move at the time was up.

London Prices, March 1974

Rolls-Royce	Bentley
Silver Cloud III—$9,650–$11,500	SIII—$7,000–$7,600
Silver Cloud II —$7,350–$10,350	SII —$4,250–$6,900
Silver Cloud I —$5,750–$9,000	SI —$3,500–$4,600

This is the percentage rise in prices in this period of about a half year:

Percentage Increase in Price
August 1973–March 1974

Rolls-Royce	Bentley
Silver Cloud III—plus 38	SIII—plus 63
Silver Cloud II —plus 18	SII —plus 42
Silver Cloud I —plus 15	SI —plus 100

The sophisticated Rolls-Royce Silver Cloud III, the last of the big Rolls-Royces, rose 38 percent; but the corresponding Bentley, which had the four prestigious headlights, rose 63 percent

—from the low level of $5,000 (or under) to $7,000 or more. The SI Bentley was priced at the level of any old car in August 1973 —$1,740 to $2,200—and rose a modest amount in dollars (or pounds sterling) to $3,500—$4,600. The Silver Cloud I Rolls-Royce was *much* more expensive than the corresponding Bentley because it had the prestige of being a Rolls-Royce, but it was only a six-cylinder car and was thought to be less sophisticated than the eight-cylinder car.

People began to turn to the next best thing as prices rose, and the less expensive Rolls-Royce and Bentley cars went to America, particularly the SI six-cylinder Bentleys. Americans are operating them today more or less regularly. In this particular boom period the Viceroy Carriage Company of London, essentially a used Rolls-Royce and Bentley wholesaler, was selling about ten Rolls-Royce and Bentley cars a week, from SI Bentleys to Cloud III Rolls-Royces.

The American market was, and traditionally has been, higher than the English market. One reason is that there are fewer Rolls-Royces and Bentley cars in the U.S., and consequently fewer offered for sale. The other reason is that Americans want left-hand drive, not right-hand drive, cars, and the supply of these left-hand drive cars available to the American market is relatively low. Americans do buy right-hand drive cars in the U.S. or in England, but they are not preferred, and they may bring $2,000 to $3,000 less than left-hand drive cars. (In fact, left-hand drive cars that happen to be offered for sale in England will frequently bring a higher price in England than right-hand drive cars, because such cars can be sent to the U.S. or the Continent for resale.)

American Prices, August 1973

Rolls-Royce	*Bentley*
Silver Cloud III—$15,000–$20,000	SIII—$10,000–$12,000
Silver Cloud II —$10,000–$15,000	SII —$ 6,500–$10,000
Silver Cloud I —$ 7,500–$10,000	SI —$ 5,800–$ 7,000

In the twelve-month period preceding these price recordings, Rolls-Royce and Bentley cars about doubled. They then proceeded upward, but at a more moderate rate of increase.

American Prices, March 1974

Rolls-Royce	Bentley
Silver Cloud III—$16,000–$22,000	SIII—$12,000–$15,000
Silver Cloud II —$12,000–$15,000	SII —$10,000–$12,000
Silver Cloud I —$ 9,000–$10,000	SI —$ 6,000–$ 9,000

In this period of approximately seven months, from August 1973 to March 1974, Rolls-Royce Silver Clouds had increased in price 14 percent and the corresponding Bentleys 70 percent. For many, if not most, buyers, the price of Rolls-Royce cars had risen so far so fast that they turned to the next best thing, the Bentley: essentially the same car as the Rolls-Royce except for the radiator which cost about $250 more for the Rolls-Royce than for the Bentley when both cars were just off the assembly line.

There was little price movement between March 1974 and January 1975, but by the end of 1976 there was a wild boom in Rolls-Royce cars. At that time we made another survey of Rolls-Royce cars in England. Laurence Kayne, the very large Bentley and Rolls-Royce wholesaler in London, advertised twelve of his used Rolls and Bentley cars in the November 1976 issue of *Motor Sport* magazine. He took an entire page in the magazine and illustrated each of the cars he offered for sale, together with descriptions in some detail. Shortly after the issue of the magazine appeared, he had sold ten out of the twelve cars, and the cars that were left were not the finest offerings.

The boom, incidentally, was almost solely concentrated in the Silver Clouds of the years 1955 through 1965, not the earlier or the later model cars.

From 1976 the market to buy Rolls-Royce Silver Clouds and Bentley S-series cars was the United States. It hardly paid to seek out such cars in England, pay the transportation and insurance to the United States, pay the import duty and the state tax, and then try to have the shipboard damage repaired and the stolen tools replaced. Damage and pilferage run very high during shipment.

The American Market—End of 1976

Rolls-Royce	Bentley
Silver Cloud III—$25,000	SIII—$18,000
Silver Cloud II —$15,000	SII —$12,000
Silver Cloud I —$12,000	SI —$10,000

As of 1981 this was the price structure in America. It is still possible on occasion to buy a Silver Cloud III privately for as low as $20,000, not from dealers, though.

The American Market—1981

Rolls-Royce	Bentley
Silver Cloud III—$35,000–$50,000	SIII—$25,000–$30,000
Silver Cloud II —$28,000–$35,000	SII —$18,000–$25,000
Silver Cloud I —$25,000–$30,000	SI —$12,000–$18,000

While Rolls-Royce and Bentley cars have a market price, it is only a general market price. For a long time the price of an average condition or average-to-good–condition Silver Cloud III ran around $25,000. Then in 1980 there began to be price breakthroughs. Some firm would offer such a car for $35,000. Then other sellers would follow. The price breakthrough was the start of an upward price movement for the particular model car.

The price of gasoline had little effect on the price of these investor-collector cars. They usually are not driven to and from the office or the supermarket. Thus gas cost is not the most important element. We do, however, know of several Silver Clouds that are still used regularly as the owner's only car.

Between 1976 and 1981 a great price disparity developed between average- and mint-condition cars, and certainly between poor-condition cars and mint-condition cars. In 1976 a fine paint job could be secured for $1,000 on any Bentley or Rolls-Royce sedan. Today, $6,000 is not an unusual price to pay for a first-class Rolls-Royce paint job. In 1976, $1,000 would buy a fine leather upholstery job; today, the job may very well cost over $5,000. Thus there is a vast difference between a mediocre Rolls-Royce or Bentley and a mint-condition one.

The Magnificent Cars of the Series

In 1959, Rolls-Royce announced the "largest Rolls-Royce ever built," the Phantom V, and this car maintained its eminent position for ten years until the Phantom VI was introduced in 1968. The Phantom V was simply a big and ultra-luxurious Rolls-Royce. Mechanically it was much the same as the standard cars, but the Phantoms had superb custom bodies built on a larger chassis than the ordinary sedans.

About a decade ago these large cars, which could cost new just under 9,000 pounds sterling ($25,000), were selling in America for under $10,000, and one in Greenwich, Connecticut, in top condition, was on sale for $7,000. By the mid-seventies these cars were selling for close to $25,000. By 1981 they were selling for $60,000 to $65,000.

There is not a great deal of difference between the Phantom V and the Phantom VI, introduced in 1968. The Phantom VI cost new the equivalent of about $79,000 when it was sold in England in 1973. Sometimes both Phantom V and Phantom VI sell at auction in America for under $30,000. But in London, a fine Phantom VI was offered for $112,000 fairly recently.

I have never seen a Phantom V or Phantom VI convertible in anything but a four-door, and a very conservative four-door at that. The two-door convertibles were confined to the Silver Cloud I, II, and III cars, and the Phantom V and Phantom VI are very closely related to the Clouds I, II, and III rather than to the later, smaller Silver Shadows or to the prewar Phantom I, II, and III.

Whatever the convertible model in the Silver Cloud series, it sells high in relation to the standard sedan. Twenty years ago, during the recession of 1962, a beautiful Silver Cloud II convertible that had formerly belonged to the actress Ira von Furstenberg, was offered for sale in Switzerland for $11,500. It was about two years old and apparently in perfect condition. At the time a standard Silver Cloud II sedan could have been bought for about $10,000, and I tried a good one out in New Jersey that was offered for $9,500. At that time convertibles were not selling at a great premium over sedans.

By 1980 the price of the convertible had skyrocketed and was in the price range of the great Phantom V and Phantom VI sedans and limousines—between $60,000 and $70,000. Once in a while a convertible could be purchased for under $60,000, and sometimes first-class dealers in New York offered absolutely mint condition convertibles at over $100,000.

As late as 1975 the special-bodied cars on the Silver Cloud chassis were preferred cars: the cars with bodies by James Young, Mulliner, and Hooper. These are tremendously impressive-looking, big cars, custom-made with fine materials and craftsmanship.

The Rolls-Royce Silver Shadows

The Silver Shadow is a very good car, but it does not stand head and shoulders above everything else in its price class. It just is not quite in the category of the Silver Clouds. The Silver Clouds are all luxury: large, beautifully finished inside and out. One simply installs a chauffeur in the front seat and, presto, the ultimate in prestige and elegant motoring! The Silver Shadow, by contrast, is a relatively small car, and it is slightly on the stubby side with little or no streamlining.

In summary, the Silver Shadows are luxury cars of relatively small size that one can drive anywhere with a modicum of trouble and a minimum waiting time for parts.

The Silver Shadow is an eight-cylinder car with overhead valves, and the engine is very much like the engine of the predecessor car—the Silver Cloud III. The displacement is identical —6,230 cubic centimeters. The cylinder heads on the new cars were redesigned and the chassis construction was monocoque, not with the body fastened onto the chassis in the fashion of the older model cars. The 1966 recommended list price was $18,676 in England with the pound sterling at $2.80. It was priced at about $2,800 more than the immediately preceding Silver Cloud III.

At the same time, a special James Young two-door custom sedan also was introduced for about $2,800 more, and this is one of the very much preferred, and premium, cars on today's investment car market.

In March 1966 another two-door custom car was introduced, this one an H. J. Mulliner, Park Ward. This car listed for about 10,000 pounds—$28,000—a good healthy price for the car. This car today is also at a great premium against the standard sedan, as is the car introduced in September 1967, the convertible by Park Ward. In October 1970, engine capacity was increased from 6,230 to 6,745 cubic centimeters, which gave the car more snap, but otherwise didn't do much.

In March 1971 the Corniche, a "special," was introduced, and these cars are very much in demand on today's market, at $40,000 up. The convertible can easily sell for twice the price of the standard sedan.

In 1978 the Silver Shadow II was introduced. It was something of an improvement on the Silver Shadow, but was far from being a newly designed car. On the rear trunk lid the Silver Shadow II designation appeared, so those looking at the car knew that the owner had the new model. The Silver Shadow started out in 1965–1966 priced at about $18,500 and rose to about $85,000 as of late 1980, when the Silver Shadow II cars were still being sold new in the United States.

In late 1980 the Silver Spirit came off the assembly line. It is a somewhat smoother, less boxy car than the Silver Shadow II. The price runs from $85,000 to about $120,000.

Prices of the Silver Shadows

The prices of Silver Shadows have increased by leaps and bounds. This price rise has by no means paralleled or been a by-product of the rise in the pound sterling. These are the English list prices of new Silver Shadows for a number of years after the car was introduced:

List Prices New of Rolls-Royce Silver Shadow Sedan

1966	6,670 pounds sterling	$18,500
1967	6,971	19,500
1968	7,960 (pound devalued)	19,100
1969	8,671	20,800
1970	9,925	23,800
1971	9,877	23,680

1972	10,550	25,300
1973	11,550	27,600
1974	13,116	31,400

From this 1974 model, prices went steadily up, until the price of the 1980 Silver Shadow peaked at about $85,000, and the new Silver Spirit was expected to sell for $85,000–$120,000 in the United States.

These rising prices tended to pull up the prices of all used Rolls-Royce Silver Shadows. The 1980 is very little different from the 1965 model. One might even buy a plate for his 1965 car which reads "Silver Shadow II" and affix it to the rear trunk lid. Not one out of ten people is going to catch you in this piece of upgrading!

In 1970 the prices of second-hand Silver Shadows probably hit their low point. One dealer had two Silver Shadows of the year 1967 for sale. He priced each of them at $8,750. This was by no means an unusually low price in this recession year. The cars were, after all, used cars, and they had little classic value three years after they came out of the factory.

Then a change took place in the market and in price levels of used Silver Shadows. To a degree, they came to be investment cars. They were not sports cars, were not yet classic cars, and most certainly were not antique cars. Nor were they particularly unique. Still, prices began to rise on the second-hand market. Brand new Silver Shadows dropped in price as soon as they were sold, but only for a time. Then prices started to rise, and they have been rising ever since. For that reason the Rolls-Royce can be considered the car with the "negative depreciation," because how many totally standard sedans are made that rise substantially on the second-hand market year after year?

As of 1981 the prices of used Silver Shadows ranged from about $22,000–$23,000 for the earliest model—the 1966—to about $65,000 for the 1979, and the newer the car the nearer the price approached the $85,000 new-car price. On the other hand, when the new Silver Spirit was announced, some dealers began advertising the 1980 Shadows brand new at something off the $85,000 list—just as new-car dealers advertise any leftover new cars once the new model car is announced. It is clear that the

1979 Silver Shadow at $65,000 is about market price, and that the 1966 at $22,000 is somewhere near a market price. But it is important to note that in 1979, $18,000 would buy a good Silver Shadow of the year 1966, but in 1980 the 1966 model price went up to $22,000–$23,000.

Now that the Silver Spirit has appeared on American highways and streets, the price of all Silver Shadow IIs may very well decline, because the Silver Shadow body model is not like the new body model and thus is somewhat out of date. At $22,000 for the 1966 model, however, the new appearance of the new Silver Spirit will not be quite so devastating!

The Silver Shadow Special Collectibles

There are a small number of Silver Shadows that are definitely investment cars. The convertibles are very much sought after. In 1967 (preceding the introduction of the Corniche in early 1971) only a few Silver Shadow convertibles could be found in the United States. In 1975 they probably hit a low point in value and could easily be bought, in good condition in England, for $15,000. By 1980 and early 1981 they were up to about $50,000 in the United States, and probably in England as well. There was a companion car, a two-door closed car, a coupe, that sold for perhaps $20,000 less than the convertible.

The Corniche coupe and convertible were built by the custom body firm of H. J. Mulliner, Park Ward. The English market version of the Corniche had 10 percent more horsepower than the standard Silver Shadow sedan and cost 10 percent more than its predecessor. Otherwise there were few improvements on the car as against the earlier model. The name plate Corniche on the back of the car did have some indefinable value, however. The convertible price in the United States at the time it was introduced was about $35,000, considerably more than for the standard sedan.

As of 1981 a 1971 Corniche convertible in fine condition costs about $60,000; the 1972 convertible costs $65,000; and the 1973, $75,000. The price does not rise greatly from this figure for the more recent cars.

The Rolls-Royce Camargue made its appearance on the scene

in 1975. This was an extremely high-priced car at the time it was introduced; it sold in the United States for about $85,000. Today the new car is quoted in certain countries, Italy included, at close to $200,000. The main feature about the Camargue is the Italian-style two-door body by Pininfarina. The body is supposed to combine the majesty of the Rolls-Royce with the rakishness of the Italian sports car. There are relatively few Camargues for sale on the second-hand or classic market, and there is not a great collector demand. As yet there is no market price, but no Camargue seems to have changed hands at under its original $85,000 price.

The Early Postwar Cars

As far as investment and appreciation are concerned, the most important Rolls-Royce cars are (1) the Silver Ghosts made from 1906 to 1925; (2) the Silver Cloud I, II, and III made from 1955 to 1965; and (3) the Silver Shadows made from 1965 through 1980, especially the convertibles.

The next type of Rolls-Royce to consider includes the models of the immediate postwar years—the Silver Wraith and Silver Dawn, made from 1947 to 1955. The Silver Dawn came out in 1949 and ended with the introduction of the Silver Clouds of 1955. Production on both the Wraiths and the Dawns ended in 1955.

Seven hundred sixty Silver Dawns were made in all, and about 1,800 Silver Wraiths. The Silver Dawn was made mainly with left drive, for export, but in 1953 it was placed in some volume on the English market. The car used a modified American General Motors Hydramatic transmission.

When the Silver Wraith appeared on the American market in 1947 (although some were certainly built in early 1946), the price was about $10,500, kept low by the fact that Rolls-Royce built the bodies itself, and did not use custom coachbuilders. This practice was continued with the Silver Dawn of 1949, and the price of this Western Hemisphere export car was about $14,000 —certainly a low price for the top car in the world.

These immediate postwar cars are not the most preferred cars on the collector-investor market. Not even the large and impressive Rolls-Royce cars of the period from 1947 to 1955 are desired; yet they are probably the most reliable, rugged Rolls-Royces ever built, and so are the equivalent-model Bentleys.

In 1970 the price range of a Silver Wraith or Silver Dawn four-door sedan in fine condition ranged from $5,000 to $6,000. The Silver Dawn might have been $1,000 more expensive than the Silver Wraith. Five years later, $15,000 was required to buy a good condition Silver Wraith or Silver Dawn. Average condition cars could be bought for $7,500 to $10,000.

By 1981 the price had risen to about $25,000 for a fine condition Silver Wraith or Silver Dawn with standard Rolls-Royce body. The custom-bodied cars sold for up to $10,000 more.

A very important collector's car is the convertible of all years of the Silver Wraith and Silver Dawn series. These convertibles, in fine condition, sold in late 1980 in the region of $60,000, sometimes a little less.

While there is certainly a new element in the standard Silver Shadow sedans (and certainly in the late model cars up to the model year 1981), there is little of this element in the Silver Wraiths and Silver Dawns. They are classic cars.

The Phantom Rolls-Royce

Many so-called new series of Rolls-Royce cars are pretty much the same as the preceding series. There are very few significant changes overall. The Silver Shadow II was not very different from the Silver Shadow I. The Camargue of 1975 was touted as something very special, but the only really special thing about it was a body much more Italian than English. Mechanically, the car was still very much the Silver Shadow.

The Phantom Rolls-Royces, on the other hand, were real innovations. They were far different from the preceding Silver Ghosts of 1906 to 1925. Rolls-Royce employed overhead valves, a more modern design than the flat-head engine: the shape of the combustion chamber is far more logical than that of the side-valve or flat-head engine.

The Phantoms had a bigger appearance, a more impressive look to them than the Silver Ghosts. They are beautiful driving cars. My first experience driving one was on a trip from New

York to Washington at night in the rain—and the body model was a town car in which the driver sits out in front, exposed to the elements. Still, even in the rain the car drove beautifully, and its operation and appearance could hardly have been improved upon. It was reliable, and the only trouble was the carburetor, whose sliding valve had to be cleaned periodically so that it would keep on sliding.

One of the finest Phantoms I have ever seen was the yellow convertible used in *The Great Gatsby*. An identical car was offered to me in 1940 for $550. The car today should sell for about $150,000.

By 1970 the Phantoms were real collector cars: a standard Phantom I sedan would bring over $5,000. An open car—touring or roadster—would bring $10,000 to $15,000, and any car made in the American Rolls-Royce plant located in Springfield, Massachusetts, would bring in the region of $10,000 up, even a limousine. In 1975 an ordinary Phantom I sedan would bring $15,000, but the Henley roadster or Ascot phaeton would bring upward of $50,000.

By 1981 a Phantom I Henley roadster sold for somewhere in the neighborhood of $80,000 and an Ascot phaeton for $75,000. The standard sedan sold in the range of $32,000 to $37,000. At this point the Phantom I was selling for a little more than the Silver Ghosts of the early 1920s, but of course the earlier Ghosts were great rarities and were selling very high. Cars from 1913 on back were selling at well over $100,000, and the earliest Ghosts approached $200,000.

The first Phantom was called the Phantom I, and it was made from 1925 to 1929, when the Phantom II was introduced. It was continued to 1935. The size of the Phantom IIs engine was exactly the same as the Phantom Is. Its springs were a bit different: half elliptic instead of the long cantilever springs of the earlier model. Many improvements, but no radical changes, were made. Anyone's opinion of an automobile must, to a great degree, be subjective. Still, after having ridden many hundreds of miles in a Phantom II, I feel that the ride of the Phantom I is better, and that the Phantom II seems heavy and a little bit harsh. Still, the II is an excellent car and, of course, a Rolls-Royce.

In 1970 the Phantom II sedan brought $5,000 to $6,000 and the convertible models about twice that figure. By 1975 ordinary Phantom II sedans were selling for about $12,000 or a little more. Exotic models, including fancy town cars and open cars, sold for at least twice this figure, and some fine-condition cars sold for $30,000 to $40,000. In October 1979, Christie's sold a Phantom II drop head coupe (convertible coupe) with Windovers body. The lines of the car were excellent, but the same cannot be said of all Phantoms. The paint, chrome, and leather were fairly poor, judging from the description of the car in the auction catalog. The car went for $50,000.

By 1981 a good Phantom II sedan was selling in the neighborhood of $35,000. A good Phantom II Henley roadster would bring $75,000.

The Phantom III was something unique: a very large and tremendously impressive-looking car with a V-12 cylinder engine. It was put out between 1936 and 1939. The total capacity of the engine was, however, roughly the same as in the six-cylinder Phantoms. The V-12 engine was a light and very compact unit apparently based on the Rolls-Royce aircraft engine. (It might also be mentioned that way back in 1905, Rolls-Royce pioneered with a V-8 engine.)

If a Rolls-Royce ever was panned by the automotive press, it has never come to my attention. The introduction of any new model Rolls-Royce is generally accompanied by rave notices. *Autocar* magazine's road test of the Phantom III concludes, "Somewhere is an ultimate in the highest expression of road travel comfort and performance, and the Phantom III is beyond question the nearest approach to it as yet." This comment appeared in the October 2, 1936, issue of the magazine.

The October 4, 1935, issue of *Autocar* says, however, "Today, what used to be called complication is of no moment; the multiplication of parts, provided it ensures their better functioning, is definitely of advantage, since we are long past the days when every single component added to a chassis was regarded as an almost certain cause of future trouble."

Herein lies the trouble with the Phantom III Rolls-Royce. It is an unusually complicated car with an unusually complicated engine. Some time ago I recommended that my friend, an aviation magazine editor, buy a Phantom III Rolls-Royce because I felt in many ways it was the ultimate car. It may well have been, but in the course of one year repairs ran to as much as the second-hand car had cost him. It was always in the repair shop and repairs were expensive. Still, complicated though it may be, I would like to own one of these machines made without regard to cost. If the car were made today, it would have to cost at least $200,000.

In 1970 a number of these Phantom IIIs were sold, and they brought about $6,000 to $8,000. There was no great demand for them as collectibles, and they were difficult and expensive to use as transportation.

In 1975 a closed car would sell for $15,000 to $20,000. A convertible was an entirely different proposition. It would bring $40,000 to $50,000. As late as 1977, I found a Phantom III town car in Norwalk, Connecticut, for $12,000. It was in fairly good condition, but the body style was by no means beautiful or usable.

By 1982 a standard sedan cost about $40,000, and a convertible sedan cost about $75,000. A boattail speedster (or roadster) could cost up to $100,000.

On July 9, 1979, Christie's of London sold a Phantom III saloon (sedan) for a little over $20,000. It had a fairly attractive Hooper body. Maintenance on the car appears to have been fairly good.

On February 25, 1979, Christie's held a sale in Los Angeles at the Convention Center. This sale included a fair-looking close-coupled Phantom III limousine with Hooper body (but not one of the finest-looking Hooper bodies). Engine, transmission, and suspension had been overhauled 1,000 miles prior to the Christie's sale, and the cosmetics were described as being generally good. The car sold for $26,000.

Christie's sold still another Phantom III December 13, 1979, in London. This was a very large seven-passenger limousine. It had a Freestone and Webb body. The car went for a little under $20,000.

The Leake sale held in Tulsa, Oklahoma, in June 1980, offered three Phantom IIIs for sale. Not one hit the reserve price of the owners, but a convertible did reach a high bid of $45,000.

The Phantom III is certainly not a car that can be used for transportation (but neither are the Phantom I and Phantom II). The Phantom III is a complicated automobile and something of a troublemaker. Still, if I could not afford one of the magnificent 770K "Hitler-type" touring cars, then I would be very nearly as happy owning a Rolls-Royce Phantom III convertible sedan. Regardless of how high in price it went, I would not be at all inclined to sell it. In many ways it is the way *Autocar* magazine describes it—the best car put out by the number one firm.

CHAPTER 4

MERCEDES-BENZ

A NEW, TOP-NOTCH SERIES OF BOOKS is coming off the press; one of the books is on Mercedes-Benz, its introduction written by the great racing driver Juan Manuel Fangio. The cover picture is of a Mercedes-Benz 500K roadster put out in the mid-thirties. The same car occupies a two-page, color spread inside the book. The inside front cover of the book pictures a Mercedes with the hood open revealing the engine. The car is a white SSK roadster; throughout the book, the SSK appears again and again.

Next, let's take a look at the Kruse Auctioneers compendium of car auction prices. One car dominates the cover of this book —a Mercedes-Benz 500K roadster.

Another important book, dealing with great cars of the golden age, has as its cover picture a 540K coming at the reader head on.

Mercedes-Benz in many ways epitomizes the great collector cars.

Quentin Craft, in his *Old Car Value Guides,* calls authentic classic cars those cars produced from 1925 through 1942. The year 1925 is pretty much the start of the great sophisticated classics, since only a few were put out a little earlier. It must be remembered that Ferrari didn't exist before the post-World War II period. Rolls-Royce was primarily a manufacturer of conservative super-luxury cars; rarely did they turn out anything that resembled a sports car. Their cars were not designed to appeal to the connoisseur of sports or racing cars. But Mercedes-Benz has turned out competition cars throughout most of the present century. Mercedes raced with enormous success in the Vanderbilt Trophy races on Long Island in the earliest years of present century. In 1926 the beginning of a great road-racing car came out of the Mercedes plant: the *K* model, for *kurz* (German for short). Its six-cylinder engine developed 160 horsepower, and the car did about 100 miles an hour. Rudolph Caracciola, probably the greatest of all Mercedes drivers, pretty much started his career with this *K*.

In 1927 the Mercedes plant turned out a car that was to make the entire reputation of the company as far as racing and sports cars are concerned—the *S* model (for sport). This car had a slightly larger engine—6.8 liters. It was known as the 36–120–180 and developed 120 horsepower without engaging the supercharger, and 180 with the supercharger. The driver engaged the supercharger by depressing the gas pedal to the floor, causing a terrible scream like an overloud siren. My first experience with true sports cars was with this model car, and I bought one way back in 1938, when Werner Maeder, the great Mercedes mechanic, demonstrated it for me.

In 1928 an even more powerful car appeared from the Mercedes-Benz factory: the 38–250 or model *SS*. It had a 7.1 liter capacity engine and may have produced 225 horsepower rather than the designated 250. Caracciola was a great success in competition with the SS. The SS was my second sports car; I owned both the S and the SS at the same time. SS stood for "super sports."

In 1928 there also appeared the crowning achievement of this series of cars—the much-celebrated Mercedes SSK, featured on the cover of many books on collectible cars, sports cars, and racing. SSK stands for "short super sports" (kurz—for short). It developed 225 horsepower from the same essential engine used in the SS.

There is still another car, an almost nonexistent ultra-ultra car, the racing SSK, or SSKL, with a large "elephant blower" that forced the engine to turn out about 300 horsepower. It is possible that the SSK exceeded 150 miles per hour; the SSKL's top speed was anyone's guess. It was on the SSK series that Rudi Caracciola rose to the top rung of the world's racing drivers. The *L* stood for "light in weight" (*leicht*).

If I were asked to pick out five of the greatest of all prewar classic cars, the SSK and the 540K (or 500K) would have to be included. The 500K and the 540K are very similar; I owned them both at the same time and drove both regularly for pleasure and on business. As far as the S, SS, and SSK are concerned, regular driving use is not possible. The chances would be very great of having a breakdown, and then being stuck with no repairs in sight. Yet of all of the series of Mercedes-Benz cars to own as investments, prime cars may well be the S, SS, and SSK series. These cars were a monumental achievement for the Mercedes company, and they established the company as the producer of race winners. At the same time, the cars were beautiful and important looking, particularly for the times. As performers, they were far far ahead of almost anything made anywhere, and their only rivals were the Italians, particularly Alfa Romeos and Maseratis.

The Mercedes-Benz Model K, made earlier than the S, SS, and SSK, occasionally appears for sale, but relatively few of this model exist. The cars earlier than the K are not on the market in any volume, except very occasionally some early car that has historical interest.

An S-Series Car as an Investment Collectible

As far as pure investment goes, an S series is one of the best —not just of Mercedes-Benz, but of all investment cars. The S, SS, and SSK cars are very much wanted by a widespread group of buyers who have the wherewithal to buy and who know the car and want it.

The car has distinctive looks. At worst, it is a rather stark-looking automobile, particularly with an Erdmann and Rossi body such as I had on my S five-passenger convertible. At best, the car is low and sleek and looks as though it is traveling rapidly even when it is standing still.

Unless the car is in reasonably good condition, it is expensive and difficult to put into mint condition *if* mechanical work is required and parts are needed. Parts are not readily obtainable for this car, and some parts may well have to be made—at considerable cost. Additionally, there are few mechanics left who can work on any of the S-series cars. This is especially unfortunate since the car definitely is not as reliable as one might wish; therefore, it is of limited use as far as long trips are concerned.

Certain components of the car are overcomplicated. The supercharger blows through the carburetors; it does not pick up the mixture of gasoline and air *after* it leaves the carburetors, but rather before it reaches them. The blast seems to get the jets "unsynchronized," particularly if there is any dirt whatever in the gasoline. There was a filter at the neck of the tank to catch dirt, but dirt still gets in the gas and gets stuck in the jets. The driver must always have with him a jet wrench, which he regularly uses to unscrew the two jets and blow them out, maybe as often as once each time the car is used.

There is no dip stick for measuring oil; instead, there is a kind of turnaround valve which leaks some oil on the ground if there is enough oil in the crankcase. This valve sometimes gets stuck or filled with dirt and won't allow a flow, even if there is enough oil. Then the crankcase must be dropped and the valve cleaned out. I learned this very quickly from Chief Mercedes Mechanic Maeder, when I bought my first S-series car.

Instead of using the time-proven Bendix drive starter, the car uses a complicated and unreliable sliding-armature starter. The key is turned on and the starter button on the dash pushed. This push moves the entire armature on the starting motor forward toward the engine and its ring gear. When the armature has traveled a certain distance, it trips a switch that starts the motor rotating—when the starter gear and the ring gear are meshed. But very often you must take up the floor boards and push in the armature with a screw driver or some other tool so that it engages and starts to turn.

The choke is something to talk about! It is simply a hand pump on the dash which pumps raw gas into the carburetors —only sometimes the packing isn't tight enough and the pump sprays raw gas over the driver who is trying to start the car.

In some ways the gearing could be better. The car goes backward almost as fast as it goes forward, and the high gear is high indeed!

When one is going along at speed, it is best to grip the steering wheel as though for grim death. If one hits a bump, the steering wheel may break out of one's grip and slam into the hand or break off a fingernail. I have broken many fingernails in this way.

The clutch requires a weight lifter to push it in, particularly if the drive is a long one and one becomes fatigued.

Still, with all these drawbacks, I believe I would rather own an SSK than any other prewar classic car; I *know* I would rather own an SSKL than any other car with the possible exception of the 540K roadster.

Price Trends of the Mercedes S, SS, and SSK

In the late 1930s these cars were worth literally nothing. Almost everyone felt they were distinguished cars and that many of them were beautiful. But they were simply second-hand cars no one wanted to buy. A few of the more exotic ones were offered for sale by the major dealers on Fifty-seventh Street, New York; these were priced at $2,000 to $3,000, in show condition.

The rest of the cars were essentially something that the dealer wanted to get rid of. My own first sports car, a Mercedes S five-passenger convertible with Erdmann and Rossi body, apparently had been taken in trade by THE Mercedes-Benz dealer and repair shop—Number One in New York. The car was in reasonably good condition and was sold to me for $350.

Less than a year later I bought an SS for $550 from the Liberty Warehouse in New York, a sales organization operated by two ex-race drivers, Ray Gilhooly and Neil Whalen. (Gilhooly was the father of the common expression, "He pulled a Gilhooly." An unfortunate accident while Ray was racing at Indianapolis resulted in the birth of this expression.)

During this prewar period, I followed the prices and sales of Mercedes-Benz cars very closely. A completely overhauled five-passenger convertible, an S-model, which was not a beautiful car but a car in top condition, sold for $500. Whalen and Gilhooly had a succession of Mercedes-Benz S- and SS-models for sale, and I inspected at least a half dozen of them. The top one was priced at $750. One even had a superb paint job that Ray Gilhooly said had cost the incredible sum of $250. It was in this period that Jim Nutman of Dean Street, Brooklyn, was junking models S and SS and selling the metal and the parts. All one had to do was to tell Mr. Nutman to be on the lookout for a good, say, SS five-passenger tourer, and presto, you would eventually get one for maybe $500.

During the war, the prices of these cars rose only a bit, and I had trouble selling my S for $500 and my SS for $750, although I advertised rather extensively. The market was no better right after the war. In the early 1950s it began to rise a bit, mainly because some of these old cars needed a rather extensive refurbishing—and refurbishing prices were rising. In the early 1950s I tried out a reconditioned SS tourer with a superb leather interior, priced at $2,500. An SS came over from Germany, a five-passenger cabriolet, not the best-looking model, priced in Queens at $1,800. Even as late as 1965, prices were not much above these levels. In fact, the collector car market as late as 1965 had not elevated much beyond war-year levels.

But by 1970, prices had risen a tremendous amount, and the S and SS models were bringing around $10,000. Restoration costs were rising rapidly also, and a mint condition car could bring an average of $15,000. Of course Jim Nutman's operation (and many other operations like his) had materially reduced the supply of these cars; also, during the war any car with aluminum in it, and copper too, tended to be sacrified to the war effort. Such cars rarely appeared on the market in 1970.

By 1975 one could still get an S or an SS with a desirable body, a car in average condition, for a little under $10,000. However, in the mid-1970s, people were restoring more and more with quality and perfection in mind, and restoration costs were rising very rapidly. The average cost of such cars in near-mint condition started at $30,000, and Quentin Craft reported a very desirable model, the S speedster, bringing $51,000.

By early 1979 these cars had come into their own. Christie's in California sold an SS roadster for $320,000, a price so high it would have been hard to forecast. This price was probably above the overall market in 1979, but as of 1982 a mint condition SSK might well bring in the neighborhood of $500,000.

The 500 Series Cars as Investment Collectibles

All cars of the 500 series are among the best investment collectibles. They are not as rare as the S series, but they are in greater demand. Like the S series, the price on every 500 series car is high, no matter what the condition of the car. Prices have tended to rise fairly steadily for at least a decade; now nothing goes much under the mid-five–figure range.

The cars are more workable than those of the S series: they are easier to work on and parts are more available. But compared with the later Mercedes-Benz cars, 500 repairs are not as easy and parts are not as readily available.

Almost every 500-series car is big and impressive, and beautiful in body design. A few, like the 500K, 540K, and even the 380K roadsters, are some of the most beautifully designed cars that ever came off an assembly line—by today's standards as well as the standards of the 1930s, when the cars were produced. They are eye-stoppers wherever they are driven or displayed.

Compared with the S-series cars, which can hardly be driven today since repairs are far more difficult, the 500 cars can still be driven. Mechanically, the 500 series is far more sophisticated and more refined than the S series, and the 500 series car is much more like the modern luxury sports car. I have had the experience of owning and driving an S and an SS in the same time period—the late 1930s. In the 1940s I owned and drove a 500K and a 540K. In each time period the Mercedes cars were the only cars I owned, and I had to use them to travel to and from the office and to make trips, some of 200 to 300 miles. The

500 series was more reliable as well as more comfortable than the S series, by far. It is just possible that a 500K or a 540K could be used for occasional transportation today, although because of the investment and the difficulty and cost of repairs, such use is certainly not recommended.

Price Trends of the 500K and 540K Series

I bought my first car of this series in 1942. These cars were turned out in Germany in some volume from 1934 until the war, with perhaps some during the early war years. *Art and Industry Magazine* put out an illustrated article on this series, and the cars deserve recognition as art. The designs were superb, and at the top of the superb group is the standard road-ster—both 500K and 540K. When it first appeared, the sports car purists rejected it as being an "overblown," overstuffed product of Hitler's Germany, decidedly inferior in body style to the great SSK. Maybe so, but people got used to the new lines and accepted them as a standard of beauty in car bodies.

In the early years of the war, both the 500K and the 540K were simply second-hand cars, and price was related to what the cars cost new. My own 540K was a coupe, and I bought it from the race car owner, Dr. Sabourin, for $1,500. He wanted more, but he took my offer with two cars in part payment, since he needed the tires on one of my cars for his Duesenberg, and such tires could not be bought during the war. At the time, I would say a fair price for a fine convertible would have been $3,500 and for the great roadster, $5,000. About a year later, I bought a fine 500K convertible with body by the English firm Corsica for $1,550. It was in very good mechanical condition. Later during the war, I sold the 540K for $3,700 and the 500K to the Chicago Duesenberg dealer for $2,400. This was the market at the time.

The predecessor of the 500K was the 380K. To find the engine displacement in cubic centimeters one simply adds a zero. The 500K thus has approximately 5,000 cubic centimeters of engine displacement. Since each 1,000 cubic inches of displacement equals 60 cubic inches, the 500K has an engine capacity of 300 cubic inches.

A superb 540K roadster in the early 1950s could be purchased for $5,000. The cars were certainly no longer second-hand cars but now were rapidly becoming collector cars. In 1970 the 500K and 540K series were still not the preferred collectibles, the S- and SS-series cars were. An average condition 500K or 540K could be bought in 1970 for less than $10,000. A mint-condition one could easily be bought for $15,000 or a little less.

But five years later, in 1975, this series car had finally taken off. An average-condition car would cost about $20,000. A convertible or cabriolet would bring $40,000, and a fine and beautiful roadster would bring $75,000. In 1979, Christie's in California hit the jackpot when a magnificent 500K sold at auction in Los Angeles for the huge sum of $400,000. The car was just right, and the market was there to pay a top price for this top car.

By 1981, 500K and 540K cars with fine bodies and in fine condition were selling for close to $150,000. Cars with less desirable bodies would sell for far less. My own 540K coupe for four passengers, which I had sold near the end of the war for $3,700, might well have sold in 1981 for $55,000!

There is one final car in the series that might be mentioned; although it does not have a "500" designation, it is most certainly based on the 500 series. This is the 770K—a 7,700 cubic-centimeter giant of a car, supercharged, the *K* standing for *Kompressor*, as in the case of the 500K and 540K. It apparently was first put out in 1935, and its production was continued well into World War II.

The 770K tourer is one of the most impressive cars ever built, and it showed off Hitler, standing in the back seat, to perfection. Hitler's car is advertised for sale from time to time, but there are really many of these cars still extant, since many high-ranking members of the Nazi party and many military personnel had them. These special display-of-might cars can sell for anything; I have seen one advertised for $750,000.

When they first arrived in the United States they were known as "The Grosser Mercedes" (big Mercedes), and they were not much favored by the buying public. Even the New York Mercedes dealer, Jacques Schaerly, manager of Charles Zumbach Mercedes, did not push them. The reason he gave was that parts never came over with the car and thus repairs were difficult and took a long time.

During the war I looked at a 770K convertible sedan for sale in Cambridge, Massachusetts. It appeared to be in good condition and was offered for $750. No one seemed to want this "great buy." In the middle of the 1970s this "Hitler" 1940 Model 770K eight-passenger phaeton sold for $125,000. The "Hitler" 1941 Model 770K eight-passenger convertible brought $125,000. Maybe they were Hitler's own cars!

In the October 1980 *Hemmings Motor News*, an individual in Stuttgart, Germany, advertised a 770K for sale. This was a 1937 two-door cabriolet, said to be the car of the former Yugoslavian prince regent—in part restored and some "negligible parts missing." It was a good-looking, well-proportioned, big car carrying an asking price of $85,000. This was a very low price for this car, almost without regard to condition of the car or parts missing.

The Postwar Mercedes-Benz Investment Cars: The 300SL Coupe and Roadster

The 300SL gullwing coupe appeared for sale in 1954 and was continued to 1957; in this period fourteen hundred 300SLs were made. They seemed to sweep all road racing competitors aside. The top speed was probably well over 150 miles per hour.

When new, the gullwing was almost certainly the greatest postwar sports car. It cost $6,820 when it first appeared, and by 1957 the price was still low at $8,905. I had the privilege of being driven in one such car by Frederick Moscovics, former president of Marmon-Herrington and of Stutz Motor Company. Fred Moscovics told me in no uncertain terms that he had driven more miles on the highway at over 100 miles per hour than any other man who ever lived. He stated that his gullwing had cost him $7,500, which seemed a big sum at the time but was not really any money for this quality car.

Over the years I have seen few gullwings for sale, and certainly few gullwings at anything like low prices. The cars were favorites of every connoisseur from the start and are favorites today. In 1970 the 300SL gullwing sold in fine condition for about $6,000, not very much less than it cost new. Five years later, the price of an excellent condition car was about $15,000. In 1977 the price had risen to about $25,000 for a top quality gullwing; by 1979 the price of a similar condition car was over $50,000. This is one car that seems to rise in price monthly, and by 1981 a mint-condition gullwing could cost $100,000.

The 300SL gullwing coupe is the most desirable and the highest-priced Mercedes of all the postwar cars. It is the most desirable because it was, and still is, a design and performance standout. The doors open upward so the car somewhat resembles a gull. There is a 300SL convertible coupe with detachable hard top that theoretically should sell at a general price level equal to the gullwing's, only it didn't and doesn't. The 300SL convertible coupe is a beautiful car that performs well. The trouble is that expert opinion favors the gullwing, which does seem to handle better than the convertible. Perhaps the unique design of the doors created a charisma that still surrounds the gullwing. The doors hinge upward instead of outward, and the gullwing is often pictured with the doors open.

One of the enormous troubles with owning high-performance sports and classic cars is their unreliability. They are temperamental, and to get top horsepower output and torque they are highly stressed in every way. Getting 400-plus horsepower out of 4,000-cubic-centimeter engines like the Lamborghini Miura and Countach requires *complication*—multi-carburetors or fuel injection, critical camshaft cut and cam overlap, very high compression, very light-weight materials, and, almost always, a multi-cylinder engine, often twelve cylinders.

On the other hand, the postwar-production Mercedes-Benz is a *relatively* simple automobile with a relatively simple and extremely rugged engine. All postwar six-cylinder Mercedes cars have rugged engines that give far less trouble than twelve cylinders, the number so popular with the late highest-performance cars. (Of course, Ferrari started with a twelve-cylinder engine very early in his career.)

The six-cylinder 300SL engine is essentially the same engine as that used in the earlier postwar 300-series passenger cars not built for racing. The engine is not large, with a little under 3,000 cubic centimeters (180 cubic inches), the same capacity as the Ferrari 250GT. The frame is extremely rigid. The output of the engine, with fuel injection, is about 243 horsepower, about the same as that of the Ferrari 250GT, and the Mercedes engine will keep on going at 6,500 revolutions per minute, mile after mile.

The transmission is a rugged, four-speed unit, and it too derives from the passenger cars of the 300 series. While there is independent suspension front and rear, the rear is a swing-axle arrangement: the axles move up and down with the wheels. Still, this swing-axle arrangement gave little trouble in the Mercedes cars that I owned. It is a rugged spring mechanism, but it works.

On March 29, 1980, Christie's auctioned a number of cars in Los Angeles. Lot twenty-two was a very attractive, red gullwing.

This car appeared to be in excellent original condition, and it looks it from the picture. The price estimate was $40,000 to $50,000 as against $20,000 to $28,000 for the poorer condition gullwing Christie's had sold the year before. In the auction, this car brought $39,000.

One cannot always expect one sale to exactly measure the market on a particular car. The price of a particular car may be more or less than reasonable price estimates would indicate to be its value. This car was simply a good buy for someone. It was bought in a down period in the investment car market, and the market did not strengthen until the fall of 1980. In March 1980 I purchased two cars, both on the bargain side, and the seller in each case was willing to make me considerable price concessions.

In 1957, Mercedes came out with the roadster (convertible), the 300SL in open form. The 300SL roadster sold for a little over $11,000 when new, and the model was continued until 1962. It drives well, although it is no great competition car and the acceleration is anything but fierce.

By 1970, $5,000 would buy a very good 300SL roadster, and at that time there were few more rakish or better-proportioned sports cars for sale. By 1975 the price had about doubled, causing more of the cars to be drawn into the market. By early 1982,

$35,000 seemed about the modal price for a good 300SL road-
ster. In the fall of 1980 a very good 300SL roadster that we had
inspected sold on the East Coast for $35,000.

The 300S

The 300S was and is unique—very different from the 300SL
although both cars use essentially the same engine. The 300SL
is a sports-competition car of the first order, and in its day it
pretty much swept the field. The 300S, on the other hand, is a
very conservative super-luxury car, a gentleman's car that the
Mercedes-Benz Company may well have considered a rival of
the Rolls-Royce—except that the series included no sedan, only
a coupe, a roadster, and a convertible with cabriole bars.

The car is absolutely top quality throughout and, in its way,
the equal of Rolls-Royce. The 300S is a classic-looking car, in its
body design really a throwback to the 1930s and early 1940s. It
looks very much like the 500K and 540K but is smaller and a
little less rakish. It performs at least as well as the 540K without
the complications of the supercharger of the 500K or 540K. It
uses three Solex carburetors; these rarely give trouble and are
almost always in synchronization.

The 300S first appeared in 1951 and was continued through
1957. In the early years the three Solex carburetors were used,
but in 1956 fuel injection was inaugurated; on today's market
the fuel-injected cars command something of a premium.

The cars sold new for about a Rolls-Royce price. As with
almost all used cars, the price declined after it was purchased
new, and in 1955 I purchased a 300S cabriolet for $4,500, about
market price (that is, my fiancée purchased the car for me as a
birthday present).

In 1955 the cars with the three carburetors were still being
produced, and the earlier 300S cars were simply regarded as
used automobiles. In 1957 I was able to purchase a 1953 near-
mint 300S roadster, not the cabriolet, for $4,000. In 1959 I pur-
chased another cabriolet in good, but not mint, condition, for
$2,800.

The price of these used 300S cars seemed to go steadily down,
although when I sold mine, I managed to make a profit. The

bottom occurred in the years 1966–1970. In both 1966 and 1970 I located very good cabriolets for sale at $1,900. I purchased my last 300S in 1966 for $800, but the car required much work, and I did a ground-up restoration. The cost of that restoration, with superb leather interior, new chrome, and a twelve-coat lacquer paint job, was about $4,000. Over the years I spent $1,700 more on the car, making a total investment of $6,500. Today the car certainly would bring at least $30,000 at auction; retail it might well bring $50,000 or more.

By 1975 the 300S was selling in the $10,000 range. By 1979 the price level of the 300S—roadster, cabriolet, and coupe—was a little over $30,000 and at times as high as $35,000. A dealer in Westchester County, New York, stated that he had sold a mint condition 300S cabriolet for $47,000.

By 1980 at least one car was advertised for $60,000, and another for $40,000. The price level was thus probably around $50,000. The level of the model 300 *four-door* convertible was a surprisingly high $25,000, for until fairly recently this car was not much of a collector's automobile. A good car, it is now very popular and much wanted. The model 300 *sedan* is not really much of a collector car but about fifteen years ago the sedan could be bought for a little over $1,000, and in 1967 I found a very good one with air conditioning—one that had belonged to a Mercedes-Benz executive—for $1,200. In 1981 these sedans averaged about $10,000.

The 600 Mercedes

In 1963, Mercedes started to turn out a super-super luxury car, the enormous and tremendously impressive-looking model 600 with, as the designation implies, a 6,000 cubic centimeter engine. This was a V-8 with one cam on each bank of cylinders, and automatic everything. It has self-leveling air suspension, adjustable shock absorbers, disc brakes all around, automatic transmission, and instead of individual electric motors, hydraulic operation of windows and everything else. The only fault is that the car is overcomplicated; another possible fault is its square shape. Over a period of time, however, one got used to the square shape and it looks rather massively impressive.

When the 600 first appeared in the United States, a team from the factory often came to the repair shops to show how to repair this very complicated car. "Above all," cautioned the factory team, "you must be patient with this car and be prepared to spend time on repairs." The team was certainly correct! It is overcomplicated and not the most reliable car ever made by any means.

At first, the car was hard to sell in the United States, particularly as it was priced above $20,000. The Greenwich, Connecticut, Mercedes dealer had one in stock for a long time and offered it to me for $18,000 in the mid-sixties. In 1970 these cars hit a low point in the market, and I found a fine one in Germany on the floor of the Mercedes showroom for the equivalent of $6,000. As late as the mid-seventies the 600 in America might have been bought for as little as $8,000 or even less.

In the mid-seventies I had a choice between buying a 600 Mercedes and a Rolls-Royce Silver Cloud. I chose the Cloud, a car that gives far less trouble than the 600 Mercedes. But by 1981 the 600 was in great demand, both the enormous Pullman and the standard four-door sedan. A car in good condition particularly a later model car, would bring in excess of $20,000. Even an older 600 would bring $15,000 or more, although once in a while a 600 in average condition was advertised at a little under $10,000.

In 1968 the Mercedes-Benz development engineer, Erich Waxenberger, on his own and in his spare time, based a car on the big engine of the 600 series (actually the engine was a 6,329, not 6,000, cubic centimeter engine, but the 600 designation was close enough, and, I suppose, the Mercedes company did not want to call their super, luxury 600 the "6.329").

The big engine was installed in a 300 sedan, and the new car was called the 300SEL 6.3. It was, in effect, a powerhouse. It was almost certainly the highest performance sedan put out at that time or previously by any automobile company anywhere —at least any production sedan car offered for sale. It sold for $14,000, then a high price, and it was good for 130 miles an hour.

In 1975 the 300SEL 6.3 sold for $8,000 to $10,000. The later models of 1971 and 1972 brought up to $12,000. The 300SEL 6.3

is one car that has actually declined in price for two or three years before 1982. Mercedes has come out with more modern-looking bodies, and the sedan body of the 6.3 looks dated. The 6.3 is now being offered for $8,000 in some cases, and even less.

One thing that hurt the value of these collector cars was the fact that Mercedes came out with an even bigger engine in the late 1970s, the 450SEL 6.9, an engine of roughly 6,900 cubic centimeters—almost 420 cubic inches. The 6.3, a sedan, normally was powered by a 4,500 cubic centimeter engine. The 6.9 possibly eclipsed the highest performing sedan ever built—the 6.3. At a price of over $50,000 the 6.9 should have been a performer! The 6.9 went out at the end of the decade, and the price of the car is still not far from what it was new.

The Cars of the 300 Series as Investment Collectibles

The investor-collector seeking some distinction can find it in the ownership of a 300 series Mercedes-Benz. These cars stand very near the top, possibly at the very top, of distinctive cars of the postwar period. Most of these cars were rising in value fairly rapidly as of 1981. The highest risers pricewise are the gullwing, the 300SL roadster, and the 300S cabriolet and roadster. Of these, the most-wanted cars are the 300S cabriolet, the 300S roadster, and the gullwing, in that order. The 300SL roadster comes last, but certainly not least. The car is not very hard to find on the market, but it is rising in value.

The 300 sedan, not a great collector item, has been rising in value. Ten years ago, the 300 four-door *convertible* was not in any great demand; today it is, and if one cannot get the conservative and elegant 300S he might then look for the four-door convertible. You might choose between this car and the 300S coupe which, until fairly recently, was not as popular as the 300S roadster and cabriolet.

Very important, the 300-series cars are reliable cars. They are not temperamental. They keep on running. They can be used for everyday transportation, although at present price levels there are few people who would want to do so. A 300S roadster sits in my garage, and I do not hesitate to bring it out to visit someone if my "for use" car is otherwise occupied or in for servicing. The 300S always starts up, runs well, and gets me there and back.

There are a few faulty parts and quirks in these cars, though they are built ruggedly for service. One problem the 300S cars have is the differential, which tends to develop a hum, particularly if at some point its lubrication was delayed. The differential is hard to rebuild, and a replacement is practically unobtainable anywhere. The body parts such as fenders also are practically unobtainable, as is the radiator cap with star. On the other hand, most parts do not go wrong, and simple substitutions can be made. Often the parts can be rebuilt.

The ride of these cars is a firm ride and the overhead cam engine is not very quiet; the Rolls-Royce and Bentley of the same years are far more quiet. The 300 series harks back to its history of competition, when performance meant more than soundlessness.

The Mercedes 220 and 220S

The 220 model was introduced in 1951, along with the 300 and 300S models. This move in effect put the Mercedes-Benz Company into high gear for the first time since the war ended. The 220 had, as the model number indicates, a 2,200 cubic centimeter engine. (This engine was based on the earlier 170S with only a 1,700-cubic-centimeter capacity, a four-cylinder car, whereas the 220 was a six-cylinder car. The 170S convertible is a classic and commands quite a premium for what the car is. I owned a 1950 model 170S in 1952, which I purchased for $1,500. It was a good-driving and a good-looking car, but very much underpowered.) The model 220 produced only 80 horsepower, but that probably was sufficient; in any event, the 220 convertible was a very well designed car and not far from Rolls-Royce in quality.

The 220 was and is quality all through, but it is not in the class of the top-quality Mercedes of the entire postwar period —the 300S. The most desirable 220 convertible to buy is the early convertible, since the lines are not far inferior to the lines of the 300S. This model was produced until 1954, when the more sophisticated 220S was introduced. The lines became a bit different and perhaps not as good or as classic as those of the 220; but the 220S was as much of a success in the market (and with collectors) as the earlier 220 cars.

By 1961 an even less-classic 220 series with a much larger body came out, and this car too is a collector's item and commands a high price.

The convertibles of the 220 series are well proportioned. The earlier 220 models and the 220S models are beautiful cars. The later cars put out in the 1960s for five or six passengers, the coupes and convertibles, are less beautiful but still very much in demand at premium prices.

The cars are very well made, very reliable, and generally not temperamental. This means that unless the investment is very great, the cars can be used for almost daily transportation. As prices rise and parts become more scarce, the cars will be used less and less for daily transportation. Ten years ago there were many 220S models used by housewives to go to the supermarket—not so today. Still, the 220-series cars are more usable than the 300-series cars, especially as second cars for occasional business or social visits.

Repairs on the 220-series cars have not been difficult or very expensive because the cars are not hard to work on and parts are still available from the dealers at fairly reasonable prices. Fifteen years ago, parts for the 300S and 300SL series were easily available at dealers' shops, and prices were not high. Today, most parts for these cars are not available. Parts for the 220-series cars are going off dealers' shelves, too. Many parts are, however, still available.

As investments, the cars on which to concentrate are the 220 of the early 1950s, followed by the 220S models of the later decade—the convertibles, rather than the coupes. The 220 models (with various letters added) of the 1960s come next, and many of these cars are usable because they have a full back seat. Still, these cars are not the collector cars that the two-passenger cars of the earlier years are.

In the 1950s these 220 and 220S models were simply secondhand cars and did not have any particular value. In 1970 they were still not in much demand, and $2,500 would buy a good one. One housewife in Greenwich bought a 220S convertible then as a present for her husband. That seemed to be the final straw and he walked out, never to return. Too bad for him! He could have stayed and seen his investment go up ten years later to at least $15,000 and perhaps to $20,000!

By 1975 the 220 and 220S cars were pushing $10,000. The later and larger 220SE was about at the same price level, perhaps a little lower. By 1980 the early 1950s cars were close to $30,000 in price, and the later 220S cars were selling for around $20,000, some lower than this figure. The 220s were in the class of the 300S for classic buyer interest.

The 450SL and its Antecedents

In the July 1965 issue of *Car and Driver* there was a full page advertisement on the inside of the back cover which read:

Men of whatever age or means might do well to stay out of flirting range of the Mercedes 230SL.

Lest they become involved.

For this classy, sporty young one knows an uncanny lot about men and what it takes to make them fall in love with a fine motorcar.

The 230SL is a two-seater roadster. And so much more!

Its loving heart of a fuel injection engine will beat all day at 125 m.p.h.

The Mercedes-Benz 230SL starts under $6,300. Model shown: $6,395.

Maybe this ad exaggerated a little as to performance, but not as to price. This car in the mid-sixties was a great buy at $6,000-plus.

The 230SL, a six-cylinder, overhead-cam sports car, was introduced at the Geneva Auto Show in 1963. It was an immediate success from design and sales points of view. The 230SL roadster began to hit the market in 1964. The 230SL has a 2,300-cubic-centimeter engine, comparable in size to the standard 220 engine. As of early 1982 a fine condition 230SL is worth $10,000 *more* than it cost new in 1964 and 1965.

The 230SL was only the beginning of this sporty series, however. These cars came in coupe and roadster form, and these two body models were made, as the series progressed, with larger and larger engines. In 1966 the engine size was raised, and the current cars were known as the 250 SL roadster and coupe. In 1968 the engine size was raised for both coupe and roadster to 2,800 cubic centimeters—for the 280SL.

As of early 1971 about 50,000 of these 230SLs, 250SLs and 280SLs had been made, with six-cylinder overhead-camshaft engines. In 1971 a new series was introduced, with a V-8 engine —the 350SL roadster and coupe. The old six-cylinder engine was placed in some of the cars sold even after introduction of the new V-8.

The present model 450SL was first introduced in 1973, and the engine was, as indicated, considerably larger than the engine in the predecessor model—4,500 cubic centimeters. As of 1980 a 5,000-cubic-centimeter engine was installed, and the series became known, at least in Europe, as the 500 series. Some of the 5,000-cubic-centimeter cars were still known and designated as 450SLC 5.0—for some reason!

Many 450SLs are on the market, and price tends to depend on how old the cars are. The newer the cars, the higher the price, because these cars are essentially second-hand cars of the model being produced now. The latest car, the 500SL, sells in Europe for over $50,000, but none seems to have been imported into the U.S. as of 1981.

In late 1980 a new model 450SLC was advertised for $39,000, about market for a current 450SL. Two 1973 models were advertised for $13,500 and $14,900. A 1976 model was advertised for $22,500; and this is the pattern.

The 230SL is a six-cylinder car. In fact many of the greats turned out by Mercedes-Benz over the years had six-cylinder engines, usually with a long stroke, an engine that was rugged and could take hard driving and even abuse. It rarely had to be taken apart, at least as compared with the Italian multi-cylinder cars.

Perhaps the 230SL was the successor to the 190SL, but the 190SL was vastly different. It only sounds as though it is the predecessor to the 230SL because of its name. The 190SL is a four-cylinder car, with engine design very much like the 300, but with two fewer cylinders. For a Mercedes, this was no high performance car, but it did manage a top speed of about 118. In 1970, $2,000 would easily buy a 190SL roadster, a pretty, simple, reliable car, but no standout for looks or performance. Incidentally, this car was the choice of the Smithsonian Museum curator of land transportation, Smith Hempstone Oliver, and he looked a long time for a suitable 190SL, which he bought in the late 1950s for about $1,600. The car first appeared on the American scene in 1956 and was continued through 1963.

By 1975 the price range of a fine condition 190SL was between $4,000 and $5,000. By 1978 prices had risen a bit, and one might cost $7,500—although average-condition cars could still be bought on occasion for $5,000. In 1981, $10,000 was the modal price of these cars, and fine-condition 190SLs sold for $12,000 and even a bit more.

The 230, 250, and on up to 450SL series of cars are quasi-investment cars. The 230SL series led up to the 450SL and finally to the 500SL, each car being something of an improvement on the former models, mainly in the form of a larger engine and finally a V-8 instead of a straight-six engine.

The earliest cars are definitely investment cars, but the latest cars are probably not. Thus the 230SL is an investment car worth far more than it cost new, while the 1980 450SL is worth less than it cost new. It will continue to decline in value for a while and then move up. In the meantime the earlier 450SL cars sell for more than they cost new. The new car price holds a price umbrella over these older cars, besides their being *something* of an investment car even though less than ten years old.

To buy a strict investment car, one should probably buy the earlier series up through the 350SL. As the next choice, one should probably buy the *earlier* 450SLs, as they are definitely moving up in price. These cars are good-looking cars and have a good reputation. In addition, they are cars of the country club set and to a great extent are considered marks of distinction and success.

The cars can and are used for transportation anywhere and everywhere—from the recent 500SL back to the 230SL. They are fairly reliable, although not in the class of, say, the Volkswagen! Repairs can be secured but are by no means as inexpensive as on less expensive cars of today. Fortunately, parts are not overwhelmingly expensive, and are not in the category of parts for, say, a Rolls-Royce.

These cars are certainly not in the class of the greats put out by Mercedes-Benz: the S series, the 500K, the 540K, the 300S, the 300SL, and many other real sports and competition cars. They are very good commercial cars. They are relatively easy to run and maintain, and they are small, so running expenses are not as great as for the larger and more important cars turned out by the firm in times past. They are also reasonably good-looking cars. Their engineering is up to date, so the cars perform very well.

CHAPTER 5

FERRARi

THE GREATEST SPORTS CAR of the postwar era is the Ferrari. It is also the most prominent road-racing car, and since Mercedes-Benz gave up producing road-racing cars in 1955, there has been little competition for the Ferrari.

Enzo Ferrari was the most innovative and enterprising automobile manufacturer in the entire postwar era. He made more automobiles of diverse design than any other manufacturer, running the gamut of four cylinder, straight-six cylinder, V-six cylinder, eight cylinder, and twelve cylinder, with single overhead camshafts and with double overhead camshafts. His latest and finest car of the line is a double overhead camshaft twelve with two banks of opposed cylinders. He has even experimented with supercharging, although he was never much in favor of it. He has experimented with all manner of suspension systems and, until recent years, virtually all of the bodies on his cars were custom made.

A Ferrari makes an excellent driver out of almost anyone, as it literally drives itself! So it is no surprise that as of 1982, Ferrari is the hottest investment car in the entire gamut of sports and classic cars—everybody seems to want one. Used Ferraris move into showrooms of dealers and quickly out again, sometimes in the space of one day.

Enzo Ferrari started his career in motorcycle racing. In 1929 he started an Alfa Romeo racing team and was himself one of the drivers. He built his first Ferrari car in 1946. In those days, I regularly had lunch with my friend Smith Hempstone Oliver, curator of land transportation of the Smithsonian Institution in Washington, D.C., almost certainly the leading authority in the United States on the history of automobiles and of auto racing. He used to say to me, then, "Alfa Romeo is winning the races, yes, but it won't be long before Ferrari will be taking over from Alfa Romeo."

How right he was! On May 25, 1947, two years after the close of the war, Ferrari won the Grand Prix of Rome; his car was driven by Franco Cortese. Since that date, Ferrari has had twenty-two world championships and over five thousand other wins.

In 1946, Ferrari came out with a car with a V-12 engine, the engine he most frequently used in his sports and racing cars. This was Ferrari Engineer Columbo's engine, a single overhead cam V-12 of very small size—1,497 cubic centimeters, or 90 cubic inches; this is quite different from say, the 8,200 cubic-inch Cadillac Eldorado engine! In 1950, Engineer Lampredi took over at Ferrari and he developed the so-called long-block engine: first, 3,300 cubic centimeters; then successively, 4,000, 4,500, and 4,900 cubic centimeters (or 4.0 liters, 4.5 liters, and 4.9 liters).

In 1951, Lampredi came out with a two-liter four-cylinder engine with dual overhead camshafts. This same engine was later expanded to six cylinders. After 1955, Ferrari came out with a V-6 and later a V-8. Virtually all of these different types of engines were used in both racing and sports cars, with the street cars (sports cars) to a considerable extent detuned.

Hemp Oliver and I traveled from Washington to Watkins Glen for all of the early car races starting in 1948, the race which he announced. It was not until 1950, however, that Ferrari made its first appearance at the track, with master mechanic Alfred Momo in command. The car was a small twelve-cylinder Inter model with roadster body, and, as I recall, it was the famous Barchetta (little boat) body. This Barchetta was made in roadster and coupe body until 1953. One Barchetta won the LeMans race in 1949. This car did not seem to be the height of reliability, and Momo was always working on it; but when it ran it really ran!

In 1952 it was obvious that *the* car in the sports category was the Jaguar. It was the most car for the money, and it certainly outperformed anything American that it met on the road, as I found out as I tried to induce drivers of American cars to race me in my XK120.

The Ferrari was a vastly better car from a quality point of view, but the Jaguar cost under $5,000 and, in New York, the Ferrari cost around $16,000. At that time Enzo Ferrari, Count Giorgio Geddes, the Italian industrialist from Florence, Italy, and I got the idea that this selling price might be lowered drastically in order to open up the American market. We discussed the possiblity of an American assembly plant using strictly American components on the Ferrari car: bearings, generator, starter, ignition system, carburetors, lights, and instruments. With these basic American components, two things would be accomplished: (1) the car could be maintained very easily in America with American standard parts, and (2) the price of the car could be lowered.

Mr. Ferrari and Engineer Lampredi almost immediately decided that American components could definitely be used without in any way damaging the quality or performance of the Ferrari. At the same time it was recognized that the American market wanted a car with far more engine capacity than the 166 and 212 Inter models. In any event, in 1954, the Ferrari 375 America appeared in this country in some force, a car with a much larger engine and vastly better performance than the small-engined cars. In 1956 the 250GT was introduced, a smaller-engined car but very reliable. It was continued to 1964. The later cars had larger engines for the most part.

But Mr. Ferrari had other ideas besides using American components; soon he dropped the idea. He concentrated on just one thing: making cars that would win races and, as a by-product, making street versions of these winners, hoping they would sell. They did sell pretty well. His marketing organization in America had never been very well developed, and the cars weren't really pushed. Ex-racing driver Luigi Chinetti handled most sales in this country, at least on the East Coast, and he knew the cars—their performance and their mechanics. The cars sold themselves because of their fantastic series of wins, and it was not until 1980 that a really sophisticated advertising program was put into place.

Count Geddes went on to become one of Italy's leading industrialists with a worldwide organization; I did some experimental work in conjunction with the Borg-Warner Corporation on supercharging the Offenhauser engine installed in an Italian sports car. Mr. Ferrari went on to build the greatest reputation ever achieved by a car builder.

The classic car historian, Rich Taylor, sums it up this way:

Tony Vandervell went racing to defend British prestige from the onslaught of papist hordes, Ford went racing to sell cars, but Ferrari went racing because, well, racing was all there was to life. And when all the dilettantes had packed up and gone home, Ferrari was still there, winning. Consistently. Not for a race, or a season, but year after year for a lifetime.

And that's the background of the Ferraris on the market today.

The Ferrari 250GT

The 250GT racing car was on the track from 1949 to 1955, so that it had a long history of testing in practice, followed by improvements to make the car more successful in competition.

The 250GT was introduced to the buying public at the Geneva auto show in March 1956, and it was continued through 1964. The later cars are more perfected; my own 1957 coupe, one of the early ones, had a tendency to leak water from the water jacket into the combusion chamber. This was not an easy fault to remedy, not even for the New York Ferrari repair establishment. My 1960 convertible had no such problem; in fact, it had very few troubles of any kind.

The "250" stands for the cubic centimeter displacement per cylinder. Since there are twelve cylinders in the car, to get the total displacement of the engine 250 must be multiplied by 12, which equals 3,000 cubic centimeters. With 1,000 cubic centimeters to the liter, this car is a three-liter car (compared with 8.2 liters for the big Eldorado Cadillacs, the last of the big-engine cars). At 60 cubic inches per 1,000 cubic centimeters (one liter), the 250GT had a displacement of 180 cubic inches. From this engine about 240 horsepower is produced, by no means a small output in relation to the size of the engine. It does about 155 miles per hour, and it has good acceleration. The *GT* stands for Gran Turismo, which means, approximately, "important sports touring car"—one that you can drive on the highway.

In many ways the 250GT is the most satisfactory all-around car of all of the Ferraris made. The purists will cry: "What do you mean? The 250GT isn't even remotely in the class of the 275GTB or, of course, the magnificent 275GTB-4 with its four overhead camshafts." Certainly the 275GTB and 275GTB-4 are more magnificent cars than the 250GT. There were fewer 275s and 275-4s made, and those who appreciate the very finest in sports cars made anywhere in the world at any time have descended on the few such cars turned out. But there are far more 250GTs available to buy.

Overall, as an investment and as a usable car, the 250GT is an excellent collector-investor car, maybe the best, for these reasons: the 250GT is one of the most reliable Ferraris ever made. It does not have any basic faults similar to many other sports cars; it generally starts when you press the starter; and it runs and keeps on running. I have owned two 250GTs; I kept the last one for ten years. I drove it everywhere, and it rarely gave any kind of trouble. When it did, the trouble was easily and inexpensively repaired.

This is an excellent automobile to drive on short or long trips; it seems to be merely loafing along at 90 miles an hour. Further, it is a very good-looking car, particularly some of the open cars and the Pininfarina coupe; these are beautiful by any standards.

Of all Ferraris the 250GT is the least expensive to buy today. Try to buy a 275GTB-4! For an average condition 275GTB-4 (with four cams) you will pay $60,000 now. For one in mint condition, you will easily have to pay $70,000. You will pay at least half this sum for a 275GT with single overhead camshafts.

As of late 1980, Motor Classic Corporation had a near mint condition 250GT two-plus-two coupe (seating two people in the front seat and two in the back) for $12,000 asking. This is a few thousand dollars over what the car cost new. The GTB-4 started out at $14,500 in price when it appeared in 1964 (much later than the era of the 250GT). It ended up in 1968 priced at $14,900.

Back in 1970 a 250GT could be bought for a few thousand dollars or less. In 1965 I bought a 250GT with Buono body, a somewhat rare coupe, for $2,700. It was in average condition and in 1965, after doing some repairs, I sold it for $3,200. In 1970 it was again for sale, this time for $500, the lowest price I have ever seen for a Ferrari in running order.

In 1967 I bought a 250GT convertible with detachable hard top in London for $2,500. It was in good, but not mint, condition. Some of the instruments had to be replaced; it had a bad clutch and pressure plate, and the paint was not the best. By 1970 my car was near mint, and it was worth about $4,000.

In the mid-seventies, a correspondent in California wrote me that a convertible in good condition with detachable hard top had been offered to him for $2,800. This was a low price, at least from the point of view of the East Coast market, so I advised him to buy it. By 1977 the market on my car, then in near mint condition with new leather, new Pirelli Cinturato whitewall tires, and new lacquer, was about $12,000.

In mid-1981, $28,000-*plus* was a fair price for a good coodition 250GT convertible with detachable hard top, with the standard Pininfarina body. If the body is custom, the price can be over $40,000. The standard 250GT Pininfarina coupe in very good, but not mint, condition is bringing around $17,000. The two-plus-two, as we indicated, is the lowest-priced model, and it is being sold now in near mint condition for $12,000 or slightly less.

In 1959 a very special 250GT appeared—the short wheelbase Berlinetta. This is definitely a connoisseur's car and commands a connoisseur's price—$35,000 or more as of 1982. It made its debut at the Paris auto show in October 1959.

There was still another very special 250GT, the Berlinetta Lusso, a docile, luxurious, but tremendously potent machine.

This is a distinctive, connoisseur's car that any car collector would place high up on the list of the finest postwar classics obtainable. These cars do appear on the market from time to time, and as of 1981, they commanded a price of about $35,000.

In 1967 one appeared on the London market in good, but not perfect, condition, for $8,000. The price of the Lusso remained at $8,000 or thereabouts for about five years; by 1975 it had risen to about $12,000, and to $18,000 in 1977. In the three years from 1977 to 1980 the car's price rose to $30,000, if it was in good condition, and in the next six months it rose another $3,000 to $5,000.

The 275GT Series of Ferraris

The 275 series of cars has only a slightly bigger engine than the 250GT but it produces more horsepower—260, 280, or 300, depending on the carburetion of the particular car. It did 165 miles an hour—at least—and zero to 60 miles per hour in seven seconds. It is a conservative, well-designed car made to be used for street as well as track use—and it still can be used for street use.

In 1970 the car was pretty well recognized as a standout, but over the last decade more and more people began to realize that the 275GTB is one of the near greats. In 1970 it cost about $7,500, which was then no small sum for any sports car on the second-hand market. In 1981 the price had risen to about $25,000 and even as high as $35,000.

The 275GTB appeared for the first time in the Paris Salon of 1964 as the successor to the Berlinetta Lusso (the very special 250GT). A convertible appeared at the same time (a spyder). In late 1966 essentially the same model car appeared, but with two overhead camshafts per bank of cylinders. This may well be the ultimate Ferrari to date (the 275GTB-4). The horsepower was increased to 300, and the car still receives rave notices. The body is by Pininfarina and is relatively conservative looking. The engine is in the front, as it is in all of the Ferraris we have described to this point.

This four-cam car (275GTB-4) sold ten years ago for as little as $10,000. Today one must pay a minimum of $50,000 for one of any quality at all, and $65,000 will hardly buy a mint-condition one. Motor Classic Corporation advertised an absolutely mint condition 275GTB-4 with 5,700 miles on it. The phone rang all one day for this car. The more the phone rang, the less the dealer was interested in selling it at all. As sometimes happens with dealers, he apparently had fallen in love with the car!

The 330 and 365 Series of Ferraris

The 250GT was the first sports car put out by Ferrari in great volume (for a small manufacturer). The next volume car for strictly street use was the 330GT. It first appeared in the Geneva show in 1965 as a replacement for the 250GTE with two-plus-two coupe body. The "330" designation meant that it was a big-engined Ferrari—330 times 12 equals 3,960; it was essentially a four-liter engine, big even by today's sports and racing-car standards. It is a good, conservative street car and is on the market in fairly good supply.

In 1970 the 330 seemed to be a real bargain. It could at times be purchased for under $5,000, in excellent condition; very often the asking price was $4,000. This bargain model was the two-plus-two, a four-seater car. In 1981, $15,000 would buy a very good 330. The coupe might cost twice as much in comparable condition, but the price of the two-seater coupe ten years ago was not very much more than the two-plus-two. This is a good, fairly reliable, conservative businessman's car, and many businessmen use the car to commute.

There is also a 330GTS (spyder) and, like all open cars, it tends to bring much higher prices than the comparable-chassis, closed cars. The 330GTS spyder today bring $50,000 and even more, in good condition.

The next model Ferrari of the street-use variety was the 365GT, and this car first appeared in 1966 at the Geneva show. It was put into limited production in 1967 and apparently arrived in the U.S. first in 1968. It is a one-overhead camshaft car. The 365 times 12 works out to 4,380 cubic centimeters or about 4.4 liters, a very big engine for Ferrari. This is a relatively big car, not tremendously preferred by sports car experts or buffs.

Five years ago a good 365 two-plus-two could be bought for perhaps $22,000. In 1981 the price had risen only slightly, to about $24,000 or $25,000.

The Ferrari Daytona

In 1968, Ferrari dropped the 275GTB and in its place produced the now famous Ferrari Daytona, completely different in appearance, using the large 365 engine. The car is a real performer and will do somewhere between 175 and 179 miles an hour. It develops 350 horsepower; yet it looks like a very refined sports car, not a racing car. This is a preferred car on today's market, preferred both by those who want a distinctive, high performance car and those who understand and love Ferraris. The Daytona is a prestige car, and its use in TV shows and motion pictures has promoted its popularity.

The Daytona first appeared in 1968, but it was only in 1969 that it came to be well known. By the mid-seventies a fine-condition Daytona 365GTB-4 coupe was selling on the second-hand market for $35,000. In 1981 the price had very nearly reached $65,000. The two-plus-two Daytona sold for about the same price in 1976, but in 1980 it had risen in price only to about $40,000. (The two-plus-two in any car is not the preferred model, and the two-seater coupe has far outstripped it.)

The Daytona spyder has far outstripped even the coupe price-wise—it is probably the highest-priced production Ferrari on the market today. Of course, a special limited-production Ferrari might exceed the price of a Daytona spyder. As recently as five years ago people didn't seem to know what to think of the spyder. It looked good, but. . . . Then it took hold, and there was a mad rush for the Daytona spyder. The average Daytona spyder in five years rose from a price level of $30,000 to $90,000. The best-condition spyder rose to over $120,000, and one was advertised in 1981 for $175,000.

The Daytona is a beautiful automobile, in a class by itself. In a way, the 275GTB and 275GTB-4 both look a little dated, but not the Daytona. There is a good deal of critical opinion to the effect that the 275GTB-4 is a better car than the Daytona. As a performer the 275GTB-4 probably is better; but for the man in the street who wants to buy an elegant car, the Daytona is the one.

The Daytona came legally (with emission controls) into the U.S. in 1970 with a price tag of $19,500. In 1973 the model was discontinued in the U.S. The price then had risen to $25,000— still a far cry from the price of just an average Daytona coupe today.

Times moves on, and opinion not only changes but matures. Now the opinion of automobile aficionados is switching to the Daytona and away from the very latest and very largest Ferrari, the 512 Berlinetta Boxer. Most critics of sports cars have the distinct feeling that the Daytona is a better-handling car than the BB.

Other Collectible Ferraris

In 1965, Mr. Ferrari began to put out something of an economy or bargain car—the Dino, named after his son. This V-6 with twin, overhead camshafts was produced until 1974. The car is designated 246GT and was put out in closed and open body type. It is a small-engined car, with just under 3,000 cubic-inch displacement. Although it is small, it is most certainly still a Ferrari, one calculated to give the owner a good deal less trouble than the bigger, more complicated, higher performance cars. Five years ago this Dino coupe sold for about $15,000 in average condition, $20,000 in fine condition. In 1981 the late-model car would sell for about $30,000; a 1976 model cost $25,000. The spyder might sell for about $10,000 more.

All of the cars discussed so far, from the 250GT to the Dino, are in the category of investment cars and have been rising in price steadily over the past ten years and are still doing so. The real collector of Ferraris would also treasure a Ferrari Super America, put out around 1960. This is a tremendously powerful, big-engine car, but maintaining it and securing parts for it are not easy. In Italy the Super America is literally off the market; the market has been bought out. In America a few of the cars come onto the market from time to time and bring under $30,000.

The Ferrari America of the mid-fifties was a fire snorter. It was designated 375, meaning that the capacity of the engine was 4,500 cubic centimeters or 4.5 liters. I like to think I had a hand in influencing Mr. Ferrari to manufacture the Ferrari America. Every other letter that I wrote to Italy in 1952 recommended that Mr. Ferrari make a large-engined car for America, as the Americans did not like small-engined cars that had to rev up high and use five gears to get up to speed. Mr. Ferrari was certainly conscious of the American market. He put out the America, the Super America, and the Daytona in recognition of the American market, as the names indicate. Still, the big-block cars (big engine blocks) have never been as popular or as successful as the small-block cars, notably the V-12s with double overhead cams. Both the America and the Super America may be bought in this country for under $30,000, which is really low for such fine quality cars.

Almost all of the present model cars turned out by the Ferrari factory are well-tried automobiles that have been produced for some time, so they are also on the second-hand market. In the Leake sale (Tulsa) of classic, antique, special interest, and sports automobiles of June 1980 several Ferraris were offered for sale. There was a featured Ferrari Berlinetta Boxer, 1979. There was also a 1978 luxury model 400, "The Boulevard Sports Car," a 1979 308GT-4, and a 1975 308GT-4. The Boxer received a high bid of $80,000 and the 1979 308GT-4 a high bid of $30,000.

The dealers who handle the strict collector-investment Ferraris generally handle the recent Ferraris as well. Perhaps these recent cars are best described as second-hand rather than investment cars. Still, they have not been declining in value markedly since they rolled off the assembly line, and the question is, how long will it take these cars to rise in price as collector cars?

The price structure of the second-hand car market is vastly different from the price structure of the collector-car market. With second-hand cars, the older the car the lower the price, starting with the current year and going on back. The new car (like a Ford) that sells for $8,000 may be worth $6,000 when it is one year old, $4,000 when it is two years old, $3,000 when it is three years old, and $2,000 when it is four years old—on the present market. The main reason is that as the cars grow older, they become more worn out. The second reason is that the more recent the particular model the more the "bugs" have been worked out and the more the car is perfected.

The following compiled figures on the 365GTB-4 Daytona represent a study of the price pattern on a recent Ferrari. The values are compiled from several sources.

1980 Ferrari Daytona Coupe Prices
by Model Year

1969	$21,000
1970	22,500
1971	31,500
1972	33,500

These values are relatively low because they are, for the most part, auction prices prepared early in 1980. As months passed, prices for all model years rose. The principle is illustrated, however, that the *late* model cars tend to be worth less the older they are; this principle holds true of currently produced Ferraris, which have been produced for several years without any basic change in the model.

Some collector-car price compilers publish three prices—for cars in fine, average, and mediocre condition. Averages have inherent weaknesses but are, nevertheless, useful summaries, and we have used them in the preparation of this book in order to keep the length of the book down to a workable size.

There are several different models of Ferrari turned out by the plant today. In fact, the plant presently turns out over ten cars in every working day and over 2,000 cars a year. It is now a production line operation—not an experimental car factory as it was to a considerable extent for many years, when different models were produced, with an eye always to producing something that would outperform all other cars. The Ferrari of those days always was something entirely exotic, something unique; something only for the very wealthy, and something for the automobile connoisseur.

Today's Ferraris

Present Ferrari production at the Marinello plant in Italy near Modena is a fine assembly-line operation. It is a compromise between the great custom-made cars that Commendatore Enzo Ferrari turned out for most of his life and the typical assembly line operation of Fiat, the organization that now has financial control of Ferrari.

Right now the one make of investment car in the greatest demand is, without much doubt, the Ferrari. There is a potential buyer for every model Ferrari ever made, and the prices of all collector Ferraris are high and will probably remain high—or rise further.

The top Ferrari produced today is the BB512—the Berlinetta Boxer with Pininfarina body, not a custom-made body, but a very good-looking, ultra-modern body. The engine is behind the driver but placed the long way in the chassis, not transversely; it faces backward. The engine is the usual twelve cylinder, but in this car the cylinder banks are horizontal, each bank of six cylinders facing the other bank—a kind of boxer (fighter) arrangement. There are twin overhead camshafts.

The mechanics of the BB512 are probably the most up to date of any car in the world. The engine is huge, with almost a 5,000 cubic-centimeter capacity—300 cubic inches. It produces 360 horsepower. It is a docile engine, and one can drive in city traffic in the car. I believe with a little "suping" it could easily produce 500 horsepower. As it is, the car will do possibly 177 miles an hour. *Car and Driver* magazine says 164 miles per hour possibly because of emission control devices.

The car sells in Italy—for export—for $61,500, which makes it a real bargain by anyone's standards. This car will not, however, meet American environmental standards, and to modify the car to do so, one must spend about $20,000 more. In the U.S. the car sells for $96,000 as of 1981, with all environmental modifications made.

The next car down the line pricewise is the 400 Automatic. It sells in Italy for export for slightly less than the Boxer: $59,000. It is a very conservative, luxury, smooth-looking car for cruising on the boulevard. The engine is slightly smaller than the Boxer engine, and the compression ratio is 8.8 to one rather than the Boxer's 9.2 to one, resulting in a smoother running engine. The engine puts out 310 horsepower, a lot of horsepower for a car as close to ultimate luxury as Ferrari will probably ever achieve.

It will do about 150 miles an hour. The 400 Automatic is a two-door closed car and seats four people; the interior is in general luxurious.

The next car down the price line is model 308; this car comes in closed- and open-body styles, seating two people. This car has a V-8 double overhead cam engine of relatively small capacity—2,926 cubic centimeters or 178.6 cubic inches—which makes the engine about the same size as the old 250GT. The engine has an 8.8-to-one compression ratio and puts out 205 horsepower. The car weighs 3,310 pounds as against 4,000 pounds for the luxury model 400 and 3,084 pounds for the performance car, the Berlinetta Boxer.

There are three different model 308 cars, all around the same price—$35,000 for export. This is a most modest price for a very well-made sports car. The 308 model is used the most in American TV shows and moving pictures, usually shown driving up to the country club or parked in front of a huge mansion. The 308GTS is the spyder (convertible) model, much sought-after, and in 1982 it could sell for around $42,000, maybe a little less.

Ferrari puts out a relatively new luxury car called the Mondial 8, with five-speed manual transmission, not automatic transmission (as in the model 400). This car sells in Italy for about $56,000. It is a good compromise between a semiluxury car and a sports car. The engine is a 3,000-cubic-inch V-8 of 214 horsepower. There are four overhead camshafts. The car looks more like a sports car than a luxury coupe.

There is even a Ferrari of smaller engine size. This is the 208GT of 1,991-cubic-centimeter engine capacity—about 120 cubic inches. The horsepower output is 160, and the maximum speed is 133 miles per hour. It lists in Italy for about $35,000. This car undersells almost all Maseratis, several models of the German BMW, most Jaguars sold on the Italian market, every Rolls-Royce, and the larger Mercedes-Benz cars from the 380SE to the 500SLC.

Ferrari seems to produce a car that will fit almost every pocketbook, from the junior vice president's to the chairman of the board's. More important, prices, comparatively, are low.

CHAPTER **6**

POSTWAR AMERICAN CLASSICS

THREE MAKES OF CLASSIC POSTWAR CAR are of sufficient importance from every point of view—quality, innovation, price appreciation, driveability, sheer elegance—to merit their separate
chapters. These are the great makes of Mercedes-Benz, Rolls-
Royce, and Ferrari. All three are innovative and great, and all
three have turned out to be good investments.

In this and the following chapters, I will consider postwar
classics other than these. I cannot consider every make that has
turned out to be a good investment, or that may do so. Instead
I have selected a group of likely cars for investment appreciation: those that are likely to go up and those that have already
turned in a good price performance.

These are the selections that will be discussed in this and the
following chapter:

AMERICAN CARS

Ford Cars and Ford-Derived Cars
  Mustang
  Shelby Mustang
  Cobra

    Thunderbird
    Lincoln Continental
    Mangusta and Pantera by DeTomaso

Chevrolet Cars
    Corvette
    Sting Ray
    Corvair

FOREIGN CARS

Italian Cars
    Lamborghini
    Maserati

English Cars
    Jaguar
    MG
    Austin-Healey
    Aston Martin

German Cars
    Porsche
    BMW

Perhaps my number one criterion for selection has been whether it is possible to purchase the car at all. One of the great innovations in sports cars was the Cisitalia of 1948. Where do you find one of these cars today? Where do you find one of the rear-engined Isotta Fraschinis, the high-performance Spanish Pegaso, a Tucker Torpedo, the rear-engined American innovation? If a make is very limited in numbers available for purchase, it is a treasure or curiosity, not a significant factor in the collector car market.

Ford Cars and Ford-Derived Cars

The Early Ford Mustang

Over the years many people have asked me, "What kind of collector car should I buy? I don't know much about cars. I do know I'd be interested in buying some kind of classic car. I can't afford a Rolls-Royce or anything near a Rolls-Royce in price. Is there anything I can buy for a modest sum; and, by the way, I don't want to buy a car whose repairs eat up my bank account!"

Today my answer would be, "Buy a Ford Mustang of the mid-sixties." The Ford Mustang of 1965–1966 is a unique car, for these reasons:

It can be purchased for little money—little money on any basis: absolute number of dollars, number of dollars compared with what one would have to put into other postwar classics, and what one gets for his money. The car is not difficult to find; Mustangs are available in almost every area of the country, not just in New York and Los Angeles. As an investment, the Mustang is not only easy to buy, it is easy to sell. Everybody seems to be at least a potential Mustang buyer.

The Mustang can be all things to all people. Some Mustangs have six-cylinder 200-cubic-inch displacement engines. These engines are certainly the best six-cylinder engines that the Ford Motor Company ever made, and they are some of the better six-cylinder engines that *any* company ever made. They have seven-bearing crankshafts, and the engine has a tendency toward long life. No matter how fast one drives the six, it never seems to be straining. With 120 horsepower it is no star performer, but it can hold its own in any modern-day traffic, and the car gets about twenty-four miles to the gallon.

The Mustangs with the V-8 engines are real performers and handle as though they were sports cars. This 289-cubic-inch engine turns out 210 horsepower, and the Hi-Performance (HP) model turns out 271 horsepower.

In the Leake sale of June 1980 a number of Mustangs were offered for sale, as they are in many car auctions. The prices received for the 1965 and 1966 models ranged from $5,500 to $7,500. Auction prices are often lower than retail prices, but these prices were high. They were also probably higher than Mustang convertibles would have brought on the East Coast. This auction was held in Tulsa, Oklahoma.

In the 1981 Leake sale a low mileage, fine condition 1965 Mustang convertible sold for the unprecedented price of

$21,500. Other of these 1964 (late) to 1966 Mustangs were auctioned in this sale for $4,600, $4,100, $5,500, $8,000, $10,750. The price trend was up as of June 1981.

Every conceivable part required can be purchased for a Mustang. The entire metal floor of the car can be purchased for under $50 a pan, and four are required if there is extensive rust. Often Mustang owners think if the floor is rusted out the car must be junked. Recently I bought an entire new dashboard for my 1966 Mustang for $15. Even carpet with the original weave can be purchased. Since the 200 C.I.D. (cubic inch displacement) engine that powered the 1965–1966 Mustang is essentially the same engine used on the 1981 Mustang, a replacement engine should be available from the Ford Motor Company for many years.

To sum up, the Mustang is probably the best buy in the entire postwar classic car area. The styling is excellent; the engine is durable and reliable; the performance is fine. There is hardly a better automatic transmission installed on any make of car. Parts are available and at little cost. Almost any mechanic can repair a Mustang, since it is a Ford. It costs little compared with other investment automobiles. There is a ready market for the car, and the price is rising.

Robert Wieder and George Hall in their comprehensive book, *The Great American Convertible* (Doubleday & Company, Garden City, New York, 1977), sum up the Mustang very well: "It's one of the few really 'bulletproof' cars, meaning almost nothing bad can be said of one. . . ."

The Shelby Mustangs

The early Mustangs—those put out in 1965 and 1966—are excellent cars, and they are strict production cars turned out by the factory. At little expense, one could "supe" them up to secure a great deal more horsepower and torque. Carroll Shelby latched onto the Mustang with the intention of turning it into an authentic sports car, in fact a competition car. Shelby is an entrepreneur with a background as a Goodyear tire dealer and the operator of a school for racing drivers. He is also something of a natural automotive genius.

Almost as soon as the Mustang came out in 1965, Shelby went to work to improve it radically as a sports and true competition car—and he succeeded. His main efforts were centered on the coupe, not on the convertible. The model he chose to work on was the so-called fastback. He took the smaller V-8 engine, the 289-cubic-inch engine that produced as a maximum 271 horsepower, changed the manifold and headers, and put on a four-throat carburetor (four barrel). The horsepower now rose to 306 —at least—and the engine could be made to produce more horsepower. He improved the brakes, put in a limited-slip differential and a heavy-duty rear axle. He changed the suspension and put on the Koni shock absorbers that everyone who wants roadability seems to install. He also put on big fifteen-inch magnesium wheels. The results were that his car, called the Shelby GT-350, won the B-production car national championship in 1965, 1966, and 1967.

These cars cost, everything included, from Shelby's Los Angeles shop, $4,500 new. He built 562 cars in 1965; 2,378 in 1966; and 3,225 in 1967—so there are still many of these cars around, the 1965 and 1966 cars being the better ones.

By present-day standards this car was, and is, a standout. It does zero to 60 miles per hour in 6.5 seconds, a good time for any of the very expensive European exotics, and its top speed is 130–135 miles per hour. With all of the Shelby features added to the ordinary Mustang, the car cost only $1,000 more than the standard Mustang and about $1,000 less than the Corvette.

In 1967, Shelby came out with a larger-engined car, 427 cubic inches instead of the old 289-cubic-inch engine. This car was called the GT-500. The smaller engine was rated at 306 horsepower and the 500 engine at 355, probably a conservative rating. The GT-500 outsold the GT-350 by a margin of two to one, although today it is by no means certain that the GT-500 is as good a car all around as the GT-350. In 1967, 1,175 GT-350s and 2,050 GT-500s were produced. In 1968, 1,648 GT-350s were produced and 2,802 GT-500s. By 1970 the market for both models had fallen off. The Shelby Mustangs had run their course, and the later models were not based on the preferred 1965 and 1966 Mustangs.

The market on GT-350s and GT-500s is an upward market,

but it is by no means a very active market, and an auto auction that offers twenty Mustangs of the 1965–1966 vintage years for sale—convertibles—usually has few or no Shelby's for sale. The price of a fine-condition 350 or 500 is about $7,000 to $7,500. Many of these cars in only *average* condition bring $3,500 to $4,000. What will happen to demand and price of the Shelby Mustangs in the future is anyone's guess. My guess, however, would be that the uptrend will continue.

The Shelby Cobra

The Shelby Cobra is an all-out sports and competition car. One way to look at the Cobra is that it consists of a great big, powerful engine in a very small and lightweight car—ergo, terrific acceleration and speed. Everything considered, the Cobra is certainly the ultimate sports-competition car that America has yet produced. It is probably the smaller-engined car—the one with the 289-cubic-inch engine—that is the better all-around car. It seems to have a little stiffer springing and handles a little better than the big 427-cubic-inch car. It is almost certainly the car with the better road-holding qualities. It is also less expensive to buy at $40,000 to $50,000 for the open model.

One of the greats of the Cobra production is the 1964 Daytona coupe. A series of six such cars were entered at Daytona in 1965. The team cars won the FIA International Gran Turismo in 1965, beating all other cars in this class. One such car is owned by Motor Classic Corporation of White Plains, New York, and this car was demonstrated for *Car and Driver* in mid-1980. The car has a probable top speed of 185 and possibly will accelerate from zero to 60 in under four seconds, thus outperforming almost any car not strictly a track car.

Plans for the Cobras were actually started by the Ford Motor Company and Carroll Shelby in 1961 using an English chassis, and by 1963 the car was operable with the 289-cubic-inch, 271 horsepower engine that was used in the Shelby Mustang. The full race version of this car turned out 370 horsepower. The car, the roadster, not the Daytona model, would do zero to 60 in under six seconds and zero to 100 in under thirteen seconds.

The 289 model was turned out between 1963 and 1965, and

655 of these cars were made. The larger-engined car, the 427, was continued until 1967. In all, 356 of this larger car were made.

By the end of 1962 a hundred 289 Cobras had been built, and these cars were priced at $5,995, an incredibly low price for what the car was. Both the 289 and the 427 cars were small and simple. They were open cars. They had independent four-wheel suspension and disc brakes all around—all standard practice for out-and-out competition sports cars. Some of the cars are quite good looking, but very unsophisticated in body design. A standard 427 roadster will accelerate to 100 miles an hour and then decelerate back to zero all in 14 seconds! With the right rear-axle ratio it should easily exceed 200 miles per hour.

The Cobra is not for inexpert drivers. It is too easy to spin a Cobra, and it is too easy to turn over. If one wants a Cobra he should place the car in a display room or space in his garage with a large sign on which are printed the pertinent facts, such as "zero to 100 and back in 14 seconds," "500 horsepower," and "the highest performer that America ever produced for sale to the public."

Five years ago prices started upward, but as recently as two years ago a good Cobra could be purchased for between $15,000 and $20,000. Today a 289 will, as we have indicated, bring close to $50,000. A good 427 roadster can bring $65,000 and up. If anyone has one of the six 289s built, the racing Daytona coupes, he can ask what he will and maybe get it—in six figures.

The Ford Thunderbird

One can probably describe the Ford Thunderbird as a sporty runabout. The classic Thunderbird produced in the mid-fifties is just that. It is certainly not a specifically designed sports car, nor is it a great treasure that one would preserve carefully in his temperature- and humidity-controlled garage to show to friends on occasion. It is a good-looking, reliable Ford, a relatively simple car that is generally trouble-free.

Why is it desirable? If one sat in my yard right now, I know I could run out of the house, jump in the car, start it, and drive anywhere I wanted to go, with no worries. By now, also, the body styling has become more or less timeless. In fact, there is a new aura about the car. Passersby in the street will sometimes say, "Look at that Thunderbird. Isn't it a gem?"

In the early 1950s public interest in sports cars started to develop. This was the era of the automobile show in which many specials were shown and prizes awarded. In some years my own cars were displayed in as many as a dozen of these shows, from Washington, D.C., to New York to Indianapolis to Philadelphia. These shows were supercolossal affairs with background music and models posing by particular cars. The major automobile companies, especially General Motors, often made special cars to see public reaction.

In the Thunderbird of 1955 the Ford Motor Company produced a car that would sell. It certainly did, with 16,000 cars sold in 1955; 15,000 in 1956; and 21,000 in 1957. The original Thunderbird weighed a very heavy 3,600 pounds and sold for a very modest $3,000. Then the small compact Thunderbird was all finished, and the car became something else—a very much larger and heavier car that was more or less of a standard convertible with the Thunderbird name. The four-passenger Squarebird was produced from 1958 through 1962, and this is not the Thunderbird we are talking about. It may become a collector's car, but it is not nearly so much of a collector's car as the Thunderbirds of 1955–1957.

In many TV shows the hero has an exotic car. The Jonathan Harts have a Rolls-Royce Silver Shadow convertible. They also have a 450SL Mercedes, and they used to have a Bentley convertible, an SIII. The hero in "Vegas" has a Thunderbird, and with this car he is not far behind Jonathan Hart in the figure he cuts. This is the status of the Thunderbird today. It is something of a prestige car, and it is certainly a collector's car. It has, in addition, proven to be a good investment and practical: almost all components on the Thunderbird are standard Ford or Mercury, perhaps modified a bit, but only a bit.

By 1970, prices had risen. Still, $3,000 would buy a fine condition Thunderbird convertible. There was also a coupe, which was selling for about the same price as the convertible. Five years later, both coupes and convertibles were selling for $6,000 to $7,000, if in top condition. Three thousand dollars would buy an average-condition car.

In 1978 a high point in price seems to have been reached, and a very good condition Thunderbird convertible would bring $15,000, and some a few thousand dollars more. Then, unusual for the present collector-car market, prices leveled off and even seemed to decline a bit to 1981. While it is true that some Thunderbird convertibles were pushing $20,000, others were selling below $15,000.

Overall, these are the pluses for the Thunderbird of 1955–1957: it is a good-looking car that is also practical; it can be used for everyday travel anywhere—unlike many collector cars. Repairs can be secured anywhere, and parts are not hard to find at reasonable prices. Finally, the car has appreciated rapidly. It has slowed down in its rate of appreciation, but there is little chance of much decline. The demand is there for the car; the price simply rose too far, too quickly.

The Postwar Lincoln Luxury Cars

The postwar Lincolns (put out by Ford, of course) are in no way sports or competition cars. They are, in general, standard sedans and a few standard convertibles. In one postwar series, though, the Ford Motor Company tried to put out a car of top quality all through, and they just about succeeded with the Lincoln Continental Mark II.

The prewar Lincoln Continental was something of a sensation. It was large and it was low. It had a kind of horizontal appearance, and, as compared with other luxury cars at the time, it had an advanced appearance, something that the industry might have expected five to ten years later. It was not priced tremendously high, but it was definitely a prestige automobile.

Right after the war, Lincoln put out essentially more of the same, but of more up-to-date design. The first series of Lincoln Continental was put out from 1940 to 1942, and the second series, not much different from the first, was put out from 1946 to 1948. These were all more or less hand-built cars based on the Lincoln Zephyr, not the greatest engined car in the world, by any means. Still, the car was thought beautiful by a number of automobile authorities, and Frank Lloyd Wright. One of these cars appeared in the exhibition, "Eight Automobiles— 1951," exhibited in the Museum of Modern Art. Of all these prewar and immediate postwar Continentals, 2,277 were convertibles and 3,045, coupes.

In 1954 the Continental Mark II made its debut, and it was a very special car. Between 1954 and 1957, when production of the Mark II was terminated, 3,012 cars were built, and they sold for about $10,000, a price very much in line with Rolls-Royce at the time. The Mark II used a refined and very reliable V-8 engine, and the whole car was quality. The only possible objection was the ride which was a bit hard and a bit unsophisticated as compared with the ride of the much later Ford products of the 1970s.

When the Lincoln Continental "postwar" went out in 1948, the car was simply another used car, and the price of the Continental went down like any used car's price. In the late 1940s neither the prewar Continental nor the immediate postwar Continental had much value, and at that time I saw good ones of both eras for about $1,500.

By 1975 both prewar and postwar Continentals (of the era of the 1940s)—both coupes and convertibles—were pushing $10,000 if in fine condition. The Continental Mark II was not in much demand at the time, and in the early to mid-seventies, I recall, many such cars were priced in the $3,000 range, very good condition cars. They were certainly not collector cars at that time.

By 1980, however, the price of the Continental Mark II of the 1950s had skyrocketed. It was a quality car, and I recall that the company advertised that the interiors could be upholstered in leather from Scotland, carefully selected so that no hide had holes in it (made from the cow's brushing against a barbed wire fence). The cars were constructed of quality materials and put together painstakingly. The performance was good, but nothing to match the quality of materials and workmanship.

By the end of 1980 the Lincoln Continental Mark II was most certainly a collector's item. There was no Mark II under $10,000, and the Kruse auction was selling them for up to $25,000 for a fine-condition car. There was a wide range in prices, depending on the condition of the car. Sometimes one could get a fine-quality car for $15,000 while a poor-quality car might sell for under $5,000. The Lincoln Continental Mark I, put out in the prewar and immediate postwar period, was selling in the same price range as the Mark II, with no very great difference in price for the prewar and the postwar Mark I cars.

The 1961 Lincoln Continental, including the four-door convertible, is in a very different class. This car was supposed to be a luxury car, and it drove and rode well, but it was no particular standout; I turned down one of these cars ten years ago, a convertible in mint condition offered for $1,200. The car is worth four times this amount now, but still it is not a great collector's car—at least not yet.

The 1967 coupe is another "maybe" collector car. It is a beautiful car, a well-made car, one that drives well and looks absolutely in date as of 1982. This car is rising in price to a degree, at least. It is most certainly not going down in value. The price level three years ago—in 1978—was about $2,500 to $3,500. It is now about at the $5,000 level.

Overall, the Lincoln Continental up through Mark II has risen a good deal in value in the past five years. That trend does not appear to be coming to an end. The car is still not expensive as compared with other collector cars. It is well made and absolutely reliable—particularly the mid-fifties Mark II with the eight-cylinder engine. Anybody can repair the car, parts are available, and the car can be used for daily transportation.

The Mangusta and the Pantera by DeTomaso

The Mangusta and the Pantera are tremendously exotic-looking cars and great performers, but at heart they are Fords. Racing driver-entrepreneur Alejandro DeTomaso built a semi–race-car chassis using a Ford V-8 351-cubic-inch engine, five-speed transmission, independent four-wheel suspension, and disc brakes all around. The chassis was driven by Mr. De-Tomaso to the Ghia body company in Italy where a streamlined body was designed by the greatest automobile body designer of any era—Giorgetto Giugiaro. Giugiaro created the magnificent steel body for the car Mr. DeTomaso called the Mangusta. The car first appeared in 1966 and was in production a few years later. The whole design, inside and out, was ultramodern from body to mid-engine; but it was essentially a Ford and was therefore simpler than the strict Italian exotics, and also cheaper—in the range of $10,000.

Along the way Mr. DeTomaso bought the Ghia company, and the Ford Motor Company bought a major interest in his company (that owned Ghia), Automobiles DeTomaso. Then the Mangusta was redesigned to be the Pantera. Ghia restyled the Mangusta by lowering the front of the car and lengthening the nose. The back line of the car (the sides behind the door) got a more broken-up look, and the whole car looks smaller than the Mangustas and is not quite as fine in design. In 1971, Lincoln-Mercury showrooms got the Pantera to sell at about $10,000. The 351-cubic-centimeter engine put out 310 horsepower. The Pantera was good for 145 miles per hour, and zero to 60 miles per hour in the very low time of 5.5 seconds.

By 1974 the car was both pretty well perfected and finished in production! In all, 5,269 cars had been built. In 1974, Ford bought out Mr. DeTomaso completely. The Mangusta is one of the beautiful cars of the recent postwar classic era. It is only 43 inches high, but it does not give the impression of being a little car. The Pantera sometimes does give that impression.

Theoretically, these cars should combine the best of both worlds: the sports-classic car world and the utility- or transportation-car world. Actually both cars fall somewhat short of this happy average. The bodies tend to rust, and, of course, they are steel. The cars should have plenty of room for the driver and his passenger, but somehow they do not, and the driver feels a bit cramped. Some owners complain that the cars have troubles, perhaps not major troubles, but annoying troubles that keep cropping up. In any event, neither car seems preferred as far as driving and reliability are concerned, at least not by some of their owners and some of those seeking to buy high performance Italian exotics.

In 1978 we found the market for these cars in Italy to be as low as $6,000 for a fine-condition car, and we located an excellent Pantera in Florence for exactly this figure. In America the Pantera and the Mangusta could be bought in good condition for $10,000 to $12,000. By 1979, prices for the cars had risen a little, to about $13,000 to $15,000, with particular emphasis on the Mangusta, the earlier and more beautiful car which was put out in smaller volume than the Pantera.

By 1980 there was considerable buyer interest in both the Mangusta and the Pantera. A very good Mangusta of top quality in a beautiful red lacquer was offered early in 1980 for $18,000. Late in the year the same quality car would bring in excess of $20,000 and perhaps as high as $25,000. The Pantera did not reach $20,000, and $15,000 to $17,000 would buy a fine-condition Pantera.

Chevrolet

Corvette and Sting Ray

In the early 1950s America began to pay attention to sports cars and auto racing. The Watkins Glen races had just started with a motley array of cars: out-of-date sports cars, some home-made cars, and some "just plain cars." General Motors decided to capitalize on this new American interest in sports cars by developing a car they named the Corvette—after a small, compact, naval vessel used in World War II. The Chevrolet Division came up with a two-seater, open car that had the appearance, and at least some of the performance, of a sports car. The trend setter at the time was the Jaguar XK120, and Chevrolet had a hard time equaling this standout.

The Corvette came out in 1953; it was small and rather neat looking. It used the Chevrolet six engine, suped from 115 to 150 horsepower. The body was fiberglass, relatively new at the time and popular. The Corvette sold for a little under $3,500—less than the price of the XK120. In 1953 and 1954 only 2,863 Corvettes were built, and the company had a hard time selling even this number. The buyers were apparently sports car enthusiasts with some knowledge of what a sports car should be. They apparently rejected the automatic transmission. They would probably have rejected any automatic transmission, but the Chevrolet Powerglide was no competition transmission by any means, and the "suped up" old six-cylinder engine apparently was not up to the buyers' expectations, since the Jaguar XK120 had double overhead camshafts and the engine of the XK looked like what a sports car enthusiast thought a sports car engine should look like.

In 1955 a big step forward was taken when a V-8 engine was put into the Corvette. In 1956 the body was restyled and became very much more streamlined and less austere. In 1957 a fuel injection system allowed as much as one horsepower per cubic inch of displacement, and this goal was long thought to be the ultimate in any sports car engine. In the same year the Borg-Warner four-speed transmission was introduced as an option. With 283 horsepower, the V-8 Corvette would apparently do 130 miles per hour, a high speed at the time. The price of the car in 1957, with fuel injection, was $3,600, not far from the price of the original Corvette.

The 1957 model was *the* car of the early series of Corvettes, although essentially the same car was produced through 1962. Even as late as 1962, relatively few Corvettes were produced; the preferred 1956 and 1957 Corvettes numbered 3,388 and 6,246 respectively, while Thunderbirds in these years numbered 15,631 and 21,380.

In 1963 a new series of Corvettes was introduced. Each time I see one of the new series, it looks better and more like a classic sports car. Two models were produced in 1963: a roadster and a hard top. This new Sting Ray did look a little like a sting ray in that it tended to be a flat car; the retractible headlights helped create the appearance of flatness. The engine was basically the same as the 1962 Corvette engine, but there was independent four-wheel suspension.

Each year after 1963 the car was improved in some way. In 1965, disc brakes on all four wheels were introduced. By 1966 the acceleration became phenomenal for any car, American production car or otherwise. The car went from zero to 60 (with certain gearing) in 4.8 seconds and would reach 140 miles per hour. From 1963 to 1967 the terminal year for this series, horsepower was raised almost steadily each year from 250 to 435. Production in each year remained about the same—a little over 20,000 per year.

This series, produced from 1963 to 1967, seems to be *the* preferred series of Corvettes or Sting Rays. The cars that came earlier were first attempts, attempts to make a standard passenger car into something of a sports car. In 1963, Corvette had arrived and was a sports car. After 1967 the purists, to a considerable extent, lost interest. Still, the present-model Sting Ray, which dates from 1968 on, is no car for anyone to shrug off, and there are many late-model Sting Ray enthusiasts—and buyers —both in the new market and in the second-hand market. I suppose this last model car dates from the exhibition car called the Mako Shark which created something of a sensation when it was displayed in experimental form years ago. It was certainly superstreamlined for the times, and there were both proponents of the new shape and opponents. The proponents apparently prevailed, and the car in essence has been produced ever since.

In 1970 a 1955–1962 model could be bought for a little over $1,000 in fine condition. The 1953–1954 models may have been poorer cars, but they often sold above $2,000. The 1963–1967 series were in the category of second-hand cars and were not much collected by collectors. By 1975 the 1953–1954 cars were selling for over $5,000 if in good condition. The series from 1955 to 1962 could be bought, in good condition, for a little under $5,000. At this time, in 1975, the now preferred, 1963 or later models could also be bought for under $5,000.

By 1981 the Corvettes and Sting Rays were getting sorted out as collector cars along the lines that might be anticipated. The older cars had become the true collectibles, simply because they were older, more classic, the original Corvettes, and fewer in number.

The Corvettes of the later years of the 1950s were bringing anywhere from $11,000 to $15,000 if in good condition. The cars produced in the early 1960s were selling around the $10,000 mark. The new series, put out from 1963 through 1967, all sold in the neighborhood of $10,000 and slightly less; the cars produced after this series closed in 1967 seemed to sell in the $7,500 range. The price of the recent used cars tended to be dependent on the price of the new cars.

Corvettes have been going up in value rather rapidly in the past decade; to 1981 they have proven to be a good investment.

The investment *per car* is not high, and in all probability the car will not decline in price in the future. There is a very good market for the car; the cars can be both bought and sold, and good cars can still be bought at reasonable figures. All Corvettes and Sting Rays can easily be repaired and by many people. Parts for Corvettes and Sting Rays are inexpensive, and they are available anywhere in any quantity required. Reproduction parts are also available everywhere, and one only has to consult *Hemmings Motor News* to learn how plentiful these parts are.

The Chevrolet engine is probably the finest American production-car engine that can be selected for any sports car—either American sports car or foreign car. It was used in the Italian Bizzarrini, the American Chaparral racing car and many other cars. It is also regularly substituted for the Italian engine in the Maserati Ghibli. One can do almost anything he wants with the Chevrolet engine, and horsepowers of over 400 are easily obtainable. The engine is very reliable, unlike many European sports car engines.

All models of Corvette and Sting Ray drive well, even the earliest cars of 1953 and 1954. Although the sports car purists do not yet recognize the classic character of the Sting Rays put out from the late 1960s to the present, they probably will in time. The car drives beautifully, particularly with its independent suspension. It is a docile car with great performance. One of these late model Sting Rays more than outaccelerated my Ferrari 250GT from the turnpike toll booth. I went by him finally —at 117 miles per hour—but I believe he permitted me to go by!

There are some annoying troubles with the Sting Ray, but not the kind that cannot be cured. The cars tend to overheat and some of them tend to develop leaks of one kind or another. Basically, however, the cars are not troublemakers and they can be used for transportation—any of them.

Corvair

The Chevrolet Corvair was a real innovation in mass-produced American cars—it was far ahead of its time. It had a rear engine that was air cooled; it had the ultimate in springing—independent suspension on all four wheels; and the whole car was of Monocoque construction (unit design for chassis and body). This rear-engine, rear-wheel-drive, independent four-wheel-suspension layout is, of course, the very latest in Italian sports car design—as found in the Ferrari Boxer, Lamborghini, and Maserati. In America we seem to be mesmerized by front-engine and front-wheel drive, particularly if it bears a Japanese label; but this front-drive layout is not by any means intrinsically better than a rear-engine, rear-wheel drive layout.

The trouble with the earliest Corvairs is that they do not drive particularly well. One cannot quite tell where the engine is or which wheels are driving, or that there is independent suspension. Theoretically, the car was ultra-up-to-date. Actually it drives like a front-engine, rear-wheel-drive car. Driving the car is no revelation; it has little acceleration.

The Corvair made its debut in late 1959, and the earliest model is known as the 1960 model. The car was continued, in evolving forms, for a decade. In 1969 the Corvair was discontinued. As time went on, however, the car got better and better. As of 1981, all Corvairs are definitely collectors' cars, and as of that date it is more than a good candidate for a rise in price. For relatively little money a very good Corvair can be acquired.

There are Corvairs and there are Corvairs, and at the extremes the cars bear little resemblance to each other in performance. There is the original car, no great standout performancewise with 80 horsepower, a somewhat uninteresting-looking stubby car, and then there is the so-called Yenko Stinger, that can easily produce 190 horsepower and has won a national championship race in addition to other races. Some of the later cars matched their performance in their appearance.

This is the way the various evolutionary stages of the Corvair sort out:

- 1959 (1960 model) produced with a few improvements through 1964 for the basic Corvair
- 1960 model year—Monza—a sporty coupe—convertible added 1962 called the Spyder—continued to 1964

- 1965–1966—Corsa, the successor to the Spyder—ended 1967
- 1965—second generation Corvairs with sleeker bodies—ended 1969
- 1962—Turbo Spyder put out by factory—essentially a Monza—ended 1964
- 1962–1964—John Fitch modified Sprint
- 1965 on—Fitch's second generation Sprint
- 1966 on—Fitch Phoenix, a super Corvair and expensive
- 1966 on—the Don Yenko Stinger, more or less a racing car —ended in 1969 with the end of the Corvair

In 1969 everything in the Chevrolet Corvair department was finished. The Monzas, the Corsas, the Spyders, and the Sprints were, and are, the premium cars and they are vastly preferred as collector cars over the standard cars, even the standard second generation cars that were put out beginning in 1965, cars that had much more pleasing body styles.

None of the basic Corvairs are star performers, nor are they rare. In 1960 possibly 250,000 Corvairs were built, and this number rose to 329,000 in 1961, then dropped after that until, in 1964, 207,000 were produced. Only about 400,000 of the second generation cars were built from 1965 until the Corvair was dropped by G.M.

By 1962 the factory offered a turbocharged Spyder for about $2,500 that had 150 horsepower and would clock about 110 miles per hour. Racing driver John Fitch's Sprint was unsupercharged, but with four carburetors the engine produced 130 horsepower. It was a splendid performer and road holder. The Corsa, in turbocharged form, put out 180 horsepower. At the top end of the performance scale, about 150 of Mr. Yenko's racing Stingers were made, and this is a premium car, if one can be found for sale. Horsepower offerings ranged from 160 to 190, as against 80 horsepower for the first Corvair sold by the factory in stock form.

In all, over one million basic Corvairs were built, and the car has appreciated little in value as compared with other collector cars. In fact, it may be that even in late 1981 the standard Corvair is not considered the best investment, but over the years I expect that all Corvairs will rise in value.

The cars that come up most at auction are the standard Corvairs and the Monzas, the Monza being more or less a fancied-up Corvair. At any rate, it is more sporty and more attractive looking than the standard Corvair. In their five years of production, there were 80,000 Monza Spyders and Corsas built. These were the years 1962–1966. These cars were probably the ultimate factory-built Corvairs, and only a few low-production Corvairs like the Fitch and Yenko Stingers are more desirable.

The price of the standard Corvair and the Monza started at about $2,500 and didn't rise much from this figure over the life of the Corvair series. In 1981 a top-condition standard Corvair or Corvair Monza still brought about this same $2,500, sometimes less. It is not hard to predict a price rise in the future. If, however, a special comes onto the market it goes at a premium price. A good Turbo Spyder of 1963 or 1964 will go for $4,000 to $5,000. The convertible is much preferred to the coupe. The racing Stinger is something entirely different from the point of view of value, and no Stinger should go for under $5,000 as of the year 1982.

The Corvair is a unique car; it was far in advance of its time as an American production car. Many things have been done with the Corvair and can be done with it; it can be turned into a highly desirable, high-performance Gran Turismo car—of sorts, at least.

Corvair is not unique as far as numbers produced go. It is unique in numbers for the refined versions put out, and these rarer cars might well be concentrated on by collector-investors. Prices are still very low, by anyone's standards, and anyone who can afford any car at all can think in terms of acquiring a Corvair of some sort. He can hardly think of a prewar Chrysler Imperial convertible at $125,000 up!

The Corvair is easy to maintain. It is a Chevrolet. Many mechanics know the car, and parts are available. In addition, there are many parts specialists who turn out good products at reasonable prices. There is an ample supply of used parts.

The later models, and certainly the higher performance cars, are pleasurable to drive, when the rear-engine, rear-drive lay-out was taken fuller advantage of. Corvairs can be used, and are used, for everyday transportation. Just recently I saw a good condition Corvair parked at my bank—no unusual sight any-where.

To date, the market for these cars has, to a considerable ex-tent, been young enthusiasts with limited bank accounts. If and when the well-heeled investors get the idea of the Corvair, prices might well take off. The Ford Mustang took off pricewise in 1979. The Chevrolet Corvair might well follow suit.

The Other American Investor-Collector Cars

This chapter has considered the main American investment cars of the postwar period, but by no means all of the cars. The task of including all cars is great and would make any book a kind of dictionary or encyclopedia. The whole job of analyzing automobiles as an investment is one of picking out (1) particu-larly significant makes, years, and models, and (2) an adequate sample of investment cars so that price levels as well as price trends can be determined.

There are other cars, some of them fairly significant from the point of view of investments, including:

- The Chrysler Town and Country "Woodies" of the imme-diate postwar period
- The Chrysler 300 series
- Many, if not all, convertibles, including the Cadillac Eldo-rado, early Packards, Hudsons, and Mercurys
- Kaiser and Frazer
- The Tucker 48, a pioneering car but one not available in any significant numbers

Early postwar Packard convertibles, Mercury convertibles, and Hudson convertibles are often bringing in five figures. Cad-illac convertibles of the early postwar years and from 1966 to 1970 are rapidly becoming investment cars and are being re-stored as "treasures" more and more.

CHAPTER **7**

Postwar Italian, British, and German Classics

THEY CAN BE COUNTED across the world on the fingers of one hand or fewer. They are the last survivors of the prestige automobile. They are by name: Lamborghini, Rolls-Royce, or Ferrari. With these one plunges into the universe of the automobile that is for the most part unknown: that of art and of the respect for tradition. Of little importance is their fantastic price, their limited distribution. They exist, and that is the essential thing for us. Classics of their kind? Yes, if one considers them to be the bridge between a glorious past and an uncertain future.

This is a translation of the leading paragraph of the article, "Ferrari 400 Automatic," written, in French, by Philippe Aubry and published in the July-August 1980 issue of the French publication *Auto Moto Retro.*

Auto Moto Retro is published in Paris, not London or Rome, but it singles out, as examples of the last survivors of the prestige automobile, two Italian and one English car.

The Automobiles of Italy

Lamborghini and Maserati

Enzo Ferrari was the greatest automotive innovator in the entire postwar period. In sports and racing cars, he had very little competition from the time his cars first appeared in the 1940s. His experimentation and innovations were prodigious. Still, there were other innovators in Italy at the same time, people who also produced epic automobiles.

One of the most significant pioneering cars ever built is the Lamborghini Miura, made from 1967 to 1972. The car is as streamlined as a guided missile, with a beautiful curved body 41-inches high. The car weighs about 2,500 pounds, and the 12-cylinder, twin overhead camshaft engine in the last model produces as much as 430 horsepower.

Although the car is low profiled, an over-six-foot man is absolutely comfortable in the car. Everything is convenient—dashboard dials, pedals, gear shift lever. When you turn the key, the engine starts instantly. It idles smoothly; the clutch is not fierce. The car can be driven docilely in city traffic. It will not overheat, and the carburetors do not overload with gasoline.

As soon as you get to the freeway (at least the non-speed-limit freeways of Europe), you step on the gas and the car takes off. It covers the quarter mile in 13.9 seconds, at which time it is traveling at 108 miles per hour. It keeps on accelerating until it gets to 170 miles an hour, when acceleration isn't quite so good, and the front wheels get a little light. One expert says it is perfectly stable at 180 miles per hour.

After a lengthy description of the car, Rich Taylor, the postwar classic car specialist, in his book *Modern Classics* (Scribner's, 1978) says:

As you no doubt realize, I'm not describing some forgotten Ferrari, although every word—excepting the compliant ride—could be used to describe a composite of ultimate Ferrari coupes. But no, this is the Lamborghini Miura, the only legitimate challenger to Ferrari for best sports car in the world honors.

But for a while there in the late sixties Lamborghini was *it*—honest and truly better than any Ferrari, no matter which way you cut it.

The car cost about $20,000 new. Three years ago, $12,000 would buy a very good condition Miura. Then demand seemed to explode. In 1981 a mint condition 1972 Miura would bring $55,000 or $60,000—if not more. The early 1967 and 1968 cars could be purchased for much less money—$30,000 or less.

Whatever model the Miura, it increased in value in 1980, perhaps more than any other collector car, modern or antique. In all, about 720 Miuras were built, and few Miuras built after January 1, 1968 were admitted to this country because they did not comply with emissions control. Thus, the supply of Miuras in the U.S. is limited to a few hundred cars. In Italy, however, demand is at least as great for the Miura as it is here, and it is difficult to locate any Miura there of any model year for under $40,000. The Italians want these cars just as much as the American collectors do.

From the Miura we move on to the "extraterrestrial" car—the Lamborghini Countach—and we can best describe this automobile as *some car*. The Miura is 41 inches high, perhaps a fraction of an inch higher; the Countach is about the same height. It is a low and very angular car, sometimes with a spoiler at the back that makes the car resemble, to some extent, a modern racing car. The doors on a Miura open the conventional way. The doors on the Countach open straight up. They are not gullwing; they simply move vertically. The interior of the car is more cramped than the Miura, and one has something of the feeling that he is at the controls of a satellite.

Whatever sports car or special car one is considering today, he often compares it with the biggest and finest Ferrari, the 512 Berlinetta Boxer. The Countach compares well in performance and roadability, and some drivers like the Countach better, including some Italian drivers and mechanics.

The Countach entered production late in the year 1973, the year after the final model of the Miura. Its engine is very much like the Miura engine—4,000 cubic centimeters (3,929 to be exact) which produces 370 horsepower. It also has twin overhead camshafts for each bank of six cylinders. There are six Weber two-throat carburetors, as in the Miura, and the two-throat feature actually means that there are twelve carburetors —meaning something of a job of synchronization. There are also independent four-wheel suspension and four-wheel disc brakes. The car weighs 2,867 pounds and is supposed to reach 190 miles per hour. In suped-up form, the car is supposed to reach over 205 miles an hour, which means that virtually nothing on the road can touch the car at top speed.

What the Countach will go for on the market is anybody's guess. Very few such cars are offered for sale. Right now this car is a living room car or a showcase garage car. It would attract too much attention to drive with any regularity. In Rome, it cannot be driven and parked. The dealer there states that it would be vandalized and parts stolen if parked on the street or in a parking lot.

This automobile requires a good deal of getting used to. It is ultra-ultra modern; but so was the Miura when it first came out. Maybe we will all get used to the Countach in time. It is also possible that production will soon stop and the car will become a great rarity at the same time that it is an experiment in futuristic automobile design. A price of as low as $80,000 is a possibility, but some Countach cars are offered for sale at $100,000 plus.

The more successful models of Lamborghini are based on the fantastically successful four-liter, V-12-cylinder engine with six double-throat carburetors, an engine that today is still of ultra-modern design. The Lamborghini Espada first made its appearance in 1967, and shortly thereafter arrived in the United States. It is a streamlined four-passenger coupe, whereas the Miura and the Countach seat only two people. In Europe the Espada is often used for transportation. In the United States the car is a rarity, and the parts are somewhat hard to obtain; so are qualified mechanics.

In 1978 a good (but not perfect) condition Espada would sell anywhere from $16,000 to $20,000. By 1981 a good condition Espada was selling at auction for $21,000 to $25,000 and the price was rising.

We might stop right here on the investment Lamborghinis. Many models of Lamborghini have been turned out, but these three models are the collectors' cars. They are all super sports cars and a little temperamental.

There are two early-model Lamborghinis which are excellent cars, but collectors seem to have overlooked them. The first car put on the market by the firm was the 350GTV of 1963, which went into production in 1964. In all, only 250 of these cars were produced, although they still appear on the market—and not at high prices. They use the V-12 engine with the very high horsepower of 360, and they will do about 160 miles per hour. The detuned version is more tractable, and it produces 280 horsepower.

In 1966 the 400GT came out with a slightly larger engine and a higher speed—167 miles per hour. It seats four people. With an engine of 3,929 cubic centimeters, this is essentially the engine used on the top performance Lamborghinis produced since that date. The firm produced only 250 of these cars as against 720 of the super-streamlined Miuras, the company's masterpiece.

Both the 350GTV and the 400 GT appear on the market from time to time, and they attract no real investor interest, although they are excellent cars. Five years ago these cars could be bought for $7,500 or even less. As of 1978 they could be bought for under $10,000. As of 1981 a good example of either car could be bought for $10,000 to $12,000.

Lamborghini has produced a welter of models, most of them using the twelve-cylinder double overhead cam engine of about four liter capacity (4,000 cubic centimeters) or *half* this engine, a six-cylinder engine installed in such cars as the four-seater Marzal of 170 horsepower and 140 miles per hour put out in 1967. Very few Marzals were produced, but every once in a while one of these cars appears for sale, in the $10,000 price range.

The Islero, the Jarama, the Bravo, and Urraco are other models turned out by this prolific firm, and while they are not great collectors' cars, they are good cars nevertheless. At a reasonable price they might turn out to be good investments, and they are good cars as far as mechanics and style are concerned.

It should be stressed that all Lamborghinis are top performance cars. They are not cars to be used primarily for transportation. They are not easy to repair and not inexpensive to repair. Parts come very high, a simple brake disc costing over $400 as compared with, say, $65 for a similar brake disc for an American car. The Lamborghini is a connoisseur's car.

Maserati

In 1967 there appeared on the market a car in many ways the quintessence of a combination of luxury and performance: the Maserati Ghibli.

Throughout the history of motor racing, Maserati has been at the forefront. In 1939 and 1940, Wilbur Shaw won the Indianapolis 500 with a Maserati. In 1957 the great road-racing champion Juan Manuel Fangio won his fifth world championship with a Maserati 250F Formula One car. In the early history of Watkins Glen, George Weaver drove his old Grand Prix Maserati to a hands-down victory. That's the history of Maserati—success even after Ferrari came along.

I took one look at a Maserati Ghibli and decided then and there to buy it. When I tried it out, I wondered why Rolls-Royce didn't produce a car with as good suspension. It was not strictly stiff, sports-car suspension. It was suspension that was firm and yet produced a beautiful, comfortable ride. At 90 miles an hour the driver is so relaxed that it is sometimes an effort to stay awake!

The Maserati Ghibli is a two-passenger coupe with two jump seats in the back. The shape of the body is streamlined and magnificent. The workmanship on body and interior are of absolutely top quality. The engine is mounted in the front with rear-wheel drive, with eight cylinders and double overhead camshafts. Performance of the car is more than excellent. It will do 170 miles per hour, and zero to 60 miles per hour in about 6½ seconds. The engine is a big 4,700 cubic centimeters, and in later models, about 5,000 cubic centimeters. It probably produces 375 horsepower.

The Maserati Ghibli coupe of 1967–1972 is by no means a difficult car to find. There are many for sale, and the Maserati Information Exchange in California often lists Ghiblis that the members have for sale. A late-model, mint-condition car can cost a little over $20,000, and an early, mint-condition car can cost up to $18,000. An average-condition car can be bought for $13,000–$14,000.

The Maserati Ghibli spyder, or convertible, is a super-super collector's car. This car may well be the most beautiful foreign postwar convertible ever made, particularly with the top down. There were probably not over 125 of these cars made. Still, they are not hard to find. In the summer issue of the Maserati Information Exchange, eight spyders were advertised at prices between $28,000 and $40,000.

The difference in price between an average-condition spyder and a mint-condition spyder is about $10,000, and the extra $10,000 is worth it. It will cost at least $10,000 to put an average condition Ghibli of any body style in mint condition.

There is another "Ghibli" called an Indy—a four-passenger car that has almost as good lines as the Ghibli, but is far less of a collector's car. Very often, fine Indys can be bought for much less than the Ghiblis and much much less than the Ghibli spyders. Motor Classic Corporation in early 1980 offered a near-mint-condition, red Indy for about $14,000, a 1972 model with the larger 5,000-cubic-centimeter, 375 horsepower engine.

Very few Indys are priced as high as $15,000, even low-mileage, mint-condition Indys. One Indy, no condition specified, was advertised in the summer of 1980 for $10,500—about market price for an average condition car. Probably the car will rise in value, but this is not the collector-investor car that the Ghibli is.

There are other very good cars that have been made by Maserati. The Mexico of the mid-sixties is one. This car has never been a favorite with collectors, though probably no more than 250 of the cars were made. On today's market, $6,000 should buy a good Mexico coupe.

The Ghibli was followed by the Maserati Bora, a rear-engined car with the engine running the long way, not transverse. This is a fine, streamlined car and a performer. The 1974 Bora sells for somewhere between $21,000 and $25,000. It is likely to rise more.

In somewhat the same price class of the Mexico is the Mistral of the later 1960s, including a spyder model. This car is not the most distinguished car in the world, and it can still be purchased for under $10,000. Distinguished or not, it is a very good car and may one day be sought by collectors.

The Automobiles of England

Jaguar

In the post–World War II period, the pioneer in sports cars was, without any question, Jaguar. Strict competition cars, top quality, top price cars, were dominated by Ferrari; but Jaguar pioneered the totally modern, highly reliable, high-performance, inexpensive sports car. No company in the world ever turned out the quality sports car for the money that Jaguar did.

The London Motor Show of 1948 exhibited what turned out to be an epic-making car—the Jaguar XK120. The body was beautiful and it was streamlined. It was quality construction. The paint was fine, the chrome was excellent, and the interior was upholstered in leather. It carried a very well-designed, sophisticated dashboard. Everything was right for the driver, including a gearshift lever in exactly the right position with short-throw gear changes and synchromesh. The XK120 body was a roadster body, and the car was meant to be driven top down.

The important part of the car, however, was the engine, and this had all of the latest features, in fact an engine not very different in design from the highly touted BMW MI engine of 1982. The MI is an enormously expensive car. The XK120 engine is a six-cylinder engine with twin overhead camshafts. For many years not even Ferrari went to twin overhead cams. The combustion chamber is hemispherical—not unlike the shape of the great Chrysler hemis. The engine could safely be run up to 6,000 revolutions per minute. Further, the aluminum XK120 is light. It is certainly good for 115 miles per hour, and at Jabbeke, Belgium, an almost stock XK120 hit 132 miles an hour.

My own XK120 was purchased in 1949, and it was well worth the purchase price of $4,700. The car was a lot of fun to drive, and at the time it was largely unknown in the U.S. Every driver on the road seemed to think he could beat it, but I usually went by motorcycles when they were flat out at 95 miles per hour, and it was not hard to get the car up to 115 miles per hour or close thereto.

Today the car is something of a treasure, and the big success character in the TV show will often be driving a white XK120. When a fine one appears in the foreign car salesrooms it usually goes right out to a waiting customer. It has not become less beautiful as the years have gone by and new models have come in from many makes of sports cars. If anything, it has become more beautiful and vastly more unique. The car is rarely seen on the road except going to and from meets, at least on the East Coast.

Some 12,000 Jaguar XK120s had been built by 1954, before the upgraded XK140 came out. The main revision of the XK140 was that the engine produced 190 horsepower instead of 160. It was possible to secure some options with the car that would push the horsepower up to 210. A Borg-Warner automatic transmission was an option on the XK140.

The XK140 appeared in 1955. In 1957 the XK150 came out— about the same car but with a still larger engine and with certain improvements. The standard version of the car produced 210 horsepower. By this time over 65,000 XK engines had been produced in all. The XK150 had cleaner valves. There was an optional overdrive and an optional Borg-Warner transmission. Perhaps the most important innovation in the XK150 was four-wheel disc brakes made by Dunlop.

The XK150 was continued to 1962 when the XKE was introduced, basically the same car and engine but with more horsepower—265—and refinements. The price of this latest model was just about the same as that of the original XK120. The essence of Jaguar was that the firm offered a tremendous amount for the money, possibly more than any other sports car producer in the world ever offered for the money. All of the series might well have sold for twice the prices. In 1964 a dealer near my home in Rye, New York, offered me a brand new XKE roadster for $4,100, quite a bargain price for a car of this quality!

To use precise dates, the XKE was first exported in March

1961 and the car was first sold in England in July 1961. In 1964 the size of the engine was increased from 3,800 cubic centimeters to 4,200. The XKE with double overhead cam six-cylinder engine held sway for ten years. In March 1971 the XKE V-12 was introduced, a twelve-cylinder car with one camshaft for each bank of cylinders. The engine capacity was 5,343 cubic centimeters, and it produced 272 horsepower. This car will do 147 miles per hour.

In its September 13, 1975 issue, *Autocar* reviewed a new Jaguar sports car—the XJ-S, a sports coupe ". . . of great refinement and high performance." The new car looked vaguely like an Italian sports coupe but with considerably less verve. The paint jobs were extremely conservative, and few people would stop to look twice at the car as any radical departure in sports car design. By September 1975 no more *E*-type Jaguar roadsters were being shipped to America, and the XJ-S was intended to fill the gap.

The XJ-S is no roaring monster. In fact it is the exact opposite, and one wonders which is more silent, a Rolls-Royce or an XJ-S. Bosch electronic fuel injection is used on this car, and the horsepower is a very healthy 285. The Borg-Warner automatic transmission is optional. The car was, and is, good for a top speed of 153 miles an hour. It does zero to 60 miles per hour in a little under seven seconds. The basic price in England was 8,143 pounds sterling—about $20,000.

This is probably the most underplayed automobile of all time. It is a performer, as the figures indicate. For the times it was not by any means overpriced. The design was sleek and graceful, but certainly not ostentatious. The advertising in the United States did nothing to indicate that this car was a star performer in the class of the high-priced Italian sports cars; yet the Jaguar is in this class.

On the second-hand market the price quickly dropped to around $12,000, and $10,000 was a good target price for this car five years ago. Two years ago prices began pushing $12,000 to $13,000, and some cars were bringing more. In the June 1980 Leake sale a 1978 XJ-S brought $14,000—at auction. Today, a good used XJ-S can still be purchased for a little under $15,000 if bought from an individual. At retail, prices of good-condition cars may well run close to $20,000 for a mint-condition model.

In some ways the public image of Jaguar is that it is a cut rate sports car on which corners have been cut to keep prices down, still a very complicated car on which repairs are costly and difficult. This picture is not entirely correct. One difficulty is that the British underplay everything.

As investments, we can start with the Jaguar XK120. Ten years ago this car, in roadster or coupe form, in good (but not mint) condition, could be bought for under $1,000. In mint condition it could certainly be bought for $2,000. So could the XK140 and XK150. The purists will swear by the XK120, and they may swear *at* the XK140 and XK150 as being too bulbous and less stark. In my opinion each car had its place, but I do know that I would certainly rather have the roadster than the coupe. It is more classic and more sporty, and, like most roadsters, will probably turn out to be worth more in the future than the coupe.

By 1975 the XK120s (coupe and roadster) were selling in the $6,000 range. The XK140 and XK150 coupes and roadsters were selling for $5,000 or a little less for excellent-condition cars. By 1980 there was a difference in the price of the XK120 coupe and the XK120 roadster. The coupe, in excellent condition, was selling for $10,000 to $11,000. The roadster was selling for $13,000 to $15,000. The XK140 roadster was selling for about $13,000 and the coupe for a little under $10,000—if both cars were in top condition. The XK150 coupe was selling for perhaps $1,000 less than the XK140 coupe, and the roadster for $11,000 to $12,000.

The six-cylinder XKE sold in the early to mid-seventies for as low as $3,000 to $4,000, and I saw a prizewinning XKE in a showroom in Greenwich, Connecticut, at that time, offered for $4,500. By 1980 the XKE six-cylinder roadster was at about $11,000 to $12,000 and the coupe at $8,000 to $9,000. The twelve-cylinder car had very much of a similar price pattern. Five years ago many such V-12 cars were for sale priced at about $6,000—in the U.S. and in England. Then prices began to climb. An XKE V-12 can easily bring $15,000 if in fine condition, and I have seen them priced at over $18,000. On the other hand a coupe two-plus-two, not such an attractive-looking car, can sell for as low as $7,500—as of 1982.

There are many other Jaguars, some of them, like the early postwar cabriolets, bringing high prices. There are also very good sedans, and some of these are not only pretty fair investments but very good cars. The main investment cars are, however, the sports cars of the XK and XJ series, both coupes and roadsters, but mainly roadsters. All are good-looking cars, and all are certainly classic cars with a definitely up-to-date look. They are up-to-date running cars as well.

There is an immense market for Jaguar sports cars, and it is an active market. The cars can be bought easily, and they can be sold easily. The price trend is definitely up for almost all Jaguar sports cars, particularly the roadsters and convertibles.

There are complaints that, although inexpensive, the car is unduly complicated, and thus expensive to repair—multiple carburetors, twin overhead cams, independent suspension, fuel injection on later models, twelve cylinders on later models. Complaints seem to be that the car is too often in the repair shop. This situation means, of course, that the car must be used little and put on nonmoving display more. But other investment cars are also often in need of repairs.

The MG

Many, if not most, of the MG cars made after World War II are small, stark machines with little or no streamlining and with a very unsophisticated engine as well as other unsophisticated mechanical components. The early postwar MG didn't even have windup windows, although the cars were certainly not strict road racing cars that had to dispense with windows. If, in the immediate postwar period, a brand new company had wanted to come out with a car that was sporty looking, simple to manufacture, and reasonable in price so as to tap the postwar market, it might well have come up with a brand new car design like the MG's.

But the MG was not a new car and not a new design. It was a very old design, put out by a firm in business since the early

1920s. The guiding spirit of MG was, in effect, a genius, even though his name is largely unknown today. The record of MG wins rivals the wins of Enzo Ferrari, strange though that statement may seem. The MG genius was Cecil Kimber, and his genius in producing cars, plus the pioneering spirit and financial backing of William Morris of the Morris Garages (MG), resulted in a tremendous amount of automotive innovation and a tremendous sales volume prewar and postwar. One automotive authority calls William Morris "the Henry Ford of the British automobile industry."

These are some of the MG records established:

- 1931—750-cubic-centimeter engine—Capt. George Eyston —103.13 miles per hour with supercharged engine
- 1938—1,087-cubic-centimeter engine—Colonel Gardner— 187.62 miles per hour, a class record with supercharged engine
- 1939—same engine in same car and same driver—203.05 miles per hour, speed record
- 1946—741-cubic-centimeter engine—Colonel Gardner— 159.15 in supercharged engine car
- 1946—500-cubic-centimeter engine (two cylinders disconnected)—118.06 miles per hour with supercharged engine —Col. Gardner
- 1949—497-cubic-centimeter engine—154.23 miles per hour with supercharged engine—Col. Gardner
- 1957—1,506-cubic-centimeter, double overhead cam engine —Sterling Moss—245.64 miles per hour
- 1959—same engine—Phil Hill—Bonneville speed record— 254.91 miles per hour

The incredible thing about these speed records is that they were achieved with tiny engines. A 500-cubic-centimeter engine is the size of a motorcycle engine, and not the biggest motorcycle engine at that. The Ferrari Berlinetta Boxer has an engine of 4,942-cubic-centimeter capacity. The Eldorado Cadillac has an 8,200-cubic-centimeter engine. The new economy imports all advertise 1,500, 1,600, 1,900, and other engine capacities. So that we are not accused of bias in favor of the MG, we must add that the gearing of the MG speed record cars was the optimum for speed (not for acceleration or road racing), that the bodies were generally streamlined, and that most records were set on tracks and on straight flats conducive to high speeds. Set up the Ferrari in that way in those places, and it too would produce an astounding speed. Still, MG was establishing these records before there was any Ferrari built, and also during the pre–World War II period.

Why consider the MG an investment car? The MG is, and has been, a steady price riser in the postwar period, particularly in the decade of the 1970s. It has risen from a price new in 1947 of about $1,600 to over $10,000 for the same car today. There is little reason to think there will be any correction in the price trend of this car. The MG never appears at auction in much volume, so that there is little chance that a large number of MGs will be thrown onto the market with a resulting price decline. True, an important auction like the June 1980 Leake auction in Tulsa will offer a number of MGs for sale, but only a few really classic postwar MGs.

If you buy a restorable Ferrari Super America, your restoration bill may run into five figures. The restoration on a classic Rolls-Royce can easily run to $15,000. The restoration of an MG can hardly run to such sums, and $10,000 would be a very high restoration figure for a really poor MG. MG parts are very easily purchased for relatively low prices. One firm advertises: "MG parts: huge stock of new factory, repro, and used parts for T.D., T.F., M.G.A., M.G.B., Midget. Direct importers, we've been a major supplier of British parts for over a decade."

Another firm advertises: "MG T.D. parts: right front fender, $350; all four hood panels, $100; three top bows, $225; intake manifold, $40; right door, $50; rear end, $250 . . ."

Repair work on an MG is not hard to secure as it does not require a particular genius. The MG is not only easy to repair, it is relatively inexpensive. It is an easy car to own. There are, for most models, only four cylinders, not twelve as in the sophisticated Italian (and English) cars. There is easy access to the engine, and there are only four spark plugs to replace, four pistons, eight valves, etcetera.

The MG is not known as a troublemaker. In fact, it is known

as the exact opposite. There is little to go wrong, and one is not generally troubled by air conditioning, power brakes, power steering, automatic transmission or, in many models, even windup windows. Also, the MG can be used. Were it not getting to be a collector's car (and now a prime collector's car) it could be used as a station car or to go to the supermarket. The car now has a classic, timeless, look about it, and there is no aging to be done.

On the other hand, the car is not strictly a utility car. It seats only two people. Many models have no windup windows, and the owner may very well get rained or snowed on. It is most certainly not a family car. It is a car that *can* be used, but it is best to use it to go for a spin on Sunday afternoon.

The first MG to arrive in the U.S. after the war was the MG T.C., and it arrived here in 1947. It is possible that one or two arrived a little earlier. The car was very interesting looking, with very large wheels and thin tires. It certainly didn't look like any Grand Prix car, but its peformance for any little four-cylinder car was outstanding. The car rode and cornered beautifully. One could take a long trip in it and still not feel fatigued. What was very important, nothing ever seemed to have to be done to the car: the spark plugs didn't need cleaning; the carburetor didn't need to be cleaned. Normal greasing and oil changes were all that were required.

It is difficult to define the place of the MG in collector car circles. The MG that was offered for sale in the United States in the postwar period was certainly not a competition car. It was not a great car for acceleration or for top speed. It would not appeal to an owner who wants to boast, "That car has 400 horsepower. It has been clocked at 172 miles per hour. The road holding and cornering are outstanding." The MG was, and is, simply a "fun car."

The model T.C. apparently went into production in October 1945. About 1,500 T.C.s were built in 1946, and one-third of these went out of England. One authority on the car reports a top speed of this model of 90 miles per hour, but I never saw 80!

Later in 1947, MG produced a coupe and a four-seater open car. There was independent front-wheel suspension, but the same small four-cylinder push-rod engine with no overhead camshaft. The body was a little different on the two-seater from the T.C., and there were a few improvements. The car, however, was pretty much the same stark automobile with about the same performance. Even as late as 1947 the car had the same general appearance as the 1932 MG Midget J2 roadster.

The similar T.D. model came out in 1949 and was continued to 1953 when the T.F. was introduced. The T.F. was about the same as the T.D., but by 1955 a big change in model was made by the company. This was the M.G.A., and this was a postwar-looking car, not so much a prewar throwback. In 1956, 13,000 of these cars were produced. They were good looking by anyone's standards. They would do well-over 90 miles per hour, and they would get 30 miles to the gallon. The stark radiator had disappeared, and the new grill fit into the overall body contour.

In 1959 a larger-engined M.G.A. was introduced—1,600 cubic centimeters, and in 1961 the new MG Midget was introduced. The MG Midget had been a popular MG in the immediate pre-war period. Now it was revived, a small-engine MG and a not particularly good-looking or up-to-date–looking car. Still, the Midget found a ready market.

In 1962 the M.G.A was turned into the M.G.B., to some degree a throwback in design to earlier MG cars, and a less distinguished car. For MG it had a big engine—1,798 cubic centimeters with horsepower over ninety and a high top speed of 105. Still, by 1964 the car was selling 30,000 copies a year abroad. In 1967 came a very much larger-engined MG, the M.G.C. with 3,000 cubic centimeters. It wasn't a popular model and it was discontinued in 1969.

By 1973 a really high performance MG was unveiled, the V-8 M.G.B. Two years later this car was still being produced as well as the smaller-engined car. The V-8 would do zero to 60 in 7.7 seconds and hit a top speed of 124. The chassis is essentially that of the smaller car, but the car obviously has more power.

As late as 1970 no postwar MG was in very much demand, and none brought very high prices. The earlier cars were the ones most in demand at the highest prices. The T.C. model, introduced to the U.S. in 1947, would bring about $1,500 in average condition and about $2,500 in fine condition, sometimes up to $3,000. A fine condition T.D. would bring $1,500 or a little more; a comparable condition T.F. would sell for under $1,500.

By 1975 a good condition MG T.C. of 1947 would sell for over $5,000, sometimes for as much as $7,500. The T.D. was selling for $3,500 to $5,000 in the same condition. The T.F. of the mid-fifties was in some demand too, and a good one would bring close to $5,000. The T.F. was put out between 1953 and 1955 and was definitely a throwback to an earlier era. Still, about 10,000 of these cars were sold. As of 1975 no one seemed to be much interested in the M.G.A., and a good one could be bought for under $2,500.

By 1980, MG had come into its own in the collector car field. A 1947 T.C. would sell, in good condition, for about $15,000. A comparable T.D. would bring $10,000. A T.F. might bring even more than a T.C., possibly because fewer T.F.s were produced than T.C.s and T.D.s. The M.G.A.s were now selling for about $7,500—ten times what they sold for ten years earlier.

The most-offered MG cars are the T.C., the T.D., the T.F., and the M.G.A. There are also a few offerings of the prewar MG T.A. and the MG T.B., and these cars bring close to $20,000 if in fine restored condition.

There is an absence of some cars on the market, among them the V-8, which is probably not considered much of an investment car—as yet. The cars on which to concentrate might well be, in order: The MG T.C.; the MG T.D.; the MG T.F.; and the M.G.A.

One thing that can be said about these collector cars is that they are still within the means of many people, while cars like the classic Mercedes-Benz and the Duesenberg are certainly not. It would be foolish indeed to buy a poor-condition Ferrari or Rolls-Royce except at very much of a bargain price, since parts and restoration for such cars are extremely high in price. On the other hand, a lesser-condition MG may still be bought and restored for a fairly reasonable sum of money. If you are a knowledgeable amateur, not a professional mechanic, you may still be able to learn enough to do restoration work on an MG.

Other British Investment Automobiles

Austin-Healey

Two other investment cars from Great Britain should be included: the Aston Martin and the Austin-Healey. If we add these two makes to the other British cars, we by no means have exhausted the possible British investment cars. There are many others, but space does not permit the consideration of every investment car.

As to the Austin-Healey: Donald Healey was a competition driver. Right after World War I he made his own car—the Healey—and brought it to the United States. It was not the greatest performer, but it was a good car. He was very anxious to prove it out on the highway, and he would motion other drivers on the road to race him. He seemed very disappointed when he found that no one actually had enough competitive spirit to want to try to beat him.

The Austin-Healey was a winning combination. The Healey started out to use the engine of 2,660 cubic centimeters from the old Austin A-90 sedan, not a very glamorous car, but apparently one with a good engine. The Austin-Healey front suspension was independent, and the car that emerged from this combination was fairly modern in design—as a sports car for two people. Perhaps the most important thing about the car is the body. It is a good and graceful one that makes the car look like a competition winner. Classic car authority Rich Taylor describes the car well: "It was a cheap Jaguar, not an expensive MG, and it rapidly got even better than that." The MG at the time was a stark little automobile, and the Jaguar was big, smooth, and relatively powerful.

The Healey 100 made its appearance in the Earl's Court Motor Show of 1952. By 1953 it was being manufactured by Austin as the Austin-Healey. By 1972, when Donald Healey and Austin parted company, 150,000 Austin-Healeys had been built, and many of them are still on the road and in the market—appreciating in value.

The basic engine is not modern. It is a long-stroke, four-cylinder affair used to power a conservative, smaller-size sedan before it found its way into the Austin-Healey, but this engine started the Austin-Healey toward success. In 1955 the 100S, a production racing car made of aluminum, appeared wtih 132 horsepower. Only about fifty of these cars were made in 1955. There was another car offered in 1955 that continued into 1956: the Austin-Healey 100M, a steel-bodied car with something of a powerful engine.

In 1956 the Austin-Healey 2,639-cubic-centimeter six came along, still a conservative pushrod engine, not an overhead cam engine. It was called the 100-6. As the years went by, the car became more luxurious with windup windows, and the horsepower was increased. The development of this 100-6 continued to 1964. In 1968 this six, known as the 3000, was dropped. The very popular Austin-Healey standard car, the 3000, could be bought in 1970 for a little over $1,000 for a very-fine-condition car. It is still in good supply.

By 1975, $4,000 to $5,000 would buy almost any good-condition Austin-Healey roadster. The four-cylinder roadsters could sometimes be bought in the $3,000 range. The 100-6 model (six cylinder) pushed above $5,000.

By 1981 *all* models of roadster seemed to hover around the $7,000 level, at least the fine-condition cars. The average-condition cars went for around $5,000, some a little less. The less important four-cylinder Austin-Healey Sprite could be bought in good condition for $4,000.

In summary, it can be said about this car that it is a good two-passenger sports car, no race winner in performance, but a very satisfactory, good-looking car that can be used, at least at times. It is easy to get parts for and easy to repair, and it should not give a great deal of trouble. In 1975 we advised the son of a friend to buy a 3000 roadster. I think he got an average-condition car for about $2,000. I see he has the same car today, and his investment has gone up about 100 percent.

Aston Martin

The Aston Martin most certainly does not belong at the end of a consideration of British sports or classic investor cars, by any means. The car qualitywise belongs very near the top, and it certainly does not occupy second place to the Austin-Healey. But not very many Aston Martins were made, and few appear on the market.

The Aston Martin was, and is, a quality car mechanically and in every other way. It is a good looking car, as James Bond (007) quickly discovered. One persistent problem with the car, however, is that it tends to be a troublemaker.

As recently as five years ago nobody seemed to want the Aston Martin. In 1970 almost any of the famous DB coupes could be bought in good condition for about $4,000. Five years later, when many cars had taken off, the Aston Martins were selling at the $5,000 level.

By 1980 the Aston Martin seemed to have come into its own. The price for the six-cylinder cars was at the $10,000–$12,000 level. The later eight-cylinder cars were at the $15,000 level. Auction prices in the U.S. were, however, by no means as high as the retail market, and many DBs still sold at auction for under $10,000. The cars offered at auction sale were about at the retail dealer level in price.

If the type body is convertible, and the car is a later eight-cylinder model, the price could be close to $20,000. As the retail price of new Aston Martins rose to around $85,000, the price of the comparable used eight-cylinder cars tended to rise. Of course the latest models were simply used late-model Aston Martins, and their price was simply a discounted new-car price, which tends to drop as the car gets older until a bottom is reached, from which the price tends to rise as the car is recognized as a classic and not simpy as a used sports car.

The *DB* comes from David Brown, who bought Aston Martin in 1947 and proceeded to make an excellent car that first appeared in 1950 and was called the DB-2. The engine was a six-cylinder double overhead cam unit of 2,580 cubic centimeters. The super engine, called the Vantage engine, turned out 120 horsepower. This car is rather conservative looking and conservative driving, but it gives one the feeling that it is quality inside and out.

Almost all Aston Martins are coupes. A few from the early 1950s are convertibles, and their styling is conservative and beautiful. Possibly the most beautiful Aston Martin I have ever seen had a Superleggera Italian body.

In 1953 the car was updated a bit in the DB-2/4, and again in 1955 in the DB-2/4 Mark II. Then came the Mark III, again a nominal advancement on the old DB-2. The Mark III appeared in 1959.

As early as 1955 the company was planning for a more powerful engine of almost 4,000 cubic centimeters, still a six-cylinder power plant with twin camshafts. In 1962 this engine put out a nominal 282 horsepower in normal form and perhaps 325 in Vantage form. The DB-4 appeared in 1958, late in the year, with four-wheel disc brakes, and in the following year the DB-4 Gran Turismo appeared wtih 310 horsepower and a top speed of 150 plus. Then came the DB-5 and the DB-6 Mark II and these cars were continued well into the 1970s.

In September 1969 came the first big change in Aston Martin cars since the DB-2 of the early 1950s. In 1969 a very advanced engine was put out in the DBS V-8. The capacity of the engine was 5,340 cubic centimeters as against 2,600 to 4,000 for the old sixes. The engine was all aluminum with twin overhead cams for each bank of cylinders. Bosch fuel injection was used. Disc brakes were used and an aluminum body. An automatic transmission was optional, and in 1971 air conditioning could be specified. In September 1973 four Weber carburetors were substituted for the Bosch fuel injection system, strange as this innovation may seem. In 1959 the Aston Martin cost a very high $10,000. In 1974 the price was up to $27,000 in England.

There is some critical opinion to the effect that the Aston Martin is over conservative. There is also critical opinion that the car is hard to maintain. Certainly the market does not reflect any wild enthusiasm for the car. Looking at it another way, however, the car is a quality automobile and good looking. For what it is, it still seems underpriced. The car to buy might well be a convertible, and some of these cars are advertised with bodies by quality British coachbuilders. It might also be a good idea to look for a V-8 in good condition, but not one so late that the price is influenced by the high new-car price. In any event, $12,000 to $15,000 should purchase a very good Aston Martin in the present market of 1982.

The Automobiles of Germany

The leading make of investment car in Germany is the Mercedes-Benz. Over the entire history of the automobile, Mercedes has been the great innovator and the great performer. In the prewar period back to the last century, and in the postwar period at least to 1955 when Mercedes retired from racing, these cars have established a standard. After producing the 300SL and the 300S in the postwar period, the company turned to transportation cars and decidedly deemphasized performance cars as well as superluxury cars. The exception is the limited production of the very complicated model 600, which is not a big factor in the collector market or sales picture of Mercedes-Benz.

We have devoted a chapter to the great Mercedes-Benz from the early collector car production times to the present. There remains the task of taking up the other collector-investor cars from Germany, and these are essentially two makes: Porsche and BMW. For the most part these two makes are limited-production, high-price-tag, performance cars, although a few cars were, and are, transportation cars. The transportation cars, as is usual, are not strictly the investor-collector cars.

Porsche

The Porsche is the most quietly effective car of the entire postwar sports car and competition car era. When Ferrari won a race the world knew it, and when they were about to enter a new model in a race, the world knew it. As a result of such publicity, when a Ferrari passed by in the street, a lot of people knew it was a Ferrari. In the great races Porsche was often absent, since the company didn't build anything like the Ferrari premier Formula One racing cars. Porsche certainly had performers on the track, and even twelve-cylinder performers; but somehow the public's attention was never quite focused on them.

The underplay characteristic also applied to the sports cars sold to the public. They are not big, impressive-looking cars.

They are not obviously streamlined cars, although they must certainly have performed well in the wind tunnel. The later semistreamlined models are smoother looking cars, but they too are underplayed. Possibly the explanation is that the cars were put out by a very small firm specializing in high performance quality cars, but not cars of great size or great engine capacity. The company certainly didn't have the money to spend on sales promotion that, say, Mercedes had and still has. They simply turned out a splendid car—in construction and in performance.

Sports car circles eagerly awaited the inauguration of the first Porsche cars in the late 1940s. The first Porsches were based on Volkswagens and utilized many basic Volkswagen parts. The engine of the 1948 car was tiny, a flat four air-cooled engine in the rear that drove the rear wheels. Its capacity was 1,100 cubic centimeters, more or less—smaller than most of the engines in the Japanese cars of today. The engine in these early cars produced only forty brake horsepower but the car, known as the Model 356, would do 88 miles an hour.

Porsche's method of developing the car was to increase the capacity of the engine gradually, up the horsepower, add a flat six engine, and then increase the output of this engine. The V-8 and V-12 cylinder engines were never used in street cars, at least to any appreciable extent.

The Porsche is a connoisseur's car. It is a strict, but docile, and very usable sports car, not temperamental. Parts are obtainable, and repairs cost a good deal less than on Italian twelve-cylinder double-overhead-camshaft-six carburetor monsters.

I was anxious to own one of the early Porsches, and I bought a 1951 1,300-cubic-centimeter coupe. The output of the engine was 46 horsepower. To see how good it was as a road car, my wife and I drove 850 miles in it in one day.

As time went on, Porsches became better and better in performance and ease of ride. They may have become somewhat more complicated and harder to repair. Still, they have remained excellent sports cars and not great troublemakers. There is the added feature that the landmark models are still not expensive to buy, even as of 1982.

The greatest performer of the whole gamut of Porsches is the street car designated as the 930 Turbo (with exhaust-driven supercharger). Modifications made by the factory to the car for racing resulted in a car designated the 935, and since 1976 about twenty-five of these cars have been delivered to customers in the United States. The latest group apparently sold for $125,000 apiece.

However, let's consider now the other Porsches that the collector-investor might buy. The 356 series of Porsche first appeared in 1948. It is a very small-engined car with only 1,131 cubic centimeters, a flat air-cooled four with rear engine, rear drive. Most mechanical components are Volkswagen components. The same essential car was produced each year up to 1964. Though the body is essentially the same, the engine was continually enlarged, and the road qualities of the car were steadily improved. Both coupes and convertibles were produced. By 1955 the engine of the model 356 was up to 1,500 cubic centimeters. In 1954 a special model "speedster" was put out, and it was continued in subsequent years. In 1956 the engine was of 1,600-cubic-centimeter capacity, and the model was generally known as the 356A. One particular model was the 356A speedster.

In 1960 the 356B model came out, a 1,600-cubic-centimeter, 70-horsepower car with the new look—actually, a more graceful, sloping hood line. The designation was continued through 1962. In 1963 the 356C appeared. There was a choice of engines in this model all the way up to 2,000 cubic centimeters capacity. The model was continued for about two years.

The early cars of the 1940s in good condition rarely bring less than $15,000, and can easily approach $20,000. The early 1950s cars, no great performers but not the early pioneering cars, bring just under $10,000. The 1955 cars up to the end of the 356 series bring from $9,000 to $12,000. As Porsche specialist dealer Guy Garrubo says, "Price in the case of Porsche depends on (1) original condition, (2) modifications along the way, and (3) degree of perfection—of the particular car."

There is, however, a bottom figure, and no Porsche of this 356 series, no matter what condition the car is in, seems to bring as little as $5,000. In 1970, by contrast, almost any of this early series car could be bought for $2,000, and a fair-condition car could be bought easily for under $1,000, even the Speedster. By

1975, however, the Speedster was recognized as a premium car, and it was selling for $5,000 to $7,000. The rest of the cars of the 356 series could be bought for $5,000 and as low as $4,000—for a car in very good condition. All unrestored models could still be purchased for relatively little money—$2,000 to $3,500

In 1965 a very new model appeared: the 911 six-cylinder overhead camshaft engine car. Engines for this series progressed from 1,991 cubic centimeters to 2,195, 2,341, and 2,687. In August 1966 the 911S with 150 horsepower appeared, followed by the 911T with less horsepower (110). Then the 911L with 130 horsepower appeared. In September 1968 the 911E with fuel injection made its debut. The 911T, E, and S all had the 2,195-cubic-centimeter engine. In October 1971 the 911T, E and S all had the 2,341-cubic-centimeter engine.

The major body-shape change came in October 1973, and fuel injection was introduced. The 911, 911S, and the Targa model were all fuel injected.

As of 1981–early 1982, all of these model cars were selling in the $9,000 to $10,000 range. The later models of 1972 and 1973 ran up to $13,000. In 1975 even the much wanted Targa model could be bought for about $5,000.

The 356 and the 911 appear on the market most frequently. When we get to the Turbo, the exhaust supercharged car, we get to modern Porsches. This car, of 3,000 cubic centimeters, appeared in 1973, and its price is related to that of the new Turbo. Two years ago a 1973 model, the Turbo-Carrera coupe, failed to sell at a high bid of $17,000 at auction.

From time to time Porsche racing cars appear on the market, and some of these cars are fantastic performers. The first was produced as early as 1953; but in 1964, the Model 904 was put out. The 904 was a landmark in racing history, particularly since the car was of only 2,000-cubic-centimeter engine capacity and cost just $7,425. The car started out as a four cylinder of 198 horsepower. Later on, the six-cylinder engine was employed at 230 horsepower. One car used the flat eight-cylinder engine of 270 horsepower; this will outperform nearly any car built. On the rare occasions when this car appears on the market, it sells for a minimum of $25,000 and could bring as much as $50,000.

This racing car series was followed by the 906, the 910, the

907, the 908, and finally the 917, produced in 1969. The 917 is a flat twelve-cylinder-engined racer of 4,500-cubic-centimeter-engine capacity later boosted to 4,900 cubic centimeters—equal to the largest Ferraris. It developed 520 to 600 horsepower. In 1972 it was supercharged, and in this form produced an amazing 900 horsepower, possibly even a bit more. The 917 weighed less than the older 904 of 180 horsepower, which gives an idea of the potential of this car for acceleration and speed. The 904 can be purchased occasionally, the 917 probably never.

There is one other racing car that on occasion appears on the market: the 550 of 1953. This is a mid-engined racing car, a four with double overhead cams and a top speed of 140. This was a very small-engined car—1,500 cubic centimeters. In 1956 it became the RS and, in 1957, the RSK with 170 horsepower. But there are very few of the 550 around to buy.

The Porsche is an excellent car, any way you look at it. Many collector cars are controversial; some are too big and clumsy, some are fine on the track but poor on the street. Some are more often in the garage than available for use. The Porsche has none of these problems—it is simply a well-made, fine-running car.

The maintenance on a Porsche is neither difficult nor expensive as compared with the more complicated exotics. Many mechanics can repair Porsches, and many official Porsche repair shops are available. Parts for the Porsche are neither expensive nor hard to find. The early Porsches were in many ways just fancied-up Volkswagens, and they had the design simplicity of the Volkswagen. Even later Porsches did not include complicated, hard-to-find parts in their mechanical features.

The Porsche is an excellent running car. It starts easily, and is reliable. It is thus at the opposite extreme from the very complicated Mercedes-Benz 600 with its elaborate hydraulic system. In fact, most Porsches can be used in everyday service, and are used this way by their owners. Also, the Porsche is an inconspicuous car that does not invite vandalism or theft.

Prices on collector Porsches are relatively low: $10,000 or less will buy a very good Porsche. The car has gone up in value, but it has not increased greatly, as have certain models of Ferrari. It thus probably still has price increases ahead. The demand for very fine, used Porsches is very strong, so that the investment can be liquidated easily, if need be.

Finally, a Porsche owner can lean on the many members of Porsche clubs, who seem to be a group extremely loyal to their cars. Members can supply help in locating cars, selling cars, locating parts and repair services, and solving problems that arise in the maintenance of the Porsche.

The BMW

The letters stand for *Bayerische Motoren Werke*—Bavarian Motor Works. The BMW is a standout from every point of view. It is a docile, reliable, luxury car to be used for transportation. It is not overcomplicated, and most of the successes of this car have been achieved with a six-cylinder engine. Today the German car connoisseur, or even the German car purchaser, thinks extremely highly of the BMW. In fact there are those who place the BMW ahead of the Mercedes in many areas of car design and performance.

BMW advertises how little their cars go down in value as time goes by and the car gets older. They point out that the 1979 Mercedes sold in 1980 for 83.8 percent of its cost new, the Cadillac Seville at 76.7 percent of its new price, but the BMW 5 series at 100.3 percent of its new cost.

The 1978 Mercedes declined to 75.3 percent by 1980, the Seville to 68.8 percent, and the Jaguar XJ-6 to 67.9 percent. The 1978 BMW, however, dropped to only 79.7 percent of its cost new.

In performance, the BMW apparently hit the jackpot with their M1. This car is the result of an effort to beat Porsche in class racing, and this was a hard job. The engine is a six-cylinder, twin overhead camshaft type with four valves per cylinder —twenty-four valves in all. The normal engine develops 277 horsepower, but the horsepower of the competition engine has been increased to 470. This car is for so-called class four racing. For class five, the displacement is altered to 3,200 cubic centimeters, and the horsepower is raised to about 800. The car weighs 2,260 pounds. The body is designed by the premier world designer, Giorgetto Giugiaro, and made in Turin by his firm of Ital Design, then shipped to Munich for final assembly. Thus the appearance of the car fully matches its performance.

The amazing increase in horsepower for the ultimate competition model BMW is achieved by supercharging, and the supercharger is an exhaust-driven turbo. How long the engine would last with this power output is questionable, but in racing, the car has held up well enough to win, and that is enough.

The first major postwar collector BMW is the BMW 507, the design started in 1955, a lightweight car of 2,600 pounds with independent front suspension and a V-8 overhead valve engine of 2,600 or 3,200 cubic centimeters, putting out 140 horsepower in the latter form. It will do about 130 miles per hour, and it cost a fairly high $10,500 when it appeared in 1956.

The 1956 BMW 507 was a car of timeless, splendid design. The car was put out from 1956 through 1959, and some models were listed as 1960s. There was not a greal deal of demand for these cars until around 1975, when they commanded a price, in fine condition, of about $5,000. Average condition 507s could be bought for half this sum and less. But by 1980 the price had tripled at least, and fine-condition cars were selling at $15,000-plus. One such car actually sold for $20,000 in 1979.

In 1965, BMW put out a small engine (2,000 cubic centimeter) four and called it the 2000CS. By 1969 the 2800CS/3.0CS coupe appeared and this was kept until 1975. It started out selling for $8,000 and ended up with a price of $11,000. The car is docile, but it will reach 130 miles per hour. Driver Rich Taylor says about the car, ". . . the CS is just about the best buy you can make in the whole collector car world. I have never, *never* driven a car that provides such consistent pleasure day in and day out."

The coupe is difficult to find. It doesn't look like a strict collector car. It certainly doesn't have the verve of a Ferrari, and it doesn't have the sound of a Ferrari or Lamborghini in action. In many ways it looks like a conservative coupe and is not inclined to attract attention. It is strictly a connoisseur's car. Perhaps it is a sleeper. In any event, I have seen these cars go as low as $5,000. It might well pay to search out one of them as an investment that will supply a good deal of driving pleasure.

CHAPTER **8**

Prewar American Classics

THERE ARE PROBABLY FEW AUTOMOBILE COLLECTORS who would not want to own at least one of the great cars of the prewar period such as the Cadillac V-16 roadster, the Packard Boattail 734 speedster and the Duesenberg J or SJ. These cars are all in the six-figure range, and a few of them may even reach the half-million mark. For the well-heeled automobile investor-collector, the prewar classics probably represent the best buying opportunities, combining investment potential with pride of ownership.

Prewar classics have risen in price far more than postwar classics—all models included. In the prewar era, simple cars were produced that are now sky-high in price compared with what they cost new and compared with their reputation as fine automobiles. At this extreme are the Fords, mainly the Model A Fords and the V-8s of the 1930s. Any convertible Model A Ford in reasonably good condition will sell for at least $10,000, as will any V-8 convertible in comparable condition. A mint-condition convertible in either Model A or V-8 can bring up to $20,000.

One of the least elegant cars in these categories of Fords is the Model A Ford two-door sedan. Still, an average-condition Ford Model A two-door sedan will bring $7,000 on the present market.

Selected American Prewar Classic Cars

Auburn-Cord-Duesenberg
Packard
Chrysler
Cadillac
Ford and Lincoln

These are selected cars, of course; we cannot review every investment make and model car, and we have obviously left out such prewar investment cars as Pierce-Arrow, Stutz, Buick, and Franklin, among others. From a market point of view, however, these latter cars are of less importance than the five makes selected.

Foreign Prewar Classic Cars

Bugatti
Hispano-Suiza
Isotta Fraschini
Bentley
Alfa Romeo

We have left out Rolls-Royce, Ferrari, and Mercedes-Benz because we have considered these three makes in separate chapters. We have left out such prewar classics as Jaguar, Delahaye, Delage, Talbot, and BMW. Why? Because in the process of picking the more important cars for the above list, our point of view was that of the market for prewar classics.

It is not clear just what the difference between a prewar classic and an antique is. Sometimes the cutoff year used is 1925; sometimes it is 1922. Some flexibility is needed in this type of definition. One make may be a classic and another make of the same year an antique. The last Ford Model T was put out in 1927. This was a two-forward-speed, four-cylinder car with about a 22 horsepower engine and a top speed of about 45 miles an hour. It had a planetary transmission and a brake on the driveshaft. To me this model Ford might well be considered an antique, even though it was made in 1927. It might be best here to try to sidestep the question of what is a prewar classic and what is an antique, and talk about individual investment cars.

Auburn-Cord-Duesenberg

Without much question, of all the prewar American classic cars, those turned out by the Auburn-Cord-Duesenberg Company of Auburn, Indiana, seem, at the present time, the most valuable collectible cars and probably the most desirable cars to own—simply as fine cars. The company concentrated on (1) style of the future, (2) styles of verve, (3) performance, and (4) excellence, and in the lesser cars, excellence *for the price.*

Duesenberg

The Duesenberg is the most valuable collector car in America and possibly in the world today. True, there are very expensive Bugattis, and the most expensive is the Bugatti Royale; but there were at most only seven of these cars produced, and one can almost ignore the Bugatti Royale as an investment. There is probably no one who would part with his Bugatti Royale!

On the other hand, Duesenbergs change hands relatively often, and a Duesenberg can be bought, if one has the money. Probably a fair average market price for the wanted Duesenbergs today—the J and SJ models—would be $200,000. Closed cars may go for less and speedsters for more than this average price.

From another point of view, if you can afford a Rolls-Royce you have a prestige builder. If you can afford a Duesenberg you have very much *more* of a prestige builder. E. L. Cord, in 1926, took over the company that produced Auburns, Cords, and Duesenbergs. The brothers Fred and Augie Duesenberg, who had developed the Duesenberg car originally, were kept in charge of engineering design by E. L. Cord, with the admonition to "produce a new car which, it terms of style, engineering and sheer panache, should rival the best the world has to offer."

The result, the Model J Duesenberg, was, in the words of the company, "the world's finest car." Maybe it was, but if it wasn't it was very *near* to being so—alongside Rolls-Royce, Hispano-Suiza, Isotta Fraschini, Mercedes-Benz, Horch, Maybach, and Minerva. In any event, the car was most certainly the best the United States had to offer, and it probably remains the greatest quality car the U.S. has ever produced.

The Model A Duesenberg was built from 1920 to 1926, the latter year being the purchase date of the company by E. L. Cord who set out to make a superluxury car. The Model A Duesenberg was the first straight-eight-engined car produced in any quantity in America. It had a fairly large engine with 4,260 cubic centimeters, somewhat larger than the top Italian sports car engines of today, but not large by the standards of the 1920s. The car had a racing background. In fact, Duesenbergs won the Indianapolis race in 1924, 1925, and 1927. The passenger car was billed as "the world's champion automobile —built to outclass, outrun and outlast any car on the road." At least 500 model As were produced.

Model A is very conservative. It has no flair, but it did earn a good deal of respect for its quality. It is not the most wanted Duesenberg on today's market. In 1982, $50,000 should buy a good condition model A, and a very fine sports roadster might approach $100,000.

The J and SJ Duesenbergs are the sought-after models. Still, it was not so long ago that these models were not at all sought after. Between 1928 and 1936 (the year the model was discontinued), 470 S and SJ models were produced. One important thing about these cars is that almost every car carries a magnificent body. The bodies were all custom-made, by the best American and European body builders. The American builders of these bodies were just as good as the European builders.

The engine was the latest design and the best that could be made at the time. It was a straight-eight with twin overhead camshafts and four valves per cylinder. The horsepower of the J was 265, and the car would probably do 115 miles per hour, perhaps a little more. The SJ, introduced in 1932, had a supercharger which increased power to 320 horsepower. The car would do a reported 130 miles per hour, a fantastic speed for any luxury car at the time—or even today!

Ken Purdy, late editor of *True Magazine,* was one of the greatest American authorities on automobiles, and he backed up his writing with ownership of some of the great classic cars. He reported that the chassis of the J, when the car first appeared, sold for $8,500. In 1931 the chassis price was raised to $9,500. The SJ chassis of 1932 listed for $11,750. The custom bodies started at $3,500. In 1932 the price of the car and body ran from $13,000 to $17,500. A few very special-bodied cars sold for $20,000, and one or two cars approached $25,000—an enormous price in the Depression.

At the outbreak of the war in 1941 the value of Duesenbergs was not high. One extremely fine convertible coupe, owned by a racing driver, was offered for $750. A dual-cowl phaeton was offered for $600. These are some of the "fish that got away" from me.

There are diverse opinions on the Duesenberg. There are those that think it is the finest car ever made anywhere in the world; others favor small high-powered cars like the Alfa Romeo and the Bugatti. My first chance to drive the Duesenberg came at Indianapolis at the time of the 1946 race, the first such race after the war. The car I drove was in perfect condition, as was to be expected, since it belonged to Jim Hoe, who was, and most certainly is, the greatest Duesenberg mechanic who ever lived. Ken Purdy states that Jim has had no fewer than 200 Duesenbergs in his shop for repairs at one time or another. At any rate, Jim chose to drive my Auburn 851 boattail speedster out to the track, and I drove his Duesenberg. The Duesenberg was a beautiful-running, magnificent-looking car, but big, heavy. The leader of our delegation from the Sports Car Club of America, Hemp Oliver, drove a Packard 1930 model 734 touring car; and this car, plus some others in the delegation, got as much attention as Jim Hoe's Duesenberg. It was much later that the Duesenberg became so choice.

Ken Purdy, writing on Duesenberg in the spring 1962 *Automobile Quarterly* (volume one, number one), estimated that at the time he wrote, the price of a Duesenberg was two-thirds of its cost new—about $10,000 in 1962.

By 1970 even the humble Model A Duesenberg was selling for close to $20,000. The J and SJ sedans were selling for about

$25,000, the convertible sedans for about $30,000, and the phaetons and roadsters for up to $60,000. The SJ Derham dual-cowl phaeton that was offered to me in 1941 for $600 may have sold in 1970 for $60,000, although I am by no means sure this was the identical car. (It should be recalled that in 1970 one could get a very good Mercedes-Benz 300S cabriolet or roadster for from $2,000 to $2,500 and a Ferrari 250GT convertible for $4,000. By 1970 many cars had not risen a great deal in value, but Duesenberg certainly had.)

By the year 1975, Duesenberg was in the price stratosphere. For $50,000 a fine Model A Duesenberg could be secured, but the J and SJ models had soared. A sedan could be bought for $100,000 or less, as could even a sports coupe or roadster at times. Once in a while a phaeton sold *down* toward $100,000, but most sold from $140,000 to $175,000, and one perfect car topped $200,000. By 1980 the old Model A Duesenberg was selling for prices up to $90,000; some cars topped $100,000.

The J model sedans now sold for about $150,000. A Bowman and Schwartz convertible sedan appears to have been sold for a price in the range of $100,000–$125,000. The rest of the convertibles were selling for prices up to $250,000 and $300,000.

In late 1979 and 1980 some resistance on the part of buyers apparently developed at auction, and some of the cars did not meet their reserves, which did not seem to be astronomically high. The Christie's sale of October 2, 1979, was not a resounding success for several reasons, although many of the cars offered were of quality. One of the cars that did not find a buyer was a J model, four-passenger sedan in apparently fine mechanical condition, with a good-condition body by Murphy. It was estimated to bring $180,000 to $250,000.

In the March 1980 car auction at the Los Angeles Convention Center conducted by Christie's, two Duesenbergs were offered for sale. One was a dual-cowl phaeton with LeBaron body. The other was a four-door convertible with Rollston body. The estimate on each car was $180,000 to $250,000. Both cars appeared to be in mint condition and had been show winners. Neither car sold, although it was likely that the reserves were not too high, considering what Duesenbergs had been selling for.

Apparently, prices of the J and SJ had risen so high as to meet buyer resistance. No other car in the world with a number of specimens on the market was selling at prices as high as the Duesenberg. In any event, at $200,000 or thereabouts, the market for any collector car becomes very thin. Few people want to invest a sum of close to a quarter of a million dollars in any one automobile.

Yet the Duesenberg stands at the apex of collector cars. It is probably the finest that America has produced. It is to all intents and purposes a superluxury car, and yet it has a racing background. In appearance, it is an absolute standout, and Duesenberg cars have been adorned with the best bodies that America and Europe have produced. If one wants to impress his business colleagues or his friends in the country club set, the ownership of a Duesenberg certainly helps!

The cars can be driven, and they are reliable. On the other hand, they are so fantastically expensive that few people would use them except on special occasions. To get them into the condition they deserve costs a great deal of money, and once they are in top condition it is best not to run them down. It is too hard and too costly to put them back in first class condition again.

As an investment, few cars have equaled the Duesenberg. From a level of $600 to $700 as of the 1940s, the same cars are now worth close to $250,000. Gold in the 1940s was $35 an ounce. As of mid-1981 it was around $415. Duesenbergs had risen in value far more than gold!

Auburn

The "replicar" industry is getting to be a big business, not only in the United States but abroad as well. In this country there are reproductions of the great classics—Stutz, Duesenberg, Mercedes, and so on. The car that has been made in replica form more than any other make or model is the Auburn 1935–1936 boattail speedster. The replica car has been based on this Auburn because of the original's popularity with buyers. The Auburn is popular with buyers because, of all American cars, it is considered to be at the zenith of style and beauty. The car was a fantastic beauty when it was first produced, and it is fantastic now.

Gordon Buehrig was a young man when I met him at the Indianapolis race in 1946, but he had already designed many great cars, and his stars were the Auburn boattail speedsters of 1935 and 1936. An Auburn boattail speedster first appeared in 1928; in 1931 the incredibly low price tag was $1,150. I recall seeing this car as the featured display in the Washington, D.C., motor show of 1931. Strangely enough, the ordinary Auburn sedans were supposed to offer competiton to Ford and they were priced at under $1,000.

The Auburn in which to invest, and the car that supplies to the possessor a great amount of pride of ownership, is the speedster. As early as 1970 this early car in fine condition would bring $12,000 or more. Over the years, the lines were improved and the engine made more powerful. The 1929, 1930, 1931, and 1932 models were bringing as much as $15,000 in 1970, and more in prime condition.

In 1932, Auburn came out with a fantastic car: the V-12 speedster of 160 horsepower and a speed of over 100 miles per hour. This car listed new for $1,495 and captured the American Stock Car Speed Championship, touching as high as 117 miles per hour, a high speed even for the Mercedes-Benz supercharged SS. In 1970 this rare speedster model was selling for over $20,000.

The ultimate in Auburn speedsters are the models 851 of 1935 and 852 of 1936, the finest creations of Duesenberg designer Gordon Buehrig. It was a crowd stopper when it came out, and it is a crowd stopper today. The engine is a straight-eight flat-head with a supercharger designed by one of the Duesenberg Brothers, the supercharger supposed to raise the horsepower of the engine from 115 to 150. This increased horsepower, plus a Columbia two-speed rear axle, gave the car, in effect, six forward speeds instead of three, and the very high speed at the time of over 100 miles an hour. Each 1935 and 1936 model had a plaque on the dash which stated that Ab Jenkins, the driver of the famous Mormon Meteor, had driven the car 100.1 miles an hour or 101.25 miles an hour or whatever. All of these cars had to exceed 100 miles per hour or they were not delivered to dealers for sale.

The bodies of these cars are fantastic. The mechanicals are good for the price, but the value of the Auburn boattail speedsters lies in the body of these cars, which, for its type, probably could not be improved upon.

In 1970, $15,000 would buy a fine-condition Auburn speedster of the 851 and 852 series. Sometimes the price was a little less and sometimes a little more. By 1975 these cars had increased greatly in value. The 851 and 852 models and the V-12 speedsters of earlier years were all selling, if in top condition, for $35,000 to $40,000. The earlier models were selling from $25,000 to $30,000, probably closer to $30,000. These speedsters are not scarce, but the fact that many companies are turning out replicas of the 851 and 852 will drive up the price of the originals. The car is not simply a rare old car to be appreciated only by sophisticated connoisseurs; it is a car that anyone can appreciate owning and driving today.

As of 1981 the end of the price rise was certainly not in sight. A fine 851 or 852 boattail was selling for $60,000 to $65,000. The V-12 boattail was selling at the same price level. The earliest boattails were selling in the low $40,000s and the later boattails, before the great 851 and 852 models, were selling in the $50,000 range. The top seems yet to come.

Cord

The most eminent of all Cord automobiles is a custom car called the Phantom Corsair. Over the years this car has received more publicity than any other Cord ever made. It was featured in the 1939 World's Fair exhibition in New York. It was featured in the film called *The Young in Heart,* a film shown again and again in the immediate postwar period; here it was called *The Flying Wombat.* Its latest appearance was in the *New York Times* of November 9, 1980, where it was labeled ". . . a 1938 Phantom Corsair." Only it wasn't *a* Phantom Corsair of 1938; it was *the* Phantom Corsair of 1939. There was only one such car ever made, and it was built by Rust Heinz of the "57 Varieties" family. The car is extremely low with an enveloping aluminum body and a sharply raked nose and windshield. The doors are opened by solenoids, one door opening out and a small door opening upward and geared to the main outward-opening door. Five passengers can sit on the front seat, three to the right of the driver and one to the left.

In the back seat, the riders face backward. On either side. there is a door which opens onto a cocktail bar. The bar lights up when the door is opened. The upholstery is pin tuck fabric and leather. The chassis is Cord, model 810, unsupercharged V-8. It is possible that the top speed is 115 miles per hour, although I rarely drove the car over 95. One trouble with keeping the speed down was that the car is effectively soundproofed with cork and rubber. You couldn't feel the speed.

The Phantom Corsair cost me $5,000 in 1947. As a trade-in on the Phantom, my Auburn 851 speedster was valued by Andy Granatelli at $1,800, leaving $3,200 for me to pay in cash. The Chicago Duesenberg dealer felt I had grossly overpaid and told me that all of the dealers on automobile row were making fun of me. Today $100,000 would not be considered high for the Phantom!

The Phantom Corsair is a very special Cord, one of a kind. The stock Cords are in a different class. They are regularly traded in the market, and they have a market price (within limits). There are really two distinct stock models, two very distinct cars. Their only common feature is that they are both front-wheel-drive cars.

The model L-29 of 1929 is a straight eight with flat head and a very long hood to accommodate the very long shift lever that connected to the front of the engine. The shift lever came through the dash board.

The model 810 of the mid-1930s is a V-8 with an electric pre-selective transmission. The hood of the 810 of the mid-thirties is of rounded box shape. The L-29 has a chrome grill that very much resembles the very impressive Duesenberg grill.

For its day, the L-29 was far ahead of most other cars in appearance and performance. It was supposed to have a top speed of 75 miles per hour. I rode in an L-29 in 1930 with the speedometer reading well over 90, and the car seemed to be doing at least that. A real trouble with the car was that it was an extremely difficult shifter, as the shift rod had to cover too great a distance and make too many turns to reach the transmission in the far front of the car.

In the famous "Eight Automobiles" exhibition at the Museum of Modern Art in New York in 1951, a Cord was one of the eight. This fact says a good deal for its design. Although it is vastly different in design from the Auburn boattail speedster, both cars were designed by the same man—Gordon Buehrig.

By 1970, Cords were on their way as "value cars." The L-29s were selling at over $10,000 for the open models—cabriolets or convertible sedans—and a little under $10,000 for the closed cars. In the 810 model, $7,000 to $9,000 would buy a car of fine condition. As of the mid-seventies, $50,000 was about an average price for a convertible L-29 in excellent condition. A few convertibles brought a little less, and the sedan brought under $20,000. At this time a good 810 or 812 phaeton of the mid-thirties was bringing $20,000 to $25,000 and a sedan as little as $10,000.

The upward climb in values continued in the next five years, to 1980.

A number of cords were offered at auction in 1979, and the L-29 model was selling in the $60,000–$70,000 range. The 810 and 812 convertibles were in the $40,000–$55,000 range, and the sedans were about $20,000. As of late 1980 a good L-29 sedan would sell for about $40,000, and any convertible could bring $75,000 if in top condition. At this time a standard 810 or 812 sedan brought $25,000–$30,000 and a convertible model about $50,000, some even more.

Packard

One might liken a prewar Packard to a painting by Renoir as far as the market is concerned. Collectors with money want both, and the market is always firm. Some Packards can be likened to Renoir paintings of little girls in a landscape setting —they both go high. Some Packards are like a Renoir still life of fruit—both are wanted, but the price is materially below the price of the most-wanted objects.

At the apex of value stands the Packard 734 boattail. In the famous Leake sale of June 1980 a 1930 Packard boattail speedster went for $125,000, certainly a high price for a prewar classic, but not an extraordinarily high price, particularly for the car. The catalogue read:

One of the six boattail roadsters in existence, this is absolutely authentic in every respect and immaculately restored. Packard considered this to be the most desirable and collectible car in the Packard line, and built this model with more horsepower to the engine and special carburetors.

There we have the value characteristics of the car: Packard considered this to be a most desirable and collectible car. So do connoisseurs, because it is immaculately restored, and authentic in every respect. There are no replacement wheels or special engine installed later, etcetera, etcetera. Also, this is one of only six such models in existence. The supply is very small in relation to demand for this car. In addition, this car had special original Packard-installed features that other Packards did not have—more horsepower and special carburetors.

As a matter of fact, the purchaser of this car got a fine buy— the retail price on the car might well have been above $125,000 even at the time the car was auctioned in the summer of 1980.

Packard produced the greatest welter of models all the way from a competitor of the Rolls-Royce to a car that could be bought for a little more than one would have had to pay for a Ford—the Model 110.

The first Packard eight really appeared on the market in 1924, when a few were sold. In 1925 more were sold, and in 1928 the company stopped building its reliable old standby, the six, or Single Six, as it was often called. This car had first appeared in 1921.

The *old* V-12, or Twin Six, was produced from 1915 to 1922; a new and vastly superior V-12 was produced from 1932 to 1939. In 1935 the model 120 came out, with a 120-inch wheelbase and independent front suspension. It had four-wheel brakes, hydraulically operated, and a straight-eight engine. With a price on the business coupe of only $990, the car sold like mad to many who had wanted all their lives to own a Packard but couldn't come near the purchase price of prior Packards.

In 1937 a six-cylinder car was added to this "cheap" line, and sales of the company hit an all-time high. The elegance and quality of Packard rubbed off on the new cheap model cars, but to all intents and purposes the finest car image was finished.

It might be pointed out that there was an attempt made to put out a reasonably priced car as early as 1932: the Light Eight. One characteristic of this car was a curved line at the bottom of the radiator. The car was well designed and a quality car, selling for under $2,000. In 1939 I located a second-hand Light Eight convertible for one of my friends for $125, a car in almost mint condition. The car drove well and was completely reliable. A year later (1933) this model was merged with the main line of cars and was simply called the Eight.

The big eight-cylinder cars were produced throughout the 1930s and 1940s with the exception of the war years, and immediately after the war both six- and eight-cylinder cars were produced. Two designations of the big straight-eight models were 160 and 180.

Whether the models 120 and 110 were tinny or not I am unwilling to say. I drove many miles in a 110 during the war with a professional airline pilot, and the car was very satisfactory if not luxurious. It was, however, no model 180 and no V-12! One variation of the big straight-eight should be mentioned, and this is the Packard Darrin, body designed by Howard Darrin. In my opinion, this car, with its cutaway doors, was one of the most beautiful Packards ever produced. This car, made in 1940 and 1941, was, and is, a very good car. It could be bought as of early 1982 for $100,000 or even a little less.

The Packard 120 (and 110), humble cars though they may be in comparison to the straight-eights and V-12s, sold, in convertible form as of 1982, for about $25,000, a price up with the larger Packards. The closed versions of the 120 and 110 sold for under $10,000, still a healthy price. The model 115, a six-cylinder car of the late 1930s, and the Packard Clipper of the early 1940s, both relatively inexpensive, sold for a little less than the model 120.

Packard has been a car of tremendous charisma, and it secured this charisma during its lifetime. The advertising and publicity put out by the company did much to create the image of a quality, dashing automobile.

In the late 1920s one referred not to the Packard, but to "the Packard straight eight." This kind of reference was like a reference to a Harry Winston diamond or a Patek Philippe watch. At the time, straight eight was *the best*. There was no question about that fact! The V-8 was definitely second best, in the popular mind.

Price Range for Packards

An open Packard is vastly more in demand, at higher prices, than a sedan or coupe. An open Packard is a car of verve and has some sporting element. A closed Packard may be elegant, but it is very formal—as formal in 1982 as when it first left the showroom. So, a Packard touring car, roadster, or convertible tends to bring a much higher price than a closed car. On February 25, 1979, Christie's had a sale at the Los Angeles Convention Center at which time a large and impressive looking Packard 1938 super eight, model 1603, four-door sedan was auctioned. The car brought $8,000. In July 1979, Christie's of London auctioned a somewhat similar closed car, this one a 1935 model 1202 seven-passenger limousine. The car was apparently well restored, and it brought 5,500 pounds sterling—$12,100 at the rate of exchange then. These were prices at the large auctions, not the specialized car auctions held here in the United States. The actual retail value of good condition sedans was about twice these prices.

The large and important model Packards of the 1930s did not vary much in price as of 1982 whether they were an early or a late thirties car. All open cars from 1932 to 1939 tended to bring somewhere in the same price area—from $55,000 to $75,000, if in top condition. The sedans brought half as much. The twelve-cylinder models are premium cars. If they are open in body model they tended to bring from, say, $90,000 to $125,000. Here, also, the sedans and even the coupes brought half as much.

In the case of Packard, the year 1926 might well be considered the start of the prewar classic era and the end of the antique era. The Packard straight-eight appeared in June 1923, and the car sold better and better as it became known; as the years went on the body became more and more sophisticated and the car more and more accepted. A few eight-cylinder open cars dating back to the year 1924 appear on the market from time to time, and these cars as of 1982 were selling for around $35,000. The price of closed models was about half this level.

The 1928 model open cars were selling for $50,000 to $75,000. The 1929 model was, and is, much favored by Packard collectors, and as of 1982 this car was selling for up to $75,000—the roadster and the touring car.

The 1930 was, and is, a much favored car as is the 1931. Then interest in the eight seems to drop off and switches to the twelve-cylinder (the new Twin Six) model. The 1930 and 1931 model Packards, the open cars, are in tremendous demand at very high prices. They range in price, if in mint condition, from $125,000 to over $150,000.

What have prices done in the past half decade? Increased tremendously for *all* Packards. In the Leake sale in Arlington, Texas, in May 1974 a 1934 Packard 1101 eight four-door convertible sedan, in good overall condition, sold for $11,000. A 1934 Packard V-12 formal sedan sold for $16,000. The convertible as of 1982 would have sold for about $50,000 and the V-12 sedan for about $40,000.

In 1974 we wrote, "For $6,000 to $7,000 one can buy a Packard six roadster or touring car dating from the early 1920s. This is a good-looking, highly desirable car. The eight-cylinder models and the limited edition models are sky high in price, as are the twelve-cylinder models." These "inexpensive six-cylinder cars from the early 1920s" now, as of 1982, bring $20,000 to $25,000.

Buying a Packard

A Packard is a collector's car, to be purchased by a knowledgeable and sophisticated investor. There is very little chance of making a "discovery" of a Packard that is worth far more than it cost. Any collectible Packard is expensive. There are no inexpensive Packards except the postwar ones, particularly the mid-fifties sedans. Maybe one day these too will become collector and investment cars, but they are hardly in this category now. The Packard car is a legend in America—a legend of one of the best cars ever produced in this country. This legend has driven up the market, no doubt, and the legend will continue to maintain a high and active market for the car.

Packards have risen to great heights in price, but there is, as of 1981, no price weakness. There is a very large market for Packards, both a buying market and a selling market. All car auction companies like classic Packards, which tend to sell, although, of course, not always at the price the seller would like. Still, they never seem to go very low.

Packards in *good* condition should be bought, possibly in *mint* condition. Mint-condition Packards tend to bring very high prices, but average-condition Packards can still be satisfactorily restored. Parts are available for Packards. Luckily, a Packard is not an overcomplicated car and is relatively easy to work on. Finding competent mechanics should not be tremendously difficult.

These are the investment Packards that might be concentrated on as of early 1982, from the most valuable to the least valuable:

Touring cars of 1930 and 1931—the big eight-cylinder cars
Convertible coupes of 1930 and 1931—the big eights
Touring cars and convertible coupes—big eights—of 1928 and 1929
Packard Darrins—convertibles
The V-12s of the 1930s—open cars and convertibles
Eight-cylinder touring cars of the earlier 1920s
Six-cylinder touring cars of the 1920s

We have not taken up the postwar Packards, because these are not important collectible automobiles. The postwar cars do not occupy the same important position in the eyes of car connoisseurs (and collectors) that the prewar Packards do. The postwar Packards are still not important collectibles, *except* for the convertibles.

Chrysler

It is somewhat difficult for anybody whose life took place mainly in the postwar period to appreciate what the Chrysler car was when it first appeared in 1924. The significant car at that time was the Chrysler 70. It had a 70-horsepower engine and would go 70 miles an hour. I owned one of these first Chrysler 70 cars, the roadster, and often saw 70 on the speedometer.

Why was Chrysler such a success and why is it such a glamour collector's car today? That it was a success there is no question. In the first year of production of the Chrysler car, 1924, sales totaled 32,000, very big for a new make of car. The basic price of the six, the big-selling new car (not the four, which was also produced, a car essentially an old out-of-date Maxwell) was a little over $1,600. The car was certainly far higher in price than the low-priced Fords and Chevrolets, but it was far under the prestige Packard. Still, when one drove a Chrysler he did not have to bow his head when a Packard drove by him!

In 1928 the Chrysler 70 was improved, and the car looked both bigger and better: the Chrysler 72. The next year the car became the Chrysler 75, and the Blue Boy, a splendid sporty medium-blue roadster, was advertised extensively at $1,555. I remember the price well. I went to sleep at night dreaming of one day owning a Chrysler 75 Blue Boy!

In 1930 three sporty Chryslers came out—the 66, the 70, and the 77. These were distinctive, sporty cars of performance. They were characterized by a narrow cylindrical chrome band for the hood—the chrome radiator trim. Other characteristics were wing-shaped louvres on the sides of the hood; the colors, which were light and sporty, sometimes two-toned and with curving breaks in the colors; and finally, the fact that the cars were real performers.

By the late 1920s the company was well on its way. From 32,000 sales in 1924, sales zoomed to 200,000 in 1927. In 1925, Chrysler had bought the Maxwell car company and eliminated their Maxwell and Chalmers cars. Sales of 200,000 put the company in fourth place in the automobile industry and, in the three-year period ending in 1927, profits were around $46,000,000. The company used the profits for modernization and expansion of plant and equipment. My own 1930 Chrysler 70 was a most sporty and satisfactory car.

The Imperial 80 of the 1920s and 1930 was a six, but a prestige six that tended to be a rival of the Packard. The eight-cylinder Imperials of the years 1931, 1932, and 1933, with their custom bodies, certainly did rival Packards in every way.

The values of the real collectible Chryslers—the open cars—skyrocketed in the decade of the 1970s. In 1970 a six-cylinder Chrysler Imperial 80, 1926 through 1930, in fine condition, could be bought for a maximum of $7,500. The Imperial eights of 1931–1933 were hovering around $15,000, some selling as high as $20,000. The highly desirable 1930 model 77 could be bought, in fine condition, for $5,000. The 1929 Chrysler 75 Blue Boy could be bought for under $5,000, and the earlier Chrysler 70 touring cars and roadsters could be bought for $3,500 or less, the 1928 model 72 being only slightly more expensive.

By 1975 the early model 70 was selling for about $7,500, with the phaeton selling for more than the roadster in many cases. The model 72 roadster of 1928 was over $10,000, and my favorite Blue Boy was about $15,000, the 1929 car. The 1930 model 77 was even higher. The six-cylinder Imperials were selling from $15,000 to $20,000; and those treasures, the eight-cylinder Imperials, were at the $50,000 to $60,000 level. Even as late as 1975 *most* postwar collector cars of all makes had still not taken off, but by 1980 the Imperial eights were in six figures. In the Leake sale of June 1980 a Chrysler Imperial roadster of 1931 did go at the relatively low price of $97,000, but this price was, of course, an auction price.

In 1980 the 1928 Chrysler 72 roadster was bringing a little more than $15,000 and the 1929 Blue Boy was bringing about $25,000. The 1930 model 77 roadster was bringing about $10,000 more than the 1929 model 75. The six-cylinder Imperial 80 open cars were all selling in the range of $50,000 to $55,000—and for this figure, as of late 1980, one might well buy a Ferrari 275GTB-4 or a gullwing Mercedes 300SL, two of the most desirable postwar sports cars! If Walter P. Chrysler is looking down on what happened to his company he should also note what has happened to the cars *he* produced—they are in great public esteem.

These are the reasons for the popularity of the Chrysler when it was made in the prewar sporting model era: the Chrysler looked like the most sporty car available. It was a young person's car. The Packard was for a more mature, wealthy person.

The Chrysler was way ahead of many other cars for the price. The early Chrysler six of 1925 was more expensive than the Ford and Chevrolet, but it was far ahead of these cars. Both Ford and Chevrolet were four-cylinder cars; Chrysler was a six. Chevrolet was somewhat boxy, pretty much a utility car. Chrysler was a beautifully bodied, luxury sporty car. Ford was still putting out the antiquated Model T in 1925—and as late as 1927. Further, Chrysler had advanced engineering features: a high speed, high compression engine and four-wheel brakes.

The car was reasonably well made and reasonably reliable. One Chrysler-made car we bought new almost as soon as it appeared was the 1929 DeSoto, a flat-head six-cylinder car. We traded in a 1929 Chevrolet six, a car far in advance of the 1928 Chevrolet four but still far behind the DeSoto in line, luxury, and smoothness.

Why is the Chrysler so popular today and why does it command such huge prices? Probably to a considerable extent for the same reasons that made the car a standout when it first appeared on the market. There may be a good deal of nostalgia to the popularity of Chrysler as a collector's car today. Still, the car was not only a standout in its time, but it is a standout in appearance today, a car as beautiful as almost any prewar classic; and the Chrysler is a car that is not hard to maintain. It is a car that can be run with the expectation that it will keep running.

Every six-cylinder and eight-cylinder Chrysler open model, prewar car is a collector car, and, to date, every such car has proven to be a good investment. The Chrysler Imperial open cars of the early 1930s, the eight-cylinder cars, are some of the most wanted and highest priced collector cars in existence. Such a car never seems to go cheap. By my writing desk are two *Old Car Value Guides* put out by Quentin Craft of El Paso. One is his

1970 issue; the other is his 1980 issue. The front cover of each issue, ten years apart, features just one car: an early 1930s Chrysler Imperial eight touring car.

The touring car or phaeton is the featured body model of collectors, and we might concentrate on just this particular car model and body model. In 1970 the phaeton in fine condition would bring somewhere around $18,000, not a low price for a fairly recent collector car in 1970. In 1970 the roadster or convertible coupe brought about half this much.

Five years later this much favored phaeton was selling for $50,000 to $60,000. I doubt whether there was any classic Ferrari in this price range at that time. In fact there are very few classic cars of any era in this price range. The roadster or convertible coupe was selling for just a little less than this price range, possibly as low as $35,000 and as high as $50,000. By 1980 the phaeton was pushing $175,000 while the roadster and cabriolet were ranging from about $100,000 to $150,000. This is the phenomenal price performance of this make, model, and body style of car.

Cadillac

It is just possible that I am somewhat prejudiced when it comes to the Cadillac car—over the years, I have owned eleven Cadillacs. I have owned thirteen Mercedes-Benz, but Cadillac still rates high in my affection. My first Cadillac was a 1918 touring car which I bought when I was in high school for $25. It was a fine running car and in very good original condition. The Leake Sale of June 1, 1975 offered a 1918 Cadillac V-8 touring car in mint condition which brought $21,000.

My next Cadillac was a 1941, 60 Special, a sedan with sliding sun roof, an excellent running car that I drove for a good part of World War II. I sold my car in average condition for $3,000 in 1945. The model thereafter declined in value as it became simply another used car. Today, in fair condition its value would be about $7,500; in mint condition, $25,000.

From this 60 Special I moved to a very special car: an Italmeccanica of 1950, into which I put a 1949 Cadillac engine. The car was a show winner and quite a performer. My next Cadillac

This museum-quality 1893 Benz, an early model of a very important make, was sold for $65,000 at a Christie's Los Angeles sale in 1979 (very few "Oldies" sell for this amount). In 1970, however, this car would have brought less than half that amount. (*Photograph courtesy of Christie's*)

This restored 1905 Rolls-Royce six-cylinder roadster was sold in Locarno on June 2, 1980—with the Tony Frey Collection—for the equivalent of $125,400. Ten years earlier the car might have brought one-fourth this sum; and in 1981 it could have sold for as much as $200,000. It is believed to be the only surviving model of that year and make. (*Photograph courtesy of Christie's*)

One of the earliest examples of the Model T is this 1909 Ford Model T touring car. In March 1980 this car sold for $14,000 at a Christie's Los Angeles automobile auction. In 1960 it might have gone for $1,500; and in 1970 it would have been sold for $5,000. (*Photograph courtesy of Christie's*)

This Bugatti 1921 Model 35 B was sold for $83,000 at Christie's Cunard International Sale (London) on December 13, 1979. In 1970 it might have been worth $30,000; in 1981 it could have sold for as much as $100,000.

This Mercedes-Benz 1929 SS roadster was sold for $320,000 at a
Los Angeles auction in February 1979. The author was offered a similar car
in 1939 for $750. *(Photograph courtesy of Christie's)*

A 1929 Isotta Fraschini convertible cabriolet with a Castagna body that sold
for $65,000 at the Christie's Leake sale (Arlington, Texas) on May 26, 1974.
(Photograph by A. C. Cooper Ltd., courtesy of Christie's)

Values of the great prewar classics have escalated: this Mercedes-Benz 1936 Model 500K brought $400,000 at Christie's Los Angeles automobile auction in February 1979—a record high and an extraordinary price. Ten years earlier the car would not have been valued at more than $50,000. Twenty years earlier the price would probably have been $10,000 or less. The author's 500K convertible was bought in 1944 for $1,550.

This 1936 Rolls-Royce Phantom III twelve-cylinder convertible sedan was sold by Christie's at the Cunard International Hotel, London, December 13, 1979. It sold for the equivalent of $41,000. In 1981 it could have brought $75,000.

The custom-built 1939 Phantom Corsair that was purchased by the author in 1947 for $5,000. It is now in the Harrah Museum in Reno, Nevada, and the value of the car today is well over $100,000.

An MG T.D. 1953 roadster that sold for $8,500 at Christie's 1981 auction in Los Angeles. In 1970 these cars sold for under $2,000. (*Photograph courtesy of Christie's*)

This mint-condition 1954 Jaguar XK120 was offered for sale in 1981 by Motor Classic Corporation, White Plains, New York, for $17,000. In 1970 the car would have valued at about $1,500.

In February 1979 this Mercedes-Benz 300 SL gullwing was sold by Christie's in Los Angeles for $40,000. The value of the car in 1970 was about $6,000. In 1974 a similar car was sold at Christie's Leake sale for $12,000. Today the car is valued at about $70,000. (*Photograph courtesy of Christie's*)

A 1955 Mercedes-Benz 300S roadster. This car, part of the author's collection, was purchased in 1966 for $800 and was completely restored at a total cost of $4,000. In 1980 a similar car sold for $47,000. A car such as this in average condition was bringing approximately $2,000 in 1970. *(Photograph by Julie Rush)*

The author's 1960 Rolls-Royce Silver Cloud II sedan was purchased in 1977 for $7,000 and restored at a cost of $16,000. Value in 1981: about $28,000.

In 1981, Motor Classic Corporation sold this 1962 Chevrolet Corvette for $15,500. In 1970 such cars could be purchased for about $1,500. *(Photograph by Julie Rush)*

A Rolls-Royce Silver Cloud III convertible made from 1963 to 1965. This car is from the William Maxwell Davis Collection, and in 1981 its value was about $125,000.

A 1964 Shelby Daytona Cobra, one of the team cars that won the International FIA Grand Touring Class in 1965. The car, which is in the Motor Classic Corporation showroom, is valued in excess of $200,000. *(Photograph by Julie Rush)*

A 1965 Shelby Cobra model 289; a model made in the years 1963–1965. In 1981 it sold for $39,000 at Motor Classic Corporation. In 1978 the car might have sold for $25,000 or less. (*Photograph by Julie Rush*)

In 1981, Motor Classic Corporation sold this 1966 Chevrolet Sting Ray coupe for $11,500. In 1970 such cars were simply second-hand, bringing about $1,500. (*Photograph by Julie Rush*)

This 1966 Ferrari 275 GTS convertible was sold in 1980 by Motor Classic Corporation for $35,000 and again in 1981 for $39,000. In 1970 the car might have sold for as little as $5,000. (*Photograph by Julie Rush*)

The author's 1966 Ford Mustang convertible for which he paid $1,600 in 1978. Similar cars were selling in 1981 for $6,000 to $9,000.

The De Tomaso Mangusta used a Ford V-8 engine and was put into production in 1966. These models were turned out for the rest of the decade and sold new for about $10,000. This 1969 car was sold by Motor Classic Corporation in 1980 for $18,000, and sold again in 1981 for $23,000. (*Photograph by Julie Rush*)

The author's Lamborghini Miura, 1967, one of the highest-performance, advance-design automobiles ever made in the postwar era. Price in 1980: $20,000. Value in 1981: $30,000.

In 1981 this Ferrari Daytona coupe of the model produced from 1969 through 1972 was sold by Motor Classic Corporation for $65,000. When new, in 1969, it could have been purchased in America for $19,000.

The author's 1967 Maserati Ghibli coupe, probably the most beautiful sports coupe ever built. In 1981 it cost $10,900. The value in 1981 was about $14,000.

Cadillac Eldorado convertible, the model that was made from 1971 through 1976. This 1974 model is part of the author's collection. It was purchased in 1977 for $5,200 and is valued today at about $6,000. *(Photograph by Julie Rush)*

was a 1950 convertible, and from here I moved back in years to the 1938 model 75 sedan, a car which cost me $195 in 1956. I put this car in near mint condition and had a total of $325 invested in it. Today's market on a fine condition car of this model is about $13,000–$15,000.

My 1947 convertible was a very good-looking and good-driving car, and from here I moved to buying new Cadillac convertibles, buying them when the new model appeared in September and selling them the following April or May when we left for Europe.

As I am writing this page, our 1974 Eldorado convertible sits outside the door, and the Eldorado convertibles from 1971 to 1976 are some of the most beautiful American postwar stock convertibles ever built anywhere. They were classic cars before the last one rolled off the assembly line in 1976 and Cadillac convertible production came to an end.

But to prewar classic Cadillacs: we might take up Cadillacs from the most wanted—and at the highest prices—down to the least wanted. Even though Cadillacs of the prewar classic era can be categorized as least wanted, this is certainly a relative term. All prewar Cadillacs are wanted, regardless of year and regardless of body style.

These are the collector Cadillacs, starting with the most wanted and most valuable models:

Cadillac V-16 Open Cars

The Cadillac V-16 is almost unique in American automobile history. There was at least one other sixteen-cylinder car of the same era, but it never created much of a lasting impression. This was the Marmon 16 with aluminum engine, one of which I owned.

The Cadillac V-16 was the last word in luxury from the highest *volume* automobile producer in America, General Motors. Cadillac entered the first year of the Depression with its new 16, and the 1930 car is probably the most wanted Cadillac 16 of all those produced. The engine had a very large 452-cubic-inch displacement. It produced a hefty 165 horsepower. The price range was $5,350 to $8,750, a very high priced car for the Depression years.

The 1930 Cadillac V-16, particularly the open model, was, and is, a tremendously impressive looking car and a well designed car that seems to look even better today than when it first appeared in 1930. It rides very well. All the Cadillacs of the era rode well and were quiet, but you cannot be sure, unless you note the designation *V-16*, whether the engine is the 16, the 12, or the 8. Many, many body models of the Cadillac 16 were made, the standard bodies being made by Fleetwood. One important feature of the car was the silent engine, silent to a considerable extent because of the hydraulic valve lifters which were self-adjusting to eliminate tappet noise.

Too many sports and European car enthusiasts think of the best American cars as being bulbous affairs with a fancy body bolted onto the mass-produced frame into which an oversize gas-guzzling engine had been thrown. The Cadillac was not quite this kind of an automobile. General Motors had purchased a Rolls-Royce and torn it to pieces to see what made it great. A Rolls-Royce engineer, Maurice Olley, worked on the Cadillac 16 suspension, and new testing methods were developed. Dynamic road tests were developed to improve the roadability of the car.

In 1930 the first production year of the V-16, 2,500 of the V-16 were sold. For the two years 1930 and 1931, 3,250 V-16s were produced. Thereafter, maximum production of the V-16 was 300 a year until the model was discontinued in 1940.

In 1938 the very successful forty-five-degree V-16 with its overhead valves was dropped, and the new V-16 had flat heads. The 431-cubic-inch engine produced 185 horsepower. Some 311 of these cars were produced, in 1938, 136 in 1939, and 61 in 1940, the final year of the V-16.

Ten years ago, in 1970, the open model Cadillac 16 of 1930 and 1931 brought $25,000 to $35,000 if in top condition. The 1932s brought $15,000 to $20,000, and prices dropped in later models. The new engined 1938–1940 model was not, and is not, the most wanted Cadillac V-16, and in 1970 a fine open car of 1938–1940 could be bought for $10,000.

By 1975 prices of the V-16 open cars were way up if the car was in good condition. The roadster and phaeton 1930 and 1931 models could sell for prices in the neighborhood of $80,000. No open V-16 of these years seemed to sell at much under $50,000. The 1932s and 1933s were selling for $50,000 up. The 1934 models were selling for $25,000 to $35,000, as were the 1935s. The 1938 and later models were selling for under $20,000.

The price *pattern* in the late 1970s was the same but the auction prices for the 1930–1931 open cars were running close to $150,000. All model year cars were scarce, and the auctions sold few of them, of any year.

In 1980 no Cadillac V-16 from 1930 through 1932 seemed to sell under the six-figure range if in fine condition. A price of $150,000 and above was no rarity. The later models, through 1935, could bring $100,000 and a little more. Even the less wanted 1938 to 1940 V-16s were selling for prices of $50,000 to $60,000.

Cadillac V-12 Open Cars

Nine months after the Cadillac V-16 was introduced in early 1930, the V-12 was introduced. This car had a scaled-down engine, much like the V-16 but with four fewer cylinders. The chassis was not the enormous V-16 chassis, but the V-8 chassis. The engine displaced 370 cubic inches and put out 135 horsepower. The bodies were smaller than those of the V-16s. The car also cost considerably less than the V-16s—$3,795 to $4,895. In the model years 1930–1931, 5,725 V-12s were produced. From 1933 on, the company never produced more than 1,000 V-12s a year. In 1938 the overhead valve V-12 was dropped. The car was finished, although the V-16 with its new flat-head engine, was continued to 1940.

To me, the 1931 and 1932 V-12 roadsters were, and are, superb cars as well as practical cars. The styling of the Cadillac V-12 in these years could hardly be improved upon, considering that the car was a luxury car meant to be used for transportation and not a top luxury car like a Rolls-Royce or a strict sports car.

In 1970 the early V-12 open Cadillacs were selling for prices in the range of $10,000–$15,000—for the preferred 1930–1932 models. The later cars in the V-12 series, through the final year of their production, 1937, could be purchased for $6,000–$9,000.

By 1975 prices were well up, as in the case of the V-16. The early models, put out from 1930 (late) to 1932, ran from $40,000 to $50,000. The 1932 model was not in as great demand as the 1930–1931 models; but the 1932 V-12 was a superb, impressive-looking car, yet not as ostentatious as the V-16.

The 1933 and 1934 models ran in price from $25,000–$30,000. All later cars ran from $15,000 to $20,000, with a few fine examples selling for more.

The rise in price of the V-12 continued to 1980, as it did in the case of the V-16. The earliest models, through 1932, ran, in 1980, from $75,000 to close to $100,000. The 1933–1935 model ran from about $55,000 to $65,000. The later cars rarely sold for as high as $40,000. It may be a subjective matter, but the last Cadillac 12 open cars were excellent looking cars and excellent driving cars.

We come now to the standby model Cadillac, the V-8. From 1933 on, an annual production of 300 V-16 models and 1,000 V-12 models was considered good for these specialty luxury cars. In each of the years 1930 and 1931, however, about 10,000 V-8s were produced—open and closed cars. In 1932 and 1933 output and sales declined to the 2,000 to 3,000 level. Sales then rose to 13,000 cars by 1939.

Cadillac V-8 Open Cars

In September 1914, Cadillac announced its V-8 engine, and this engine was to replace the four-cylinder engine. The company never went through a six-cylinder engine phase. Every year since the first sales of the V-8 car were made in 1915, the company has had a V-8. Until 1949 the engine configuration was flat head (side valve). In the 1949 model the overhead-valve engine was the pattern, and it has been continued ever since.

In prewar classic cars we might start with the early classics produced around 1925. This particular car, in touring, five- or seven-passenger form, was greatly publicized in the moving pictures as the "gangster" car. It was impressive looking, big, fast, and reliable.

The open cars of the middle 1920s in good condition could have been purchased in 1970 for $6,000 to $8,000. A roadster might go a bit higher. The car improved in looks every year to 1928 and 1929, and the 1929 Cadillac V-8 touring car was very impressive looking and reliable. The preferred years are 1929 to 1932, and these cars ten years ago sold for $10,000 to $13,000. The later models, produced until the war cut off production, would usually sell for $5,000, sometimes a little more.

By 1975 the "gangster" car of the mid-twenties was way up in price—$15,000 to $25,000. The 1928s and 1929s were close in price to $30,000. The 1930–1932 models often ran to $40,000 and even above. The later cars, through 1935, sold for prices up to $25,000, and the still later models brought only $15,000 maximum. The 1938 model 75 was an excellent car, and in 1956 I bought one, a sedan, for $175 at retail—from a dealer. The car started easily and the engine was almost noiseless. The ride was about as good as that of the latest model Cadillac.

By the year 1980 the mid-twenties Cadillac V-8 open car was selling for $25,000 to $35,000. The 1928 model could bring $40,000, if in good condition. The 1929 car could bring $50,000 or $60,000. So could the V-8 open cars through the model year 1932. Some particularly desirable open models could push $70,000. Almost all of the later cars could be bought for $30,000 top.

The La Salle

In the mid-thirties Packard put out an inexpensive car that in essence traded on the quality name of Packard. This was the model 120, which sold for a little over $1,000. The models 110 and 115 were even less expensive cars. All of these cars sold because, for a relatively low price, a person could own a Packard, the car that was synonymous with quality—and wealth.

Cadillac never put out a really inexpensive model to compete with the lower-priced Packards. The La Salle, the junior partner of Cadillac, was put out from 1927 to 1940. By the year 1929 more La Salles were sold than Cadillacs. In the depression year of 1930 almost 15,000 La Salles were sold—in contrast to the very limited sales of the V-16 and V-12 Cadillac! The La Salle had a flat-head 340-cubic-inch V-8 engine that produced 90 horsepower. In the depression La Salle was given the 353-cid (cubic inch displacement) engine. The price of La Salle was $2,500 to $3,000 for the models with Fisher bodies, and up to $4,000 for the cars with Fleetwood bodies.

In 1934 everything was changed for the La Salle. The car was made very different in design from the Cadillac. A straight eight-cylinder Oldsmobile engine was installed, and prices were a low $1,595 to $1,695. The car and its price were the same for 1935 and 1936. In 1937 the car was made longer, and a Cadillac V-8 engine was used. The 1937 model sold for as little as $1,155. In 1938, 32,000 La Salles were sold, and after 1940, Cadillac dropped the La Salle.

Up until fairly recently, no one seemed to want to collect the La Salle car, particularly the closed models, even the fairly good-looking coupe model. Then collector interest developed and values rose rapidly. In 1981 all La Salles in good condition, closed as well as open models, were in demand. A good early La Salle car can bring close to $70,000. Interest in the La Salle is expressed in cars all the way up to 1933, and an open car of the model year 1933 could bring $60,000. Cars produced after this date could often be bought for $15,000, particularly at auction.

Ten years earlier, in 1970, $10,000 would buy an early La Salle convertible, roadster, or phaeton in excellent condition. A few open cars of the early years could reach prices a little over $10,000. The 1930 and later cars rarely achieved a price as high as $10,000, and $7,500 would often purchase a good example. The mid-thirties to 1940 cars could be bought for the bargain price of under $3,000. In fact I saw so many La Salles in this price range that I wondered what was basically the matter with the car that no one seemed to want one. Actually there was nothing wrong with it (any more than there was anything wrong with the Aston Martin, which ten years ago sold for next to nothing). Demand hadn't developed for a very good automobile.

By 1975 prices of the late model La Salle convertibles had

certainly risen, but by no means to great heights. Cars from 1935 to the final model of 1940 could be purchased for $6,000 or thereabouts, with a few cars selling for as much as $10,000. The 1927 and 1928 convertibles, roadsters, and phaetons were selling in the $25,000 range, and the later cars to the mid-thirties were selling for $15,000 to $20,000.

The Ford Model A and V-8

By the year 1927 it became obvious to Henry Ford that his old Model T had seen its best days and a brand new car was required of the Ford Motor Company. The Model T was a two-forward-speed affair that was inexpensive to buy (some of the Model Ts were advertised at less than $250). It had 22 horsepower; was hard to start (particularly in winter); had one drum brake on the driveshaft, not even two wheel service brakes; and had a top speed of about 45 wide open, perhaps a little more. It was cheap to repair, and almost any roadside mechanic could do the work, provided the owner didn't do the work himself. This car in its last years had to compete with the four-cylinder Chevrolet with three forward speeds and drum brakes on the wheels, and with a more sophisticated body.

In 1928, Ford put the Model A on the market. The "New Ford," as it was called by everybody, had all of the simplicity of the old Model T but it was better in every department. It always started, even in cold weather. The starter was up to the job at all times—which it certainly was not on the Model T. The distributor rarely gave trouble, whereas the timer on the Model T always seemed to require dismantling, cleaning, and filing. There were no bands in the planetary transmission to wear out (which they regularly did on the Model T) since the planetary transmission was replaced by a thoroughly modern and trouble-free, conventional, three-forward-speed transmission. The carburetor was better. The buzz coils were eliminated, and the car was essentially a good, inexpensive, dependable, easy-to-repair piece of transportation that at the time was rather sporty and modern looking.

The Model A Ford was more than an improvement over the Model T—it represented a revolution for the Ford Motor Company. It even inspired the very popular song, "Henry's Made a Lady Out of Lizzie."

On the other hand, the Model A Ford was far from being a Lincoln V-12—or even a Lincoln V-8—put out by the same company. It was a humble car. It had none of the attributes of greatness in an automobile that makes a car a collector's automobile. It was an economy car with a low price tag. Even the last four-cylinder Ford of 1932 (and this car was actually called the Model B) carried a price tag of $495. In that year the V-8, another milestone for the company, was introduced with a basic price of $505.

One means of assessing investment value is to determine how many of a desirable car were produced, as there can be no more of the model car on the market today than were produced originally. In 1955 there were exactly fifty-five of the great Mercedes-Benz 300S produced, so price is high.

In 1928, the first year of production of the Model A Ford, 820,000 of the cars were made. Before the Depression year 1930 was finished, four million Model A Fords had been produced and sold. In 1931 about one million were produced, a year when the American economy was going downhill rapidly.

In the Depression bottom, 1932, 133,500 Model B four-cylinder Fords were produced and almost 300,000 of the new Ford V-8s. In 1933 over 500,000 V-8s were sold. In June 1934 one million Ford V-8s had been produced in all. One year later, an additional million had been produced, in a year very close to the bottom of the Depression from the point of view of U.S. unemployment.

Despite the enormous original production of Model As and V-8s, recent prices of these cars have skyrocketed. The reason is that people like the cars, and the cars do not come onto the market in the numbers that these production figures might suggest. One might expect to find Model A Fords and V-8s come regularly onto the used car lots, but they don't, although they do appear in numbers at important auto auctions—where they always seem to bring very substantial prices.

Ten years ago, in 1970, a deluxe roadster could be bought in fine condition for $4,500. The touring car sold for about the same figure. For $1,800 to $2,500 most other body model cars could be purchased, cars in very good condition. The Model B four-cylinder cars sold for about the same thing. A few sporty V-8s sold for $4,000 and a little more. The rest of the V-8s of all years hovered around $1,500 to $2,500.

There was something of a jump in the price of a Model A between 1973 and 1974, but it was a jump up and not a jump down into the recession to accompany the stock market. In 1973 a 1931 cabriolet, a very desirable and late model car of the series, in totally restored condition, would have brought $4,500—with side-mounted tires, rumble seat, and roll up windows. In good but unrestored condition it would have sold for about $2,000, and in average, but unrestored, condition, about $750. In December 1974 this exact model car, restored, was advertised for $9,500.

In December 1974 a four-door phaeton, with spotlight, side mounts, trunk, and all curtains, presumably in fine condition, was advertised for $10,500. In 1973 this same car would have sold for about $8,500.

As late as 1975 few Model A Fords (or Model Bs) had hit $10,000, no matter how fine. In 1975 the V-8 from 1932 through the 1936 model tended to parallel the Model As in price. Only a few later cars approached $10,000. The 1939 to 1942 model was closer to $5,000. In the next five years, prices rose, but not a great deal. Prices tended to level off, particularly after 1977, and the period 1977–1980 was a period of rise for many things, cars and real estate among others.

In the June 1980 Leake sale in Tulsa, a 1928 two-door sedan reached a high bid of $13,000, and a 1929 roadster sold for $9,200. The V-8s were doing well pricewise as compared with the Model As. A 1934 cabriolet actually sold at the auction for $18,000, and a 1934 sedan brought $12,250. A 1935 roadster achieved a high bid of $19,000. A 1937 cabriolet convertible found a buyer at $12,750. At retail, in this period many cars topped $10,000 and a very few topped $20,000.

The best cars to buy are: the late Model As; the early V-8s; the deluxe roadsters and phaetons, Models A and V-8. As far as model As are concerned, every year and body model is a collector car and in demand, even the early and modest two-door sedan.

For what these cars are, and considering how many were made and how many still exist, the rise in price in the past ten years has been phenomenal. Yet there is a rise to come in all probability. While prices are not now low, they are still within the means of many collector-investors, and a sum under $10,000 can still purchase a good Model A or V-8 if one looks hard and long enough. For example, unrestored cars are easy to find at fairly reasonable prices. If the buyer can restore carefully and do some of the work himself, or at least shop around to get the work done, the costs can still be low. There are many mechanics and body shops that can work on Ford cars, and parts are available everywhere and at reasonable prices.

The cars are reliable, so they can be driven regularly, particularly since repairs and parts do not cost a great deal. The Model A can be driven only around town—it is not good for constant turnpike speeds. But the V-8 can be driven anywhere at any time. While neither car is in the category of the Duesenberg or the V-12 Lincoln, for instance, it can be a very desirable investment that provides both growth in value and ownership satisfaction. And since there is an immense buying market and also an immense selling market, the Ford in a sense is a liquid investment.

Lincoln

The Continental

The most celebrated Lincoln ever produced was the Continental, produced just before World War II, again just after the close of the war, and in the mid-fifties as the Mark II. All later Continentals—Mark III, IV, etcetera—are simply deluxe models of the standard car. These early Continentals were more or less monumental cars as far as American automobiles go.

In the fall of 1951 the Museum of Modern Art in New York selected eight automobiles for display, eight "statement" or "milestone" cars. The Lincoln Continental of prewar days was one of the eight, along with Cisitalia, the supercharged Mercedes-Benz SS and the Bentley. The museum brochure describes the Lincoln in this way: "Like the Cord, the Lincoln

Continental is, basically, a box to which fenders have been added." The box design of this car was prophetic in that today's Rolls-Royce, Mercedes-Benz, and Cadillac Eldorado (up to the latest design) are all essentially boxes.

On the other hand, the Lincoln Continental used flat surfaces, mainly horizontal flat surfaces, to give an ultramodern look to the car. It is seventeen-feet, eight-inches long, a big impressive car, yet a fleet car, not a "truck."

The prewar Lincoln Continental first appeared in 1939, but it didn't hit the salesrooms in volume until 1940. While the Lincoln Continental was based on the less expensive Lincoln Zephyr, it was put together with care and quality materials. Essentially it was a refined Zephyr, with four inches cut from the doors and body to give a low, flat line that turned out to be a sensation.

The power plant was a flat-head V-12, not a very great engine, but adequate, and the car rode well but not wonderfully. Its looks were the secret of its success. Essentially the same car was produced from 1939 through 1948, with some body updating after the war. In all of these years, 2,277 cabriolets and 3,045 coupes were produced, not a great number—and not a great supply available for the market of 1982! Of course, the war cut off all production.

In 1970 the cars were in the $3,500 to $4,500 price category. While Lincoln Continental has certainly risen in price since then, it is still probably underpriced as compared with many other collector cars. In 1975 the open models were at the $10,000 level and the closed cars at the $6,000–$8,000 level.

As of 1982 there is little difference in price between a 1940 Lincoln Continental and a postwar Lincoln Continental. They all run around $20,000–$25,000 with the open models bringing the most money, but not a great deal more. Closed models can still at times be purchased for a little under $20,000.

The Lincoln Zephyr, Lincoln V-12, and Lincoln V-8 Open Car

The Zephyr was something of a landmark car when it first appeared. In 1936 a streamlined car was produced by the Ford Motor Company with a twelve-cylinder flathead engine of only

110 cubic inches. The body was semiunit construction and the car sold for a low $1,275. In my marketing class in the Amos Tuck School of Business Administration at Dartmouth College, the Professor, Al Frey, asked the class to indicate what automobile body style represented the car of the future. Almost everybody in the class said Lincoln Zephyr. Professor Frey thought the Cadillac 60 Special represented the car of the future. Of course he turned out to be right! The 60 Special was a refined box design, but a very smooth-looking car.

In 1936, 19,000 Lincolns were produced, of which 17,700 were Zephyrs. Zephyr dominated sales as far as Lincoln went; then sales gradually declined.

In 1970 no one seemed interested in a Zephyr, not even in a convertible, and $2,000–$3,000 would purchase a car in fine condition of any body model. By 1975 the convertibles were at the $5,000–$6,000 level and the closed cars at the $4,000–$5,000 level.

The Zephyr, until recently, has not been a connoisseur's car. It was not thought to have the quality of the big Lincolns or the Continentals either. Now, in ten years, the whole picture has changed on the up side. As of 1981 open Zephyrs were about at the $20,000 level, and sedans could be secured for a bit under $10,000. Coupes were halfway between the top prices for the open cars and the sedans.

The Lincoln V-12 is an entirely different proposition from the point of view of mechanical design and construction. It is a quality car by connoisseur standards. The English car magazine, *Autocar,* raved about the quality of the "new" Lincoln V-12 of 1932. It was called the KB model, and it developed a very high 150 horsepower. In one form or another, this V-12 car was continued until the war.

In 1970 almost no open model Lincoln V-12 sold for over $10,000, and the late model open cars could be bought for $5,000 to $6,000. The late model sedans could be bought for under $5,000. The Lincoln V-12, especially the custom-bodied convertibles, skyrocketed in one decade. In 1975, $40,000 would buy a *custom*-bodied early Lincoln V-12 convertible in fine condition, and $20,000 would buy an *ordinary*-bodied convertible in fine condition of the early years of the V-12. The later convertibles could be bought for $25,000 and the late model closed cars for $10,000.

As of 1981 an early V-12 in fine condition would bring up to $100,000, particularly the 1932–1934 models, which were splendid-looking, top quality automobiles. The later models were more in the $50,000 range, with some later sedans selling for prices in the $15,000 range. The convertibles are obviously very much the preferred models.

My own Lincoln was a V-8 of 1930, a phaeton that I purchased in 1939 for $50. I thought I made a very good buy at the time! It was an aluminum-bodied car in very good, but not mint, condition; the car was good looking and it ran extremely well. This car in 1982 would sell quickly at auction, in the condition it was in at the time I owned it, for $30,000, more or less. Quentin Craft, the price analyst, quotes a price for this model car in fine condition, as of 1980, at $77,500. I guess I should have kept this car!

In 1975 the same car would have brought under $25,000, and in 1970 about $15,000, still not a low price, and not low as compared with the Lincoln Continental and the Lincoln Zephyr in 1970.

All Lincoln V-8s from the mid-twenties on are in approximately the price range of the 1930 that I selected to trace price. The earlier cars may be in the $50,000 range, if open cars, but rarely less, and $55,000 and more is not at all an unusual price. A 1932 open car can bring from $85,000 to $100,000. In 1939 and 1940 only 120 of the big Lincoln V-8, called the model K, were sold, and the big cars were dropped in 1940, prior to the outbreak of World War II.

It may be that this diminished production at the end of the run of V-8s was responsible for the flat price curve regardless of year produced—from 1932 to 1940. The postwar V-8s were very different, standard transportation automobiles, with the exception of the Continental and the Continental Mark II of the mid-fifties. Columbia House's *Illustrated Encyclopedia of the Motor Car,* 1974, captioned its section devoted to Lincoln as "Lincoln/The Great Cars—Faultless, Swift and Luxurious," and this appellation applies very well to the V-12s and the V-8s, the early classic cars.

CHAPTER 9

Prewar French, Spanish, Italian, and British Classics

THERE IS AN ALMOST ENDLESS VARIETY of prewar classic cars, those produced from the mid-twenties until the Second World War. The European prewar classics, however, do not come onto the American market in any great numbers, with the exception of Rolls-Royce and Mercedes-Benz, to which we have devoted complete chapters.

Other than these, we have selected the following makes of prewar European classics to trace in this chapter for price trend, including present value in the market:

- Bugatti
- Hispano-Suiza
- Isotta Fraschini
- Bentley
- Alfa Romeo

The above list is a sampling of the greats from Europe in the prewar period. As far as Italian cars go, we could well have included Lancia and Fiat; and for English cars, MG and Jaguar and its predecessor SS cars. In France, we might well have included Delage, Delahaye and Talbot.

Bugatti

The Society of Automotive Historians (of America) has prepared a list of the thirty most significant figures in automobile history. Henry Ford stands in number one spot because he developed the enormous mass market for the automobile, and he got the price down at one time to something just over $200 a car. F. Henry Royce is the first foreigner on the list, and he occupies place number sixteen for developing his car into the Rolls-Royce and subsequently making a progressively better and more modern luxury car. Carl Benz is number nineteen, and Ferdinand Porsche number twenty. In place number twenty-six stands Ettore Bugatti. He is among the few foreigners on the list.

Plans were made for the production of what Mr. Ettore Bugatti no doubt felt should be the finest car in the world. These plans were made in 1926, and thereafter an experimental car was made, followed by six actual production models of the car, the type 41, known as the Royale. The wheelbase of the car was an enormous fourteen feet two inches, and the track was five feet three inches (as compared with four feet 8½ inches between the standard railroad tracks—to give a comparison). The engine was a huge, straight eight with single overhead camshaft and with three valves per cylinder. The capacity of the engine was a fantastic 12,763 cubic centimeters (as compared with the biggest Cadillac Eldorado that "advertised," on the side of the car, 8.2 liters—8,200 cubic centimeters). The engine was a low-speed engine, but at 1,700 revolutions per minute it had a power output of 300 horsepower.

It is hard to describe how you feel when you first look at the engine of a Bugatti Royale. You almost have to turn your head one way and then the other to take in the whole engine.

It is a car of top quality, a big, tremendously impressive looking car, and it probably overshadows even the Duesenberg SJ dual-cowl phaeton. For its size, it is a great performer. It is also a car that would sell today, if it were offered for sale, at a higher price, in all probability, than the Mercedes-Benz 500K or 540K with roadster body—like the Mercedes that sold in California at auction in early 1979 for $400,000. The Bugatti Royale would probably bring more than an SSK Mercedes-Benz roadster, or even the ultrarare SSKL.

A Bugatti Royale with cabriolet body by Weinberger, Munich, on chassis number 41 121, was apparently the first Royale chassis sold outside of France and it was sold to a Dr. Fuchs of Munich.

Some of the Bugatti Royales are just plain massive. This cabriolet was massive but beautiful. The front fender curves beautifully and then reverses to form the running board, reversing once again to form the rear fender.

This is the car I saw in New York for sale in 1940, and the garage that had the car on display advised me to talk to Dr. Fuchs in his office if I was interested in buying it. I met him, but I felt the car was just too much for me to get into condition and to keep in condition, although at the time it appeared to require very few important repairs and restorations.

What happened to this particular car has been set down by Paul Kestler in his excellent book, *Bugatti, Evolution of a Style* (Edita Lausanne, 1977). He says on page 98:

Photographs of the cabriolet, with rare exceptions, show it painted pearl grey with dark green mouldings, head and trunk.

The Weinberger Cabriolet, of all the Royales, is the one best known to the general public, thanks to numerous photographs that have been recently published, and to the Lindberg plastic models on sale in every toyshop. This was the most successful Royale body built outside Molsheim.

Today, after following its owner to Shanghai and to the United States, where it was scrapped, the car is on view in the Ford Museum at Dearborn, Michigan, to which it was presented by its restorer, Charles Chayne.

This was the car I saw. It was offered to me by Dr. Fuchs for $600. Had the car been bought at the time by Charlie Chayne I would have had no regrets. We can always look back to the house we could have bought for $60,000 that now is worth $600,000 or the Rembrandt that we could have bought for $30,000. My only regret is that I did not buy the car and save it from scrapping. Parts were lost in the scrapping and it has never been restored to its original condition. This scrapping I could have avoided—if only I had had the $600 offering price in 1940!

In 1955, Russ Sceli, one of the founders of the Sports Car Club of America, and a big dealer in exotic cars in Hartford, Connecticut, called me on the phone in Washington, D.C., and told me he thought I might be interested in a car that he had just taken in trade. It was a two-passenger Bugatti 57 convertible of 1937. The engine was a straight eight two-overhead-cam unit of 3,200-cubic-centimeter capacity. The car had a top speed of about 125 miles per hour and it appeared to be in fine condition. We took a long drive in it as I wanted to get the feel of the car. The engine was in perfect shape but was naturally noisy. The clutch was effective enough, but it required very careful handling. It was either in or out, and there didn't seem anything between. Unless the clutch was handled with great expertise the car jerked ahead. I turned the car down for $1,500. Today it would be worth about $100,000, perhaps as much as $125,000.

It should be pointed out that, although Ettore Bugatti was born in Milan, Italy, and has an Italian name, the car is a French car and was made in Molsheim, France, not far from Strasbourg. The name Bugatti is well known in art and antique circles; Carlo Bugatti, Ettore's father, was the designer and maker of the famous and distinctive Bugatti furniture.

Ettore Bugatti was born in Milan in 1881. In 1900 he built his first automobile by hand. In 1909 he set up shop in an old dyeworks in Molsheim in the province of Alsace, then a part of Germany, now a part of France. Bugatti was no large producer of cars. In fact, the total output of the Bugatti plant was very small, with many different types produced.

In many ways, Ettore Bugatti stands at the top of esteem by automobile aficionados. Why? In his book, Paul Kestler explains exactly why:

Thanks to his artistic training, and his gifts as an engineer, Ettore Bugatti may be considered one of the masters of modern industrial aesthetics. The architecture of his eight-cylinder engines with single overhead camshaft is so pure, so free from nonessentials, that it is impossible to divine their internal structure . . . that elegance as well as practicality. . . .

After 1929, Bugatti's son, Jean, made his ideas more and more felt in the design of both mechanics and bodies, with twin overhead camshafts, supercharging and beautiful bodies.

Kestler continues:

Although his total production did not exceed 7,500 vehicles in forty years, no other make has earned such a reputation nor aroused such fanatical devotion. Bugatti owners' clubs exist throughout the world.

In racing, Bugatti was a standout. In 1925 the great type 35 appeared, and this model was produced through 1930. It was a car of approximately 2,000 cubic centimeters with a single overhead camshaft and three valves per cylinder. Some of the cars were supercharged, some not. The 35B and 35C were supercharged. Top speed was about 125 and the cars were, and are, beauties. Of great importance was the ultimate in design, the famous Bugatti "horseshoe" radiator and grill. The car was an open two-seater, essentially for Grand Prix use. The type 35B with 2.3-liter engine and supercharged, is probably the standout of all the type 35 cars.

The type 37 looked about the same as the type 35, but used a four-cylinder engine, later supercharged. This car appeared in 1926 and was produced through 1930.

Up through the years, Bugatti produced epic car after epic car. From 1930 through 1933 he produced the big engine (4.9 liter) type 50, one of which raced in an early Watkins Glen race, a beautiful, big yellow car, and I think this car was equipped by the owner with an automatic transmission. This was an eight-cylinder twin overhead cam car, supercharged, and if there was any Bugatti that I wanted at the time it would have been the type 50. I was a flagman on the Watkins Glen course, and I watched the car go by time after time.

The final really important types were the 57, 57S, 57C, 57SC, and 57 S 45. These were, and are, all twin-cam eights, all but the type 57 S 45 being 3,200-cubic-centimeter engines. The 57 S 45 had a 4,700-cubic-centimeter engine. The C, SC, and S 45 were supercharged. One of the most unique-bodied and valuable Bugattis is the streamlined type 57 S Atlantic coupe. The car was for sale many years ago. Today it would bring perhaps $300,000, perhaps as much as $500,000.

Ettore Bugatti died in 1947, after the death of his son, Jean, an eminent engine and body designer. When the type 101 appeared in 1951 (to 1954) it attracted little interest in the auto shows. It had all the features of the great Bugattis except a unique body design, but times had moved on and Bugatti was not at the helm of the company to innovate.

As collector-investor cars, *any* Bugatti is important and valuable, any antique or prewar classic Bugatti. In some ways the cars we have described above are particularly important collectors' automobiles.

As late as 1970 the prewar classic Bugattis were not tremendously high in price, although they were certainly not at the 1955 level of $1,500 for a fine condition drop head type 57. The 1970 price level was about $10,000 to $12,000. The car in *average* condition could be bought for $5,000 to $7,000.

On March 20, 1975, Christie's in Geneva sold a 1.5-liter, 1923 Brescia racing two-seater Bugatti, completely overhauled, and returned to original specifications in the restoration. The body was a replica built to Bugatti specifications. In automobiles of vintage years, replica bodies may not be as good as original bodies, but they do not seriously damage the value of a car. This Bugatti brought the equivalent of $13,200.

The same sale offered one of the Bugatti greats, a type 35 two-liter Grand Prix two-seater, 1925. The car was original and in overhauled condition throughout. It brought the equivalent of $28,000.

In Christie's sale at Beaulieu, Hampshire, July 10, 1975, lot thirty-four was a three-liter type 44 sports tourer, a rather good-looking car, but not one of the best-looking bodies, a 1927 model. It sold for about $17,500.

In the July 1974 Beaulieu sale, a two-liter four-passenger type 30 touring car, not a beautiful car by any means but one in fine condition, brought the equivalent of $19,200. A rather well rebuilt 1927 type 35A Grand Prix two-seater brought $26,400, although there were some replacements of parts.

Between 1970 and 1975, Bugattis skyrocketed in price in the U.S. Many type 57s were sold, and prices ranged from $17,500 to $46,750. *C.A.R. Values* reports one Bugatti type 57 coupe sold at auction for $32,000 in 1979. Four type 57 convertibles received high bids of $37,000, $40,000, $20,000, and $31,500. In 1980 the type 35 was selling for close to $30,000. The type 50 was close to $40,000. The type 57 in fine condition started at about $40,000, and the types 57S and 57SC were bringing over $60,000. Even the postwar type 101s were bringing about $25,000 at auction.

If any Bugatti is bought, it should be a car in very good to mint condition. Trying to restore a Bugatti in poor condition could turn out disastrously. Costs of parts are sky-high, if they can be obtained at all, and the more nonoriginal parts, the less the value of the Bugatti. It would be better to buy a type 35 Bugatti in mint condition for $100,000 than one in average condition for $50,000.

Hispano-Suiza

The Hispano-Suiza was Spain's first automobile, and it was produced in Barcelona in 1901 by Marc Birkigt, a Swiss born in Geneva in 1878. In 1912 a plant was opened in Paris, and two years later the operation was moved to larger quarters. This plant produced the great and expensive cars of the 1920s and 1930s, although the Spanish plant continued to produce Hispano-Suiza cars, but mainly the less expensive ones. In 1938, Birkigt stopped production of automobiles in order to concentrate on military hardware. He died in 1953. Like Le Patron Bugatti, Birkigt *was* the car he made.

As in the case of Bugatti, any Hispano-Suiza is a collector's car. There are, however, three models which should be mentioned, as they represent the best produced by Hispano-Suiza. The H6 model was first produced in 1919, and the chassis was French-made. The engine is of 6,200 cubic centimeters. It has an overhead camshaft and is of light alloy. The brakes are excellent, unlike the brakes of many other luxury cars of the era. This model is also known as the 32CV, and it develops 135 horsepower, a high engine output at the time. It has six cylinders. Essentially, the same model car was produced up to 1934. The price of this car was approximately the same as the Rolls-Royce, and the car was sold to the King of Spain, to other royalty, and to the Hollywood film set, equipped with bodies from the finest coach builders.

Toward the mid-twenties a big engine was put into the same chassis, this one with eight-liter capacity, about the size of the big Cadillac Eldorado. It won the sports car race at Boulogne, and thereafter was known as the "Boulogne." Its official designation was 46CV. In 1924 a tulipwood streamlined body was fitted to a 46CV Boulogne model, and the car was raced in the Targa Florio road race in Sicily, but it did not win. Should this car ever come onto the market it might very well be a contender for the most expensive car ever sold. The 46CV was continued to 1934—as was the 32CV.

In 1928 a memorable race was held at the Indianapolis track. A Boulogne 46CV was pitted against an American Stutz Black Hawk straight eight with 4.9-liter single overhead cam engine. Frederick Moscovics, president of Stutz, bet $25,000 on the Stutz. In Mr. Moscovics's own words, "The Stutz swallowed a valve." It lost the race and he lost his $25,000.

Another great car built by Hispano-Suiza was a V-12. This was to be a quiet car, and it had one camshaft that opened overhead valves with pushrods—as most V-8 engines have today. This was the type 68 or type 68 bis. The first had an engine capacity of 9,400 cubic centimeters and the second, 11,300 cubic centimeters—both huge engines. In France the car was called the 54/220 CV, and the second model was called the 54/250 CV. This latter car appeared in the Paris Salon in 1931.

Hispano-Suiza has been known as a top quality car ever since it came out, and through the years it has never lost this position. Relatively few Hispanos come onto the market. In fact, few were on the market even when these cars were second-hand and not yet collector cars—in the late 1930s and the war years. At the bottom of this used-car period one might have been bought for as little as $500.

By 1970 the cars were selling for fairly substantial sums of money. In 1970 the H6 model (32CV) was selling for $12,500 to $16,000 if in top condition. The V-12 cars were selling for

$18,500 to $35,000. Unrestored cars were something else, and they could be bought for under $7,500; Quentin Craft records one at $3,000. Even ten years ago, cars in fine condition sold at big premiums.

By 1975 a number of Hispano-Suizas had changed hands in the marketplace as compared with 1970. The H6 was selling for $35,000 to $40,000. The V-12 closed cars were bringing about $30,000 and the V-12 convertibles about $50,000. The Boulogne cars brought prices between these two figures. The Boulogne brought about the same price relative to the H6 and the V-12 in 1970 also.

In 1979 one auction house sold an H6 drop-head coupe for $60,000, and Kruse sold a Boulogne convertible for $81,000—relatively huge auction prices. Kruse's Official Price Guide shows no Hispano going for a price under five figures, and some well into five figures, for 1980. In 1980 an H6 open car would bring $65,000 to $75,000 and a Boulogne model close to $100,000. The V-12 was bringing anywhere from $50,000 to $100,000, the cabriolets bringing top figures.

The Hispano-Suiza is a strict collector's car—a wealthy collector. The car is not widely known to the general public. The Flying Stork figurehead is in a sense the trademark of Hispano-Suiza. It is tremendously prized by collectors of the marque. Hispano-Suiza will have to take its place along with the Duesenberg J and SJ, the Bugatti Royale, and the Mercedes-Benz 500K, 540K, and SSK as a top collector car.

Isotta Fraschini

Isotta Fraschini is one of the most flamboyant cars ever made. In 1929 I saw a particularly flamboyant one in Hartford, Connecticut. The outstanding feature of the car was the running boards that looked exactly like the wings of an airplane viewed from the end. It is possible that these "wings" could be adjusted to act like the spoilers on modern racing cars—but I doubt it!

The radiator ornament (not the mascot) resembles a chrome-plated bolt of lightning, so the car looks as if it is traveling at 100 miles an hour even when standing still with no driver at the wheel. This ornament is particularly successful in giving the car the appearance of dash and speed.

In the pre-World War II period, there is little doubt that Isotta Fraschini was Italy's absolutely top luxury car. It was in the class of Rolls-Royce and Hispano-Suiza, among European cars. An Isotta Fraschini caps an automobile collection. It sets the tone of the collection. It also sets the tone of an automobile auction, and, no doubt, people will visit the exhibition of the cars for sale as well as the auction itself just to see the Isotta Fraschini and what it sells for.

Christie's October 2, 1979, sale at Madison Square Garden had a number of buy-backs (non-sales). The capstone car was a 1930 Isotta Fraschini type 8A 2/4 passenger convertible. It had a body by Castagna of Italy, one of the finest body companies in the world at the time. The catalogue description starts out, "The United States was the principal market for Italy's Rolls-Royce, the eight-in-line Isotta Fraschini . . ." The car brought the record price of the sale—$110,000. This is about the present market price for these standout cars.

On December 13, 1979, Christie's held a sale of cars at the London Cunard International Hotel. Lot 38 was another of the great type 8A cars with body by Castagna, only this was a seven-passenger landaulette. The chauffeur sat out in front, and the top of his compartment could be removed. The very back of the rear seat folded down by means of cabriole bars, as used in cabriolet models. The car brought only $65,000—the dollar equivalent of the pounds sterling. Had the car been a convertible coupe or tourer or roadster, the price might have been close to the price of the cars sold in America at about the same time.

Five years earlier, on July 10, 1975, another type 8A was sold, only this car was a limousine, a body style far less in demand. Coachwork was not by Castagna but by Cesare Sala. It brought about $14,000. In Geneva on March 20, 1975, still another type 8A was sold, this one a very desirable torpedo sports four-place tourer. It brought $40,000—and this price can be used in 1975 to compare with the 1979 and 1980 prices of $110,000 each reached at Christie's auctions in New York and Los Angeles for two type 8A cars.

In 1970 the type A roadsters and cabriolets were bringing about $15,000 to $18,000 if in fine condition. The price rise of these cars in the decade was high. The *Old Car Value Guide* for 1980 reports five Isottas, going for $105,000, $120,000, $115,000, $120,000, and $135,000.

Messrs. Cesare Isotta and Vincenzo Fraschini started to produce IF cars in the year 1900, although they were in the car import business in 1899. Their plant was located in Milan, Italy, and here they operated until the original company closed down in 1935. The aero manufacturer, Gianni Caproni, took over then and made aero products throughout the war, but the old car company was essentially finished.

As was the case with Bugatti and Hispano-Suiza, one engineer was, to a considerable extent, responsible for Isotta Fraschini right from the first and up to two years before the close-down of the plant in 1935: Giustino Cattaneo. Right from the start Cattaneo was an innovator. In 1905 he produced a car with a huge engine of seventeen liters—twice the size of the big Cadillac Eldorado engine, and with an overhead camshaft. It produced 120 horsepower.

By 1908, Cattaneo was producing 7.9-liter, overhead-cam-engine cars that won a great many races in Europe and in the U.S., thus establishing the make as a car that merited serious attention by luxury automobile buyers as well as racing enthusiasts. In 1909, Cattaneo came out with four-wheel brakes, although there were few four-wheel brake cars in the U.S. even in the early 1920s.

While Bugatti turned out any number of different model cars, Cattaneo turned out in essence one car. This car was announced in 1919, and it actually appeared for sale about two years later —the Tipo (type) 8. This was a straight eight-side valve engine with rocker arms—no overhead camshaft. It had an engine capacity of 5,900 cubic centimeters and produced only 75 to 80 horsepower at 2,200 revolutions per minute. Ronald Barker in *The World of Automobiles* (Columbia House, New York, 1974) has this to say about this model car, which is now one of the greats of automobile collecting:

> With neither the power nor maneuverability of the Hispano nor anything approaching Rolls-Royce unobtrusiveness, it is difficult to understand how the Tipo 8 was such a success. It was not even a pleasant car to drive. The answer probably lay in the huge chassis, with its 12 ft-plus wheelbase, which formed a wonderful platform for the specialist coachbuilders of Italy and the USA in particular.

The great Packard Straight Eight of the 1920s had the same kind of side valve, straight eight engine. So did the famous Auburn 851 and 852 speedsters; and a low compression side-valve engine is infinitely quieter and more docile than an overhead cam engine.

By the end of 1924 about 400 Tipo 8 cars had been sold by the factory, and the Tipo 8A appeared, an altogether more powerful car. It had an engine of 7,400 cubic centimeters that produced 110 to 120 horsepower at 2,400 revolutions per minute. Higher compression ratios and other changes were made to the Tipo 8A, apparently to match the Hispano-Suiza 46CV with its 8,000-cubic-centimeter engine. One car was called the Spinto and another the Super Spinto, and a sporting 8ASS was turned out that could top 100 miles per hour.

In April 1931 the Tipo 8B was launched. At 3,000 revolutions per minute, this engine produced 145 to 160 horsepower, and a Wilson preselector gearbox was optional. Only about thirty of this model were sold before the plant closed down in 1935.

After the close of World War II, IF again tried to get into the car business, this time with a much different car, a rear engine V-8 with overhead camshaft. There was four-wheel independent suspension. The engines were fairly small, some being as small as 2,500 cubic centimeters and some as large as 3,400 cubic centimeters. Perhaps sixteen of these cars were built, and I have seen just one. In Italy, however, I have never been able to locate even one of them, at least one that could be purchased.

With the right body, like the 1931 8S with Worblaufen of Berlin coachwork, the car can be a sensation. There are relatively few of these cars; and they are tremendously impressive looking machines. They will no doubt always be sought after by collectors who want the unique and the imposing.

Bentley

Over the last twenty years the pre-World War II classic Bentleys have risen in price from "nothing" to staggering amounts —at least staggering in comparison with what they brought as recently as 1960. Today there is essentially no difference between a Bentley and a Rolls-Royce, but it wasn't always so, and in the pre-World War II period Bentley was one of the greatest sports cars, and at the same time greatest competition cars, in the world. Today there is no Bentley sports car or competition car, nor has there been since the war.

In 1924 a Bentley, driven by John Duff, came first in the Le Mans race. This was a three-liter Bentley. In 1929, Bentley came in one-two-three-four in Le Mans. In all, the make had victories in the great Le Mans race in the years 1924, 1927, 1928, 1929, and 1930, as well as in other events.

There is a sharp distinction made by Bentley purists between those cars made by W. O. Bentley up to 1931 and those made after that date—when the company was acquired by Rolls-Royce.

Kevin Brazendale's *Great Cars of the Golden Age* (Crescent Books, New York, 1979, page 77) says:

Total output of Bentleys was 3,051—ten more were to be built after 1931 from spares.

Rolls-Royce pre-empted Napier Motors in acquiring Bentley, and from then on the marque inexorably moved towards being merely a Rolls with a different badge and radiator grill.

Gianni Rogliatti's *Great Collectors' Cars* (Grosset and Dunlap, New York, 1973, page 132) says: "Bentley cars are remarkable for their longevity, and of the 3,061 built during the lifetime of the make, well over 1,000 survive today . . ."

On the other hand, *Automobile Quarterly*'s "Great Cars and Grand Marques" (Bonanza Books, New York, 1979, page 164) says at the outset of the illustrated article on Bentley:

It actually seems that there is a certain element among Bentley enthusiasts which likes to pretend the marque literally died in 1931, upon acquisition by Rolls-Royce. Like a proud family which tends to overlook the fact that one of its members has been committed, these types regard the Derby- and Crewe-built Bentleys as subjects definitely not for discussion. This is silly, of course, for in fact the Bentleys that Rolls-Royce built are outstandingly fine automobiles, in virtually every way better than their predecessors, and through the years have been the embodiment of just about anybody's idea of what a truly great high performance passenger car should be.

. . . no one who knows them can say that they are not bloody good cars, because they are.

This taking of sides is probably the nearest two groups of Englishmen can come to emulating the American Hatfields and McCoys!

From a collector's point of view, and from the point of view of the market for Bentley cars, it is clear that the former group, the real Bentley purists, will not be in there bidding up the price of Bentleys made after the Rolls-Royce takeover of 1931.

Whatever the year of the car, the Bentley is characterized by ruggedness, dependability, and long life. The same cannot be said about many, if not most, other exotic cars, and certainly not about the highest performing ultramodern cars.

Unlike Bugatti and Ferrari, there were relatively few Bentley models made in the era of the kingpin of the company, W. O. Bentley, and even after the Rolls-Royce takeover, from 1931 to the onset of the war.

In 1919, Bentley introduced the three-liter model at the Motor Show at Olympia. The car was first sold in 1921. It was a four-cylinder overhead-valve model, and its performance at the British Brooklands track in 1921 was outstanding. This was the dominant car put out by Bentley until 1925, when the larger engined, 6½-liter was introduced, a six-cylinder version of the three-liter-four. In 1926 work was started on a 4½-liter car, which was the 6½-liter, six-cylinder car less two of its six cylinders.

In 1929 the 6½-liter, six-cylinder car was made somewhat more sporty and less luxury than it had been and was known as the Speed Six. Production of the three-liter car ended in 1929, and the 4½-liter car production was gradually curtailed almost as soon as the car was introduced. In 1929, 129 6½-liter cars were produced and 260 of the 4½-liter cars. In 1930, 126 6½-liter cars were made and only 138 of the 4½-liter cars. In 1930 a number of high performance supercharged 4½s were built.

At the end of 1930 the great 8-liter Bentley was on the market, and it replaced the 6½-liter car in that year. The early 1930s, under Rolls-Royce ownership and direction still led by Sir Henry Royce, brought out a good Bentley, the 3½-liter model. The engine of this new car was actually Rolls-Royce from the model 20/25 Rolls-Royce car. In competition, driver Eddie Hall proved the car in the class of the old Bentleys. In 1936 the engine was increased in size to 4¼ liters (4,257 cubic centimeters). The 3½-liter engine was also put in some Bentleys for a time. Van Vooren of France produced at least two streamlined, 4¼-liter coupes of top performance.

To my way of thinking, the 3½-liter and the 4¼-liter Bentleys of the mid- to late-thirties are superb-looking machines and superb-driving machines. Twenty years ago few Bentleys of any model were worth anything much. The June 1959 *Antique Automobile* advertised a Bentley which looked fine for $2,500. Six years later a 1935 Bentley 3½-liter car was offered to me for $1,500, a car in apparently very good condition and a convertible.

By 1970 a Speed Six tourer was bringing about $15,000; a 4½-liter tourer of 1929 was bringing about the same. The smaller and earlier tourers, 3 liter, were bringing half that much. The huge 8 liter was bringing close to $15,000. The mid-thirties 3½-liter open car could be bought for about $8,000, and the 4¼ liter for about the same price.

On July 12, 1972, Christie's at Beaulieu, England, sold a very fine 1931 4½-liter, supercharged four-passenger drophead coupe with vanden Plas body, apparently in top condition, for the equivalent of $36,000, no small price at the time. In the same sale a 1929 Speed Six with vanden Plas body—all original—four-door touring, brought $25,200. The very next car in the sale was a 1930 Speed Six in somewhat nonoriginal condition. It brought $18,000. The star of the sale was a 1931 4½-liter supercharged replica four-seater like the car that was on the

Birkin-Paget Bentley racing team. The body was not original, but a good copy. The car realized $40,800.

By way of contrast, in the same sale a very standard 1934 3½-liter Bentley sedan, in apparently good condition, *but* a Rolls-Royce-made Bentley, brought the very low price of $1,080—450 pounds sterling. The car was anything but a collector's car in 1972.

In March 1974, in Geneva, Christie's sold a somewhat similar standard sedan for about $5,500, still not a very high price, and not high in relation to the collector Bentleys of the era. This too was a "Rolls-Royce" Bentley.

In the Leake sale in Texas in May 1974 a superb eight-liter Bentley, four-passenger, sport touring car of 1931, one of the last "Bentley Bentleys," brought $70,000. In the same sale one of the late Rolls-Royce Bentleys, a 1935 four-passenger Continental tourer of 1935, brought $22,000. It was apparently in top condition.

In the Beaulieu sale of July 1975 a fine-looking 1931 eight-liter replica, four-door tourer in outstanding condition according to the sales catalog, brought close to $40,000. A 1930 Speed Six convertible coupe, an excellent-looking car in fine condition, brought about $35,000.

In the Beaulieu sale of July 9, 1979, the featured car, frontispiece in color, was a 1928 6½-liter (just prior to the Speed Six). It was a two-door coupe with body by Martin Walter of Folkestone, England, a firm with which I have had contact for over twenty years—without knowing that they ever made automobile bodies! The car was in fine condition and brought about $60,000. In the same sale an ordinary-looking 4¼-liter, 1938 sports saloon brought about $12,500—a Rolls-Bentley.

One market trend seems clear, and that is that, although the pre-Rolls-Royce era Bentleys are certainly the preferred Bentleys, the gap is being closed and the Rolls-Royce era Bentleys are rising in price fairly rapidly.

Alfa Romeo

We pick Alfa Romeo as representative of the smaller, higher performance Italian cars of the prewar era. We might have picked the Italian Lancia and we might have picked Fiat; but Alfa Romeo is a top quality, smaller, high performance car and very much of an investment car.

The 1930s were the years of the Alfa Romeo, certainly as far as road racing went. Of course the team had the best drivers: Nuvolari, Caracciola, Chiron, and Fagioli. Nuvolari probably goes down in the racing hall of fame as Italy's finest driver, perhaps the world's finest driver. Caracciola, despite his Italian name, was probably Germany's finest driver—on Mercedes-Benz. In the hall of fame he might be right up there with Nuvolari. In 1934, Alfa Romeo won fifteen races, and in 1935, thirteen. In 1935, Alfa Romeo won the German Grand Prix against the great Germany cars that were to dominate racing in the later years of the 1930s.

The little Alfas were too small and too highly stressed for the Indianapolis 500. In fact they were too small and too highly stressed to compete against the 4,500 Ferraris that were soon to dominate road racing in Europe.

From the day I first set eyes on an Alfa Romeo, I was more than impressed. It was a bright red, 2.9-liter, double supercharged Alfa Romeo roadster of 1938, which cost $10,500—a fantastic sum at the time for any two-seater. For years I tried to buy this car, or one like it. I thought it was the most beautiful car I had seen; only the Mercedes-Benz 500K or 540K roadster compared with it in beauty. There were not many of these 2.9 twin supercharged cars made, but they were superb in appearance and in mechanical excellence.

In some ways, the Alfa Romeo might be considered the forerunner of the Ferrari. Enzo Ferrari was the manager of Alfa's racing team as well as a driver. Engineer Colombo was with Alfa Romeo before he became Ferrari's first chief engineer. Vittotio Jano was the kingpin of Alfa Romeo. Between the mid-twenties and the mid-thirties, Alfa Romeo produced a superb series of sports (or road) cars, in addition to racing cars.

In 1927 the firm put out the first of these street greats—a small-engined (1,500 cubic centimeter), six-cylinder single, overhead-camshaft touring car. This car was followed by a similar design of 1,750 cubic centimeters. Then two more cars came out of the factory—a 1,500 and a 1,750 cubic centimeter with two overhead cams, and some of these cars carried a supercharger. They too were six-cylinder cars. Bodies were made by the leading Italian coachbuilders.

Then followed straight eight-cylinder cars, supercharged, of 2.3-liter engine capacity. Six-cylinder and eight-cylinder cars, unsupercharged and supercharged, were built for street use, many with rakish bodies, and all excellent and reliable pieces of machinery.

In the last year before the war, the basic road car was the 6C2300, a six-cylinder model, but along with this car went the 8C2900, the great supercharged eight. This was the car that won the very first Watkins Glen road race, a blue coupe from the prewar years, and it won easily, driven by Frank Griswold.

All Alfa Romeos are collectors' cars, and, for some reason, all of them tend to bring the same general price—unless, of course, one of the great 2.9, twin supercharged cars comes along— painted a bright red!

In 1970 a fine Alfa could be purchased for $10,000 or less. The 2.3-liter roadster would go for well above this figure as would the 1938, 2.9-liter, approaching $20,000.

In Christie's Geneva sale of March 21, 1974, a very simple, unassuming four-door close-coupled sedan, a 6C 2300 of 1934, brought about $8,000. The car was in excellent condition. In the very same sale, a 1930 6C 1750 two-seater cabriolet with a rather stark-looking body by Brichet of Geneva, brought the very respectable sum of $35,000. This was another car in splendid condition. This car sold for more money than a Phantom II Rolls-Royce convertible of 1931 with Freestone and Webb body —also in excellent condition.

In the Christie's sale at Beaulieu, England, in July 1974 a splendid and sought-after eight-cylinder Alfa was sold, this one a 1932 8C 2300 short-chassis Mille Miglia sports two-seater—a twin-camshaft straight eight with supercharger. The body was, however, a replica or reconstruction. The car was in excellent condition and brought $33,000.

On July 9, 1979, Christie at Beaulieu sold an almost identical car, and this too had a replica body—a roadster body, whereas the original body was a drophead coupe. This car brought exactly twice what the similar car brought in 1974—in pounds sterling. It was even the same year—1932—and an 8C 2300.

Kruse Auction house reports two twelve-cylinder competition cars going in the year 1980, one for $30,000 and one for $40,000, the first being a 1939 model and the second a 1938. All models of open Alfa Romeo cars from the 1920s and 1930s seem to go in the region of $30,000 to $50,000, some fine cars higher. But whatever model the Alfa Romeo, there seems to be some collector who wants it and who will pay a good price.

CHAPTER **10**

Antique Cars

Antique cars can rarely be used for transportation. About twelve years ago I called my friend, Smith Hempstone Oliver, a great authority on antique cars in the United States, for his advice on whether I should buy a 1909 Maxwell roadster. His first comments were, "I don't see why you would consider that car. It has only two forward speeds, and you can't cruise at much over 30 miles an hour. You can't keep up with turnpike traffic."

Hemp Oliver was right, of course. The car wouldn't keep up with turnpike traffic and could never be run on a turnpike. It was so slow as to be a definite traffic hazard. In fact, the car could not be used for transportation at all, not even once a week or once a month. It should probably not even be driven over the highway to old car meets.

Antique cars should not be thought of as a means of transportation, although many cars that are now antiques were originally driven every day. My first investment car, a 1921 Studebaker Special Six touring car, could actually keep up with turnpike traffic, cruising at 55 miles an hour; but why do it? A steady 55 miles an hour will strain many old cars; and for many other old cars, 55 miles an hour is an impossibility.

Use—any use—of antique cars results in very high maintenance, almost prohibitive in cost. If a clutch went on a 1921
Studebaker Special Six, parts could not be secured easily or at
reasonable prices. Very often parts must be specially made, and
time is required for the manufacture. Sometimes a car is laid up
for years waiting for hard-to-find and hard-to-make parts. Old
Fords are the only possible exception to this rule.

One might, of course, buy an antique that can occasionally be
used to go on an outing or to a meet. The Packard Twin Six can
certainly be placed on the highway on occasion, as can many
Packards made in the late teens and early 1920s. The same for
the big Cadillac V-8s like the 1918 Cadillac touring car that I
once owned, or my 1923 Buick six touring car.

Storage must be very special and well protected for an antique car, or the car may very well be fooled with or vandalized.

Complete insurance that will cover vandalism, theft, fire, and
collision without restrictions on the use of the car is hard to get,
and extremely costly. Often satisfactory settlements from the
insurance company may be difficult to secure.

Skilled quality mechanical work on a Stanley Steamer is not
readily available. The car may have to be moved some distance
to a qualified repair man. A Stanley originally was not difficult
to repair—troubles could be located easily. Now, however,
there are few available steam car repair men.

Most important from an investment point of view, there is
not a big market for antique automobiles—to sell or to buy. One
may well look a long time before finding a good Mercer Raceabout or a good Stutz Bearcat. When one is located, the cost
will now be well into six figures. Furthermore, there is no definite market price, or even a close market price, for many antiques. One car may be offered for $50,000 and a similar model
car for $100,000.

Price trends are somewhat hard to determine when only a
few cars are sold. What is a two-cylinder Rolls-Royce worth?
What is Peter Helck's Locomobile "16" racer worth? Is it worth
$150,000? Is it worth $550,000? These are unique cars and they
have unique prices. For some antiques, of course, the price may
be much more easily determined, as well as price trend.

Increasingly, unique cars are being displayed in more or less museum surroundings. Dr. Samuel Scher of New York once had a fine display floor for his collection, very much like the display rooms of a museum. Each car had a card in front of it explaining just what the car was, and I recall the Renault staff car of General de Gaulle.

Many old cars deserve to be displayed along with art and antiques, and they possibly belong in the category of art and antiques. It is enough that they can be owned and displayed occasionally; and if they appreciate in value and thus turn out to be good investments over a period of years they have fulfilled their function as investment automobiles.

The Important Distinction: Large Cars and Small Cars

While there is some disagreement as to the exact definition of an antique automobile, a common definition is those cars produced up to the year 1925. Prewar classic cars are those produced from that date to World War II, and postwar classics are those produced after the end of World War II.

There is a division of antique cars into the large and the small cars. The collectors of large cars tend to be different from the collectors of small cars.

There is a vast difference in the two categories of cars other than simply the number of cylinders. The one- and two-cylinder cars tend to be very small and very simple machines. Many of the multicylinder cars tend to be very large and vastly more complicated machines. The one-cylinder Brush is a modest and, perhaps, cute little car. The Pierce-Arrow 48 is literally a living room on wheels. The one-cylinder cars tend to lope along at 30 miles an hour or thereabouts, while the Mercer Raceabout and the Stutz Bearcat roar along the road at speeds that are respectably high even by today's standards.

Today's collectors certainly include the "nostalgic buyers" going back well before the start of World War II and to the antique car era. One motive for buying important antiques is that these were the cars of the wealthy and otherwise important people at the time when the cars were new. Buying such cars today gives the buyer a second chance to own what he couldn't afford at the time, probably because he was too young to own any car! This motive seems very important in antique car collecting.

The big, multicylinder cars sell for disproportionately high prices as compared with the simpler machines—those we sometimes refer to as "the oldies." If often seems that the bigger and noisier the antique, the more it sells for. If one settles for few cylinders, however, $10,000 will still purchase a one-cylinder Curved Dash Olds or Brush, or a two-cylinder Maxwell, in excellent condition.

In some ways the standard cutoff date between prewar classics and antiques—the year 1925—is unfortunate, and it is unfortunate that we have to pick the year 1925 or *any* particular date. What is the difference between a 1927 Ford and a 1922 Ford? Very little. They both have the same four-cylinder engine of about 22 horsepower, the same planetary two-speed transmission, the same simple braking system.

Or take the Rolls-Royce: the 1918 car was a six, of 114 by 121 millimeter bore and stroke. The wheelbase was 12 feet 6½ inches; the length of the car was 16 feet 4½ inches. The chassis weighed 3,800 pounds. The 1926 car had precisely these specifications, even the Rolls-Royces made in the United States. Now which is really an antique car: the 1927 Ford or the 1918 Rolls-Royce? I have driven both, and I would have to say that the Ford is really the antique—as late as the 1927 model.

From a strictly market point of view, antique cars might be divided into the following categories:

• The small antique cars made from the beginning of the automobile until about the end of the first decade of the present century—and even for a short time into the decade of the teens. These are the one- and two-cylinder cars made for the earliest and most primitive transportation. A few very simple four-cylinder cars of the same era also fall into this most primitive category—the category of the so-called oldies.

• The more sophisticated, larger, higher-priced cars of the same era or a bit later in the timetable of automobile production, but still clearly antiques.

• The real performance cars of the first two decades of the present century, probably the most sought after of all antique categories today—the Mercer Raceabout, the Stutz Bearcat, the Simplex two-seater, etcetera.

• The superluxury cars of the late teens and of the twenties until the cutoff year 1925—the Rolls-Royce, the Pierce Arrow, the Bentley, the Locomobile, the Isotta Fraschini, and the Hispano-Suiza, and more. In essence, these cars differ little from the prewar classics, and in many cases the same car was made before as well as after the magic cutoff date of 1925.

• The Model T Ford—a car in a class by itself. This is the car that put America on wheels and that established the automobile industry. It was, and is, a humble car. The car was little changed during its entire history from 1908 to 1927, during which time fifteen million Model Ts were produced.

There is certainly no shortage of Model T Fords, even today. Still, the car has become a collector car, and despite its numbers has risen greatly in price in the past decade. This one make and model is so important in the collector car market that it forms a category of its own, and a price trend for the car can be established.

Deciding Whether to Invest In Antique Automobiles

In some ways, the small one- and two-cylinder cars (and a few small fours) have seemed to hold back in market price rise in the past decade. They are still not beyond reach as of 1982. The market is not as strong for these older, simpler cars as it is for other areas in the investment car market. It is somewhat harder to sell these cars.

To a degree, you get what you pay for. These cars are simple in construction and do not consist of very much metal and other materials. The bodies are not elaborate, and no coachbuilders bothered with many of these cars.

On the other hand, a work of art does not always have to be large and detailed to be important and valuable. A small Breughel painting is important and valuable. So is a Pollock, although it does not seem to involve a tremendous amount of labor and craftsmanship. These old cars may simply not yet have come into their own in the market.

The cars are not complicated and thus are not so hard or time-consuming to repair. But parts and components may be unobtainable at any price. On the other hand, it is legitimate to make new parts without seriously diminishing the value of such cars. Even entire bodies can be constructed without ruining the value of such automobiles. This work will, however, be costly and the artisans may be hard to locate.

These cars are so underpowered, as well as so fragile, that they even have to be trucked to meets. However, since they are small, their paint and leather can be easily refurbished. They can be put on display anywhere without taking up too much space: in the garage, in a special building, even in the home. Cars of this age and size are sometimes placed on display in stately homes in England.

The larger cars are more in demand by car collectors. There is no lack of these cars at present. As time goes on, they will tend to get much scarcer than many other categories of collector-investment cars.

The larger cars are harder to work on than the simple oldies and parts are just as difficult to obtain. Very often, if a part or component has to be made, the cost is much more than in the case of the simpler one- and two-cylinder old cars because more has to be made. A crankshaft for a six-cylinder car is much more complicated than a crankshaft for a one-cylinder car. There are of course more parts and components to go wrong than in the simpler automobiles.

Not only is mechanical work harder to perform on these cars, but the large cars cost very much more to buy than the simple cars. An investment in one of these cars can take up a good deal of cash, as can restoration.

The real performance cars of the first two decades of the century are some of the most sought-after cars in the entire market. Prices have been in a steep uptrend for over a decade. The cars are relatively scarce, and they will likely become very much scarcer in the years immediately ahead. There is absolutely no weakness in the market for these cars, even though the Mercer Raceabout is now well into six figures and the Stutz Bearcat not far behind.

These performance cars should be in original condition. Replacements are not tolerated the way they are in the first two categories of car. The cars should be as near to their condition when they left the factory as possible. Spare parts are by no means easy to locate, and parts and components will have to be made in many cases, at considerable expense.

The cars can occasionally be driven, but these are not cars for use. They are too valuable and fragile—at least too fragile to have to pay for any repairs necessitated through their use.

There are plenty of superluxury cars of the late teens and early twenties around, and there is little chance that the market will dry up or even get tight. Market trend and price trend are up and strong, but not equally or for everything. In fact, the up-trend in prices is not as strong overall as it is for the sports cars. Depending on what a particular car is, parts and components can be more than hard to locate and very expensive. Parts may have to be made, as in the case of some Bentleys, and these are usually very expensive.

The cars in the sports car category just discussed are very liquid. They are not hard to dispose of at good prices. The superluxury cars are a kind of conglomeration of cars, and unless one picks cars the market wants, it can be hard to dispose of the cars at good prices. They are not all Renoirs. The sports cars of the antique era *are* all Renoirs.

The market for Model T Fords is a peculiar one. There are relatively many Model Ts available for sale, or potentially on the market, but the price over the past twenty years has been rising steadily, even for the 1925–1927 models which were turned out in tremendous numbers.

The Model Ts that actually appear on the market are far fewer than the numbers made and sold when new might indicate. For this reason, prices have held firm and have risen, so there is anything but price weakness; the market is there to buy and it is there to sell. Sometimes Model Ts at auction do not sell, but very often they do find a buyer. A collector still has his pick of good Model Ts if he wants to collect the car, including the much wanted early Model Ts, particularly the brass-radiator models.

If you want to collect Model Ts now, you should concentrate on the early models in good condition, because such cars do not yet seem to command huge premiums compared to cars in average condition.

Parts for the Model T Ford are readily available. They do not cost a great deal, and there are no parts that can't be found. Labor to repair the Model T is not hard to locate. It is even possible to do all one's own work. The car is simple, and almost anyone can learn its construction and how to repair it—even its planetary transmission.

The car should probably not be used except to go to meets, but it can be used for short drives. If something goes wrong on short drives, it can be fixed fairly easily and inexpensively. Even for prime early Model Ts no great investment is required, and the Model T might be the place for a beginning collector to start; you can work up from there.

The Small Antique Cars

In general, the small single- or two-cylinder antiques are not preferred cars in today's market, and they do not bring the big prices that cars with four cylinders and up do. A rough correlation in price might be made for antique cars according to weight: the heavier the car, the higher its market price; the smaller and lighter the car, the less its value.

Another correlation might be made in price with number of cylinders. The one-cylinder car would stand at one end of the price scale, the sixteen-cylinder car at the other. Of course we have to move up at least to the late 1920s to get any sixteen-cylinder cars actually. But the Packard Twin Six appeared in 1915.

So, generally at the bottom of the price scale stands the one-cylinder car and perhaps the two-cylinder. From another point of view, you get what you pay for. A one-cylinder car isn't very much of a "piece of transportation." Nor was it even when it was new. It should, therefore, cost little. In general it did, and still does, cost little.

However, even the categorization of the one- and two-cylinder cars as little cars or inexpensive cars or oldies is not strictly accurate. Many of the early four-cylinder cars are little more than two-cylinder cars with two more cylinders added. They still are little, inexpensive-when-new, low-performance cars—and certainly nonluxury cars. One such car was the lot number one in the March 29, 1980, Christie's sale in Los Angeles. This was a 1907 Franklin 12 horsepower, two-passenger runabout, a car that still bore a faint resemblance to a carriage. It was supposed to embody the manufacturer's principle of "Scientific Light Weight," and this it did, including the absence of any windshield! The engine was four-cylinder and air-cooled, in the Franklin tradition.

For its age this model is a very good looking car, and this example was in excellent condition, with gas head lamps, gas side lamps, and an oil tail lamp. This car sold for $18,000.

Two cars later, the same auction featured a four-cylinder oldie, a rather attractive looking Hupmobile two-passenger runabout, a 1910 model car. In this model there are no doors, and, to a degree, the car resembles a carriage, even this car made as late as 1910. It brought $11,500.

In the Leake auction in Tulsa in June 1980 a highly interesting, very early, very primitive car was sold. It was a 1904 Stevens Duryea, a little carriagelike affair with a two-cylinder engine. This was one of the pioneering American automobiles. The car is without top or windshield, and there is a tiller instead of a steering wheel. The only deficiency in this particular car offered for sale was that it lacked a transmission. The car brought $4,750, a car that required a great amount of restoration plus the substitution of new parts for the originals, since, in all probability, original parts could not ever be found anywhere.

In the Bud Cohn car sale held by Christie's in February 1979 one of the most primitive cars made was offered for sale. Lot fifty was an extremely early pioneer car by the firm that probably developed the automobile in the first place. This was a Benz of the year 1893, a single-cylinder 1½ horsepower "velo two-passenger sociable." The catalog describes the car well:

One of the earliest automobiles still in operable condition, this car is in the true horseless carriage idiom with rear mounted motor started by rotating the flywheel. The wire wheels are of unequal diameter front and rear, and the simple two-passenger coachwork has neither doors nor top.

The car was used in the seventy-fifth anniversary ceremonies of Daimler-Benz and was displayed in the Ford Museum in Dearborn, Michigan. It took the Veteran Car Club of Great Britain's Wellington trophy for its performance in the London-Brighton commemoration run. This price was a very high $65,000.

As we move back in time (in the market for these old cars), prices were less by a good deal. On July 10, 1975, Christie's held a sale at Beaulieu in which a 1900 M.M.C. Princess, four-seater was sold, a rather high-wheel, buggy-looking car with a very high folding top with cabriole bars of sorts. It was a two-cylinder car driven from the *back* seat. The folding front seat had only a footboard between passenger and the open country ahead. The engine was in the rear and was mounted horizontally. The lights actually were candle-powered. The engine was described in the sale catalog as noisy, although in 1974 no less than 700 pounds sterling was spent for a complete mechanical overhaul. Today the engine overhaul might have to add another zero! The car brought the equivalent of $10,350.

Another old car went for exactly the same price in the same sale—a 1903 Panhard 7 horsepower two-seater with two-cylinder engine. There were no doors, no hood, and no windshield. Condition was described as "fair."

One year earlier, in Beaulieu, prices seemed still lower. On July 11, 1974, Christie's at Beaulieu sold a splendid, more or less epic-making car, a Leon Bollée 1896 tandem tricar, chassis number five and engine number five. The engine was single cylinder and horizontal. It was air cooled. The drive was by belt, and the brake was on the flywheel. The car would do over 30 miles per hour, and this model was used for early voiturette racing. The driver sits in the rear. The car was reported in excellent condition with an up-to-date engine overhaul. The price realized in 1974 was $7,680. Today the car would bring well over twice this amount.

Prices in 1970 were not a great deal lower than they were in

1974–1975. In the July 13, 1972, sale at Beaulieu, England, a very similar Renault, this car a 1910 two-cylinder two-seater, said to be "in good condition," brought the equivalent of $6,240.

In America in 1970 a 1904 two-cylinder model K Auto Car was reported by Quentin Craft as bringing $6,500 in restored condition. A 1903 Baker electric was reported at the same price, and a 1905 Binford two-cylinder roadster brought about $6,000.

A single-cylinder 1907 Brush, a very nice car, was bringing about $3,000.

The 1901 Cadillac roadster might have been bought for $6,500 or thereabouts. The early Maxwells were bringing under $4,000 —1902 to 1912 models. Even the famous Curved Dash Olds of the earliest years of the century were bringing only about $3,000. The Sears Motor Buggy, a very primitive-looking car, was bringing even less.

Ten years earlier—in the 1959–1960 period—the old, simpler cars in good condition were almost at the giveaway level. In late 1959 my wife and I took off from London for New York in a then recent Boeing 707 plane. After we were off the coast of England and heading west we noticed the plane dumping fuel into the ocean. Trouble had developed in one of the engines, and we turned back to London. When we landed we were informed that we would be sent out on the next available flight; but we had a better idea. We would go to the Earl's Court Motor Show instead!

At that show there were several old cars for sale, one of the most notable being a very early four-seater Cadillac. It was priced at about $2,600, and it was in near mint condition.

The May 1958 issue of *Antique Automobile* advertised a 1902 Invincible Schacht auto runabout high-wheel car for sale, complete with the exception of fenders, but not restored. The engine was two cylinder opposed. It was a distinctly buggy-type car, and it was priced at $750.

A 1909 Buick model 10 touring car, with $400 just spent on the engine and four new matched tires, was priced at $600. Paint and upholstery were reported as not good.

As late as 1965 you could buy a very fine early car for little money. John Oldrin of Darien, Connecticut, offered for sale a fine 1909 two-cylinder Maxwell two-seater in very good condition for $1,200. I looked and looked at this car, and then started to bargain—which was my mistake. When Mr. Oldrin saw my attitude, he quickly put things into reverse gear and announced that the car was reserved for another prospective buyer. He obviously wanted the car to be loved by somebody, and he had decided I wasn't the person to assume ownership of his car.

I followed this car, and similar cars, over the years. In 1975 the car would have brought $5,500, and I found this or a similar car advertised at just this figure. In 1980 I saw another similar car advertised, maybe the same car, for $11,500. This is the way prices for these old and simple cars have moved.

The Larger and Higher-Priced Cars of the Early Years

In the Christie's July 11, 1972, sale at Beaulieu, England, lot nineteen was the first car offered for sale (lots one through eighteen had been motorcycles, fire engines, steam rollers, and caravans). Lot nineteen was not only the first car offered, but it also was featured in color. It was certainly an early car—a 1903 Panhard et Levassor 10-horsepower, rear-entrance tonneau, a four-cylinder car.

From collector and price points of view, this car, although as early as the one- and two-cylinder "oldies," was an automobile, not a buggy with an engine in it. It was sophisticated, a large and impressive-looking vehicle. It was also apparently in superb condition. These are the value elements.

The car had large front and rear seats. The engine was in the front, covered by the hood. The transmission was in the center of the car, and the drive was to the rear wheels. These are tremendously important elements in value. This is the modern automobile layout until almost 1980, with the exception of inexpensive foreign imports and the imported supercars like Ferrari and Porsche. The Panhard in 1972 brought the then very substantial price of $16,800.

In America in 1970 a 1909 four-cylinder Locomobile was reported to have sold for $17,500, and no early Locomobiles were reported as selling for as low as $10,000 if they were in good condition. The early British Napier was selling in the same price

range. So were the Great Arrows of 1907 and later—the predecessors of the Pierce-Arrows. So was the early Pope Hartford
and the Pope Tribune, and the huge Thomas as well as the
Winton.

In Geneva in March 1974 two early "sophisticates" sold for
identical prices—$13,500. The first was a French Darracq 15.9-
horsepower, four-seater double phaeton of 1910, a four-cylinder
car of "modern" design. The car was reported to be in excellent
condition. It was a big, impressive machine.

By 1980 these more sophisticated early cars were selling for
prices far higher. In the Leake sale of June 1980 a little known
but elegant French coupe in fine condition, a Unic of 1912,
brought $20,000.

In 1980, Buick touring cars of early vintage were selling at
prices ranging from $15,000 to $20,000. Some of the early four-
cylinder Cadillacs were running above $20,000. Four-cylinder
Packards were selling around $30,000. Even the one-cylinder
Packards were at this price level, if not higher, in the Kruse
Auction sales. Great Arrows were bringing as high as $50,000.
The enormous Thomas sixes were selling for as much as
$50,000. The big Wintons did not, however, touch $20,000 at
auction.

The prices of these sophisticated early cars are far higher than
the price of the one- and two-cylinder early cars. On the other
hand they are by no means as high as the prices of prime prewar classics or even the great cars of the early 1920s. They are
certainly not of the level of the sportsmen's early cars including
the Mercer Raceabouts and the Stutz Bearcats.

The Performance Cars of the First Two Decades of the Century

The real performance cars of the early years of the present
century are far different from the simple early cars or even the
sophisticated cars—in what they are like, in who buys them, in
their prices. These performance cars are some of the most
sought-after collector cars in the world, and at extremely high
prices.

At the very top of these cars stands the legendary Mercer Raceabout. Even we kids in high school who didn't follow races closely were tremendously impressed when one of the stark 1913 Mercer Raceabouts pulled up at our school and parked. We all came out to admire it, though at the time it was already fifteen years old.

The car has two bucket seats, no top, no doors, no starter. It has a rudimentary "monocle" windshield, something like a big magnifying glass. It weighs about one ton, and its 55 horsepower from a four-cylinder engine allowed it to cover one mile in fifty-one seconds. Its top speed may have been 89 miles per hour, an enormous speed at the time. New, it cost $2,250, not a low price.

The Mercer was driven to victory by the greatest drivers of the era: Barney Oldfield, Ralph de Palma, Hughie Hughes, Spencer Wishart, Ed Pullen. The car even placed second at Indianapolis and won the American grand prize at Santa Monica, a 403-mile race that had traditionally been won by the very large Benz and Fiat racing cars.

The Mercer Raceabout first appeared in 1911, the type 35. By 1920 a new Mercer Raceabout was produced, but it seemed to have little relationship to stark model 35. The 1920 car was refined in appearance and not much different from other roadsters of the period. Anyway, in 1914, Mercer's chief engineer, Finlay Robertson, had left, and the character of the company and its products changed.

In 1970 the early Raceabout could have been purchased for around $40,000. Sometimes lower prices were realized in that year. By 1973 prices of the car had risen overall to about $45,000; the 1975 price was about $50,000.

In October 1980, Karl Darby advertised an original completely restored 1912 Raceabout for sale, the car that had won national first place at the Hershey, Pennsylvania, meet in 1958. His asking price was $125,000 or best offer. Actual prices as high as $140,000 and $160,000 for this model car have been recorded.

The next most wanted and most valuable car of this type and era is the early Stutz Bearcat. This is the same type of stark, four-cylinder open two-seater speedster that the Mercer Raceabout is, and it was produced at approximately the same time.

The Bearcat first appeared in 1914, a few years after the Raceabout came on the scene. These cars, like the Raceabouts, also won races, even coming in second in the 1919 Indianapolis race and second in the 1916 Vanderbilt Cup race. It was pretty much of a 1916 stock Bearcat, which its owner thought was "gutless," that Cannonball Baker drove from coast to coast to establish a new transcontinental speed record—eleven days, seven and a half hours.

Like Mercer, the Bearcat had become by 1923 more conventional, still fine but far less stark. The average selling price of the early Stutz Bearcat in 1970 was $22,500, against $40,000 for the Mercer Roundabout. By 1973 the price of the Stutz Bearcat had risen to $29,000, against $45,000 for the Raceabout. By 1975 the gap between the price of the two cars seemed to be closing, with $45,000 for the Bearcat and $50,000 for the Raceabout. By 1980 the price was up to a range of from $70,000 to $85,000 for Bearcats in fine condition, but very few of these cars came onto the market. By 1982 the price was well over $100,000.

There are other sports-competition cars of the early period; the 1912 four-cylinder Simplex was one of the most outstanding of this type car. This was a very large, enormous-engined car with a ten-liter-capacity engine—10,000 cubic centimeters. It produced 75 horsepower, and was reputed to be the last chain-driven American car. On a slightly lower price level is the Pope-Hartford speedster of 1913, a very similar stark automobile.

Other countries put out these early sports-competition cars. One such car that might be mistaken for a Simplex from a distance is the early Lancia. Another is the British Napier. The Gordon Bennett Napier of 1903 was a sensation, and it is still a byword in British racing circles. The car won the Gordon Bennett Cup Race. One of these greats is in the Arkansas Museum. The later (1907–1912) speedsters will bring $25,000–$30,000. The early and greatest ones are to all intents and purposes off the market.

French Renault too made a Grand Prix model, two-seater car, essentially for the U.S. market. These export cars were based on the Renault that won the French Grand Prix in 1906 and finished second in 1907. The export models had four-cylinder, thirty-five horsepower engines.

In the October 1979 sale at Madison Square Garden in New York, held by Christie's, lot twenty-seven was such an early sports car, a 1904 Peerless two-passenger, four-cylinder roadster, and it was correctly described in the sale catalog as a "unique monster. . . . it is a formidable vehicle, cruising effortlessly at 55 miles an hour, and capable of 80 if pushed." It had an enormous engine of 11,000-cubic-centimeter capacity. The car won a national first prize at the Hershey, Pennsylvania, meet in 1974. It did not, however, find a buyer in the Christie's sale, although it was estimated to bring $90,000 to $120,000.

One other of these early great sports-competition cars might be mentioned, the Thomas Flyer model F of 1908, a large four-cylinder car. This model car was offered for sale in early 1981 by Sam Gurnee of California. This was the model car that won the famous New York–Paris race in its era. The car will apparently cruise all day at sixty miles per hour, and can hit 70. The drive is by twin chains. Apparently this particular car has won all shows that it has ever entered, which is quite a record. The asking price for the car was $115,000.

The Superluxury Cars—Late Teens to Mid-Twenties

The most notable example of the superluxury cars in this category is the Rolls-Royce. The great Silver Ghost was put out throughout the decade of the teens and up to 1925. In fact, essentially the same car was put out as early as 1906. We have devoted a chapter to Rolls-Royce, and we will not take up the car in this chapter.

When we traced Rolls-Royce, Mercedes-Benz, and Ferrari, we traced unique cars, and there are many of these makes on the market. The Mercer Raceabout and the Stutz Bearcat also are unique automobiles. True, there are not enough of these great cars for sale today to make much of a dent in the antique car market, but some are for sale from time to time; these two makes of sports-competition cars tend to measure the market for many such cars: for two-seater early performance cars, such as the Thomas Flyer offered for sale in California in early 1981. Though some other sports-competition two-seaters are lower in price than these makes, these leaders tend to influence the market.

It is very difficult to pick one or a few makes of the superluxury cars of the late teens and early twenties and record prices through the years to determine whether, and by how much, market price rose. There are few, if any, single makes sold in great enough numbers over the years to have a large enough sample to use in recording market price and price trend. The best we can do is to take a sample each year (or each few years) of these big luxury cars and see their level. We can do this because the big luxury cars have at least some tendency to move together in price and to have something of a common price range in any one year.

Which are the big luxury cars of this period? These are some of them:

Packard—especially the early Packard Twin Six
Locomobile
Pierce-Arrow
Cadillac
Hispano-Suiza—a car we have already taken up
Isotta Fraschini—another car already taken up
Minerva—a Belgian car
Renault—the large models
Mercedes-Benz—a relatively few large, non-sports models

We have not given particular attention to Hispano-Suiza and Isotta Fraschini in this section because we have already taken up these two makes in the chapter on prewar classic cars, and for these two makes the year 1925 (the official dividing line between antiques and classics) is not particularly significant.

We stress the original Packard twin six that came out in 1915 because this car is exactly what we mean by a big luxury car of the period. In the decade of the twenties, the Packard sixes and eights were slow to arrive at superluxury status. They arrived only very late in the decade—1928, 1929, and 1930.

The Duesenberg from 1920 or 1921, when it first appeared, to 1926, was not quite a superluxury car. The later models J and SJ were at the top of the superluxury class.

Cadillac was struggling to get into this top class and arrived there for sure about 1928. Still, the 1918 model that I owned was in something of the luxury class.

Lincoln might have been included, but the Lincoln car, like the Packard straight eight, seemed to become big and luxurious mainly in the late twenties and early thirties.

Bugatti arrived in the classic period in 1926 with the luxury car to end all luxury cars—the Royale. Earlier big cars were very much less stressed, and the company specialized in compact very high performance Grand Prix and sports cars.

Then there is the big and super impressive Renault that seldom reaches the market today, and this car was certainly a rival of Rolls-Royce for prestige.

These are not all of the superluxury cars of the period, by any means. In fact there were superluxury cars even earlier in Europe, where, in many ways, pioneering in this price-level car started, probably with the "Invisible Engine" and "Legalimit" Rolls-Royce V-8s of 1905 and 1906.

There are other very early superluxury cars, such as the Delahaye of France, model 32, and this big and impressive car came out as early as 1908. The early Delaunay-Belleville was in this class without any doubt. So was the very early, very rarely seen English Dennis, a huge car even in 1909. There are many others.

It is probably most significant to take a sample of the prices of several of these luxurious cars over the past decade or two to see price trend and actual price level.

One such car, not the latest or most outstanding luxury car of the period, was offered in October 1979 by Christie's at Madison Square Garden, New York. It was early—a 1913 Benz 39/100 touring car with body by Kellner, Paris. It had an enormous 10,000 cubic-centimeter engine and was reportedly in excellent condition. Although it was estimated to bring $90,000 to $120,000, it failed to find a buyer.

Lot twenty-five in the February 1979, Christie's sale in Los Angeles did find a buyer. This was a 1914 Minerva five-passenger touring car with four-cylinder engine. The car was reportedly in good condition. Price was $22,000. The Kruse auction reported that they had sold no fewer than sixteen Packard twin sixes in 1980. Prices ranged from $24,000 to $50,000, and clustered in the $30,000 range. The model years ranged from 1915 to 1919. Pierce-Arrow models 38, 48, and 66, as well as the later 33, 32, and 80, ranged in price from about $25,000 to $50,000. The roadsters brought the high prices. The high for a Cadillac V-8 was $20,000 in good condition, the low, $8,000 for a closed car. The important, large, Renaults brought $25,000 to $30,000. The Mercedes limousines and other closed cars brought around $25,000. The rakish open cars went as high as $80,000, the mid-twenties car. The later model Locomobiles ran around $25,000, those of the mid-twenties bringing amounts somewhat above $30,000.

For something of a contrast in prices we can go back about two decades. Prices then were almost at the giveaway level, especially when one considers the price of these cars today. At that time, when one drove around in one of these big once-luxury cars, he was asked bluntly, "What do you want to drive in that old thing for?" The June 1959 issue of *Antique Automobile* advertised a 1922 Winton big six for sale; this model was a big six! The car was a "four door sedan, [with] 38,000 actual miles. Almost fully restored, firm $800."

An early Locomobile was advertised in the same issue for $1,450. A 1923 "Pierce-Arrow dual valve enclosed-drive limousine, model 33, like President Coolidge used" was advertised with all details. Asking price was $790.

A 1922 Cadillac V-8 seven-passenger touring car, "an excellent tour car," was listed for $1,850. A 1917 Hudson seven-passenger car was advertised for $875—"ready to roll." A 1915 Simplex seven-passenger touring car was offered for $5,000—a high price, but the car was described as "in mint condition."

By March 1974 prices of this type of superluxury car had risen over their 1970 level. A very large and very impressive Renault 45 horsepower JV-type, seven-passenger landaulette, 1922, with body by Kellner of Paris, brought the equivalent of $16,200 in Geneva. It was a huge formal chauffeur car with a huge engine of 9,123 cubic centimeters. In the same sale an earlier car, a big 1910 Darracq 15.9 horsepower four-seater double phaeton, four cylinder, brought the equivalent of $13,500.

The Model T Ford

As recently as twenty years ago, the Model T Ford was no distinguished car for collecting, and was hardly an investment. The *Antique Automobile* issue of June 1959 certainly recognized the Model T as an antique car and carried several advertisements of Model Ts. There was a 1926 Model T two-door sedan in "A1" condition advertised for $250. A 1915 Model T touring car said to have "run less than 100 miles past 28 years," was advertised for $1,095. A 1921 "trophy winner," completely restored, a roadster, was offered for $900. A 1925 touring car was offered for $650 and a 1926 roadster for $750.

In many cars the later models are more valuable. They are more sophisticated; better mechanically; finer looking; they have the early kinks ironed out. In the case of Ford, however, the earlier the Model T the more it was, and is, worth. The Model T of 1927, the last year the Model T was made, is essentially the same car as the first car of the Model T series put out in 1908. The early car was more vertical looking. It had a brass radiator instead of the later painted radiator. It had no self-starter. But fewer of the early models were made, and far fewer remain in existence. The Model T was discontinued in May 1927, and between 1908 and 1927 over fifteen million Model T Fords in all had been produced. All had four-cylinder, flat-head engines with a power output of about 22 horsepower. They started out with a price tag of about $800 and got down to a price in the mid-$200s, before rising somewhat.

This inexpensive car revolutionized the automobile industry in the United States. It was cheap enough for many people to buy. It was easy for almost anyone to repair, and parts were dirt cheap. You could order whatever you wanted from the Sears-Roebuck or Montgomery Ward catalog, or from any number of automobile parts catalogs. You can still order inexpensive parts from parts catalogs today.

The car was good on back roads and in hilly country. It was rugged. It had enough speed and acceleration for its day—a top speed of about 45 miles per hour. The starter did a reasonably good job except in winter, when a fire sometimes had to be built under the crankcase to thin out the oil, and hot water could be thrown on the intake manifold so the gasoline would vaporize. With modern gasoline and multigrade oil, maybe the starter would even have worked in winter in our part of Connecticut. But that didn't matter. The car had a crank in the front and a choke wire in front for the cranker to use. We cranked when we had to. We took it for granted that we would have to, frequently.

With all of the Model Ts produced, and many still in existence, one might imagine that Model T Fords would not be worth anything, particularly in view of the fact that the Model T was nothing but a strict utility car all through its history. This is not quite the case. In 1970 the last model—1927, the least desirable one to own because it had few of the characteristics of a rare and fine antique car—brought about $2,000 for the touring car.

The 1924 touring car, in good condition, brought perhaps 10 percent more than the 1927 model—$2,250 or thereabouts in 1970. The 1918 model didn't seem to command much more money. The 1916 model brought a bit more; but the 1915 model was bringing about $3,500. The 1914 was just a bit higher in price and the 1913 a bit higher still, by a few hundred dollars. The 1910 model brought about $4,000, and the 1909, one of the first Model Ts produced, approached $6,000.

In the Christie's Los Angeles sale of 1980, many Model T Fords were offered. In this sale we note two market facts: (1) the Model T was selling for fairly substantial sums of money, and (2) the market was moving up. The same relationship existed with regard to year of manufacture; the earlier the model year the more valuable the car.

Lot eleven was a 1923 Model T two-passenger runabout, a standard roadster. "The car is sold as a runner, and rates as a good older restoration. Paint is good except around the cowl, where there is some 'orange peel' effect," to quote from the sales catalog. The car sold for $4,800.

Lot nine was a very much older Model T, the last Model T with the brass radiator, and this brass radiator is a very desirable feature as far as value in a Model T goes. It was a 1916 runabout, or roadster, with a pickup body added. The engine had a later head for greater power. A two-speed rear axle was added later. A new and modern coil had been added. The old rear deck accompanied the car. The car brought $7,000. Had the car been all original it, no doubt, would have brought more.

Lot five was a very much better, very much more unique and very much more original Ford. The condition was good. It was a 1911 two-passenger runabout, one of 69,762 Model Ts made in 1911. The body was attractive and the car looked like a collector car. It brought $9,000.

Lot two was by far the best Model T offered in this sale. It was very early—1909—a touring car, with an "older" restoration. It brought $14,000.

The general public knows the Model T Ford. It also knows the Model A and the V-8. These are about all the models of Ford cars that the public ever sees. Henry Ford, however, made numerous other cars leading up to the Model T. His first car was called Model A—a turn-of-the-century, two-cylinder water-cooled car of 8 horsepower that would go nearly 30 miles per hour. This car was followed shortly by a very much bigger and more sophisticated car, the Model B, which was priced new at a very high $2,000.

A Model F was produced about 1905 as well as a Model C. The Model N was a four-cylinder affair produced around 1906. The Models R and S were produced around 1907.

The Model K of 1906 was a very important looking, high performance, six-cylinder car. The touring car was large and good looking. The roadster was not far behind the Mercer Raceabout and the Stutz Bearcat, at least in appearance.

Most of these cars, when they appear on the market, are in the $10,000–$12,000 price class, with the exception of the Model K, one of which was recorded at a price in 1980 of $42,500—a price almost in the class of the Raceabout and Bearcat. The A, C, and F were two-cylinder cars; the B, N, R, and S were fours.

What about all of the rest of the makes built from the inauguration of the automobile to the cutoff year 1925, the cars that do not fall into any of the above categories? In a sense these other cars are in a stage of transition from being simply old cars to investment antiques. We'll see how they emerge from this transition stage. In all probability all of them will rise in value as time goes on, and at least some will emerge as definite collector-investment cars.

CHAPTER 11

Selling Investment Cars

FROM TIME TO TIME an automobile collector can look at one of the exotic car value guides and determine what his car may be worth. He can also check auction results, if the make and model car he owns has been sold recently at auction. Occasionally an extremely high price is secured for a collector car, and such a sale is reported in the metropolitan newspapers. If the car collector has a somewhat similar car, he can be fairly certain that his car has gone up in value. One can also visit foreign car dealers and ask prices, or review newspaper classified ads under such headings as, "Imported and Sports" Cars or "Antique and Classic Cars" to see asking prices.

Seeing what a car *may* be worth is, however, a vastly different thing from realizing cash through sale of the car; almost no one receives his asking price for a car. The actual price at which the car changes hands is almost always less; not even a dealer can always receive his asking price. Over the years, I have bought and sold almost one hundred automobiles of all kinds, and I don't believe I ever paid or was paid the asking price. Auctions do report actual prices received for cars, so you can get at least an idea of the "wholesale price" for your car. The really definite way to determine the value of your car is to offer it for sale; then you will see what actual offers you get.

There are numerous reasons for selling a car. You may want to realize cash to upgrade your car or cars. You may want to sell in order to get another make or model car that you desire more. You may want to sell to get cash to put into something besides a car. You may be moving to another part of the country where parts and mechanics are scarce, or moving out of the country altogether. Or you may want simply to get rid of some of your belongings and pull in your horns, moving perhaps to a smaller home with less garage space.

Most important of your selling aims, however, is to realize a capital gain. This is the usual objective of investing in anything; investment implies financial returns.

A landmark case in taxation as it relates to investing in art, antiques, or other collectibles is the Charles Wrightsman case. Charles Wrightsman is a great collector of art and antiques, and he has given several period French rooms to the Metropolitan Museum of Art in New York. When he was on the witness stand in his case (which he brought to court to establish the fact that his art and antiques were investments) he was asked the question by the attorney for the Department of Justice, "Do you ever intend to sell any of your art and antiques, Mr. Wrightsman?"

Mr. Wrightsman replied, "No, I don't." He replied not simply in these words but in even stronger terms. He lost the case. The conclusion seems to be that in order to have your investment viewed as a capital gain, taxable at preferential capital gains tax rates, you will have to sell an investment (car) from time to time at a profit. If you have collected cars for a number of years and never sold anything at a profit, which profit you would have reported on your tax form 1040 as a capital gain, then the Internal Revenue Service may decide that your cars are not investments. The preferential capital gains rate may not apply in your case, and you may have to add the profit to the rest of your income and pay the much higher regular income tax rate applicable to a person in your tax bracket.

In addition, the expenses of maintaining your classic and antique cars may not be deductible as legitimate expenses incurred while maintaining your investments, and these deductions can become important as a means of cutting your year-to-year reportable income.

Selling Cars by Advertising in Newspapers

Advertising in the newspaper is probably the first marketing method that an automobile investor should think about.

The big metropolitan newspapers have carried advertisements for specialized automobiles for sale for many decades, the *New York Times* leading all other newspapers by a wide margin. The sports section is read by many many car aficionados, not simply sports enthusiasts, and the sports section contains a section on antique and classic cars, another section on imported and sports cars for sale, as well as a section on ordinary cars.

Illustrating the coverage of the *New York Times* are the results I got selling three cars through the *Times* in 1977: a 1960 Rolls-Royce limousine with James Young body, a 1960 Ferrari 250GT convertible, and a 1967 Maserati Ghibli coupe. The Rolls-Royce was sold to a Rolls-Royce collector from Pennsylvania. The Maserati was sold to an individual from New Jersey, an auto enthusiast who apparently had never owned a foreign sports or classic car. The Ferrari ad was answered by a dealer from Chicago who flew in immediately to see the car, but we did not arrive at a deal. Then the *Times* ad for the Ferrari was picked up by a publication specializing in Ferraris. They reprinted the essence of the ad, with the result that Motor Classic Corporation of White Plains, New York, came over with cash and drove my Ferrari away within an hour of arrival!

Over a period of forty years I have sold almost one hundred automobiles, and the majority of these cars were sold via ads in the *New York Times*. Sometimes I placed the same ad twice, once in the imported and sports car section and once in the antique and classic car section. A repeated ad usually hits the potential buyer twice, and he tends to remember it. If the potential buyer reads only one of the two sections, then you are still reaching him.

The wording of an ad can be made effective by giving a full description of the car offered for sale. For example:

Ferrari 250GTE two-plus-two sports coupe. Mint condition. 23,000 miles since new. One owner car. Off white paint in perfect condition. Chrome wire wheels. All chrome perfect. Leather interior original and as new. One of later cars of this model made 1965. White Plains, New York. (914) 946-0242. Call up to 6:00 P.M. week days. Price $12,500.

It must be remembered that, as a rule, a car sells best where it is located and can be easily inspected. If a Maserati Ghibli 1967 coupe is advertised for sale in Los Angeles for $13,000, it is not likely that it will be bought by anyone from New York.

The *Wall Street Journal* can be a very effective means of reaching a segment of the high priced collector car market. The *Wall Street Journal* often contains ads for million dollar homes, yachts, and airplanes. A very recent issue contained a half page ad for new Ferrari cars, a very simple ad with a photograph and a few words that left one with the impression, "This is the finest. You must be a real sportsman to own such a car—and you must have money." An ad for a real investment car like a Rolls-Royce convertible, a rare Ferrari, a prewar Mercedes-Benz convertible like the 500K or 540K, should get responses in the *Wall Street Journal* no matter what the price!

Advertising in the Specialized Magazines and Newspapers

One of the most unique advertising media in the area of specialist automobiles is *Hemmings Motor News* of Bennington, Vermont. As far as format and style go, this publication is in the category of the *Farmers Almanac*. The cover is relatively heavy brown paper with line drawings of three old trucks. On the side of each truck is a sign advertising *Hemmings Motor News*. The June 1981 issue claimed "paid subscribers over 199,000," and it is steadily growing in circulation.

The latest issue of *Hemmings Motor News* is the 330th such issue in twenty-eight years, and it contains 496 pages of advertising. A late issue advertised, with illustration, a 1912 Mercer Raceabout, possibly the most desirable antique in America, for

$125,000. There was also a 1935 Mercedes-Benz 500K cabriolet for $175,000. There was a Ford Mustang convertible for $1,400. As a rough guess, there might be 10,000 automobiles and parts advertised for sale in each issue.

Of the popular car magazines, probably *Road and Track* is the best advertising medium. For some unknown reason, few auto magazines have much of a cars for sale section. *Road and Track* does, in its Market Place, and here there are well printed, easy to read explicit ads, and many of them have pictures.

Classic and antique cars have plenty of outlets for advertising, and it is just a matter of picking the most likely medium or media to locate potential customers. If one does not secure a customer, then a second choice can be made, and so on. *Old Cars Weekly* is a good size and very readable car newspaper with a very large car advertising section. The emphasis is on prewar classics and antique cars.

Auto Week might be used to advertise exotic cars. It is another very good weekly newspaper. For subscriptions, write to 740 Rush Street, Chicago, Illinois 60611. For advertising, write to Classified Dept Auto Week, 13920 Mt. McClellan Avenue, Reno, Nevada 89506.

Cars and Parts is put out monthly, and its address is Post Office Box 482, Sidney, Ohio 45367. The magazine is almost all advertisements of cars for sale—just under two hundred pages. The circulation is large—120,000.

Car Exchange is put out at 700 East State Street, Iola, Wisconsin, by Krause Publications, Inc. The specialties of this monthly magazine are prewar and postwar classics of the less expensive variety. The circulation is 27,000, which is good, particularly as the magazine only started several years ago.

The big monthly car magazines usually carry few or no car ads of any kind. *Car and Driver* is an important monthly magazine. Its classified ad section is small, but the ads seem to get results as far as the high-priced exotic cars go. Most ads are placed on the one page "car and driver market place."

One classic and antique car sales organization, Motor Classic Corporation of White Plains, New York, runs a heavy advertising program regularly for its cars. The firm reports best results as far as customers go from the *New York Times*, *Hemmings Motor*

News, Car and Driver, Auto Week, and *Road and Track.* The *Wall Street Journal* is effective for them, but they feel they cannot afford the high cost of the ads in that daily.

There are a few publications devoted strictly to antique cars. Probably the best advertising medium to use for this type of car is the *Bulb Horn.* This is a bi-monthly magazine, a publication of the Veteran Motor Club of America, 15 Newton Street, Brookline, Massachusetts 02146. The circulation is about 5,000, but most antique car collectors read the magazine and belong to the club.

Sales to and through Dealers

It is, in general, not easy to sell collector cars to anyone. It is time-consuming and often exhausting to sell to individuals via advertisements. There are many lookers and very few potential buyers. Even potential buyers are difficult. They, of course, will bargain, and the bargaining and repeat-looking can go on for days, weeks, and even months.

Even though advertisements for the car do result in interminable delays at times, still advertisements are for various reasons the best place to start in the disposal of a car.

An obvious market for collector cars is, however, the specialist car dealer. From the point of view of the dealer in collectible cars, the main source of his cars is the individual who wants to dispose of his car. While there are auctions for automobiles, these auctions are not the main source of the cars for most antique and classic car dealers. This is different from the situation with most other antiques and collectibles, where auctions play a much larger part in the marketplace, particularly for dealers.

The seller knows the dealer secures cars from individual sellers, and that the dealer can size up the car quickly. He knows that the dealer will not haggle, and that he will not call on the phone a dozen times before he makes up his mind to make an offer. He also knows that the dealer has the cash and will pay in cash, even greenbacks on the spot, if the seller wishes.

For too long a time the policy on the part of the dealers has been to "steal" a car so that now many individuals who advertise their cars for sale add the words, "no dealers, please."

There are certain advantages of selling to dealers, however, and those advantages become greater the harder it is for dealers to locate good collector cars. If the seller can possibly get the interest of more than one dealer in his car, and indicate to each dealer that the other dealer is very interested, then he may get a fair price. In these circumstances a seller may dispose of his car to a dealer, and these are some of the advantages of direct selling to dealers:

• The car may well have a clear market price. A Maserati Ghibli, 1967, may have a market price as of early 1982 of $14,000 to $16,000 if in above average condition (but not in mint condition, in which case the price might be as high as $18,000). In this case the seller might stick to $12,000 or even go as low as $10,000, thus allowing the dealer to make a fair markup. He might sell the car to the dealer only after trying to sell it to an individual buyer.

• The car may be in great demand, and the demand is felt by both dealers and individuals having such a make and model car for sale. In the case of the Ghibli, many were being bought to send out of the country, and at good prices.

• You are sure of your money if a dealer buys your car—at least in most cases. The dealer may very well bring all cash with him when he makes the offer.

The dealer must make a markup, and the price you receive must really be under market in order to allow him his markup. He also usually has to do something to the car to get it ready to sell, and the seller always tends to think of his car as in far better condition than it is. Today, dealers may pay you more than you think, and their offers may come closer to market price than just a few years ago.

• You can be fairly sure that a dealer is going to stretch himself to make a reasonable offer on a very desirable collector car, such as one of the following:

   • Any Ferrari convertible of any year if in good, not necessarily mint, condition.
   • Ferrari Super America, Ferrari America, 500, 275GTB, 275GTB-4, Daytona.

- Duesenberg—any model in any condition.
- Rolls-Royce convertible—any model—in good condition, particularly Corniche.
- Lamborghini Miura.
- All supercharged Mercedes-Benz cars—in any condition.
- All Cobras.
- If your car needs rehabilitation, the dealer can do the work quicker and at less expense than you can. If your car has a value of $10,000 to you and needs $5,000 in work to get it into mint condition, the dealer can do the work for $3,000, possibly less. He may be able to net you more than if you put the car in condition for $5,000.
- Strange as it may seem, if you sell your car to a dealer under market you have established a good relationship with him—at least in some cases. I asked $12,000 for my Ferrari. The dealer paid me $7,700 for the car. Years later, the dealer had a Maserati Ghibli for sale, a car that I very much wanted. Right off the bat he took $2,000 off his asking price, and we bargained from there. He also does repair work for me at close to cost, as he still remembers that I gave him a good buy.
- All the car-transfer headaches are eliminated when one sells to a dealer. He does not have to go back to get a clear and certain title to the car. He does not ask questions about why the battery died a week after the car was bought by him. He does not tell you that on close examination the car obviously needs valve guides. When the dealer has bought the car and taken delivery and you have your money, that is generally the end of him. You are likely to hear no complaints, unlike when you sell to an individual.
- If the dealer has a potential buyer for the car he can, and probably will, pay you more than he otherwise would. The good prospect means a quick sale and a good price for the dealer, so his funds are not tied up for long. There are many potential buyers, and the car dealer usually knows some and how serious about buying they may be.
- The dealer can finance the sale of the car, thus getting a good price. The individual seller usually cannot get bank financing, and he usually will not finance the car over a period of months or years himself. If you have a $100,000 car, it is hard to

locate a buyer with $100,000 that he is willing to plunk down on the spot. But if the dealer knows a customer who wants the car and will pay $100,000 on the time payment plan, or at least feels he can locate such a customer, then the dealer can secure bank financing to buy the car from you and then turn around and sell it on the time payment plan. The individual cannot usually reach the $100,000 buyer. The dealer generally can, because of his financial connections.

• At the other extreme from the car that is in good or mint condition, the car you may want to sell may be in almost hopeless condition. An individual buyer-collector is often unable to undertake the restoration of a car when the cost would be staggering. A dealer, with his repair and body connections, or his own shop, can put the car in condition for much less money and resell it at a profit. The alternative for many poor-condition cars, maybe Mustangs included, is the dealer or the junk or parts yard.

• By working with a reputable dealer, you can avoid real ripoffs. The most obvious ripoff is the bad check, and more and more bad checks are being given. Not even cashiers' checks can be trusted any more, as these are being forged regularly. All checks must be verified. It is almost a rule that no one selling an automobile should take anything in payment but cash.

One way to secure the benefit of dealing with dealers is to consign the car to a dealer to sell. You indicate to the dealer what you want for the car and get him to agree that the amount you want is realistic. Title remains with the seller until the car is sold. The car is always the property of the seller until the seller is paid by the purchaser of the car. If the car is not sold, then it is returned to the seller (owner). The dealer might make a cash offer on your car to buy it—his highest offer—of, say $7,700 for my Ferrari convertible. I want $12,000 for the car. So I propose that the car be consigned to the dealer, not sold to him. We agree that $12,000 is a reasonable price, but this is the retail market price of the car, so I agree to receive a net of $10,000, allowing the dealer a profit of $2,000.

Such a plan has advantages to the dealer, the main one being that he does not tie up his cash. The second is that he runs no risk of having eventually to sell the car at little profit to himself, possibly no profit, and possibly at a loss to himself. It is not all one way as far as dealers go; they do not always make a profit on a car.

Guidelines and Cautions about Consigning Cars to Dealers for Sale

There is no guarantee that the dealer will keep the car in the condition it was in when the owner delivered it to the dealer. A number of years ago, I consigned a very much wanted model car—a Mercedes-Benz 1950 Model 170S convertible—to a dealer to sell. I heard nothing from the dealer for many weeks. I thought it advisable to pay the dealer a visit to see what was going on. The car was displayed on the showroom floor, according to the agreement, but it had become covered with a heavy layer of dust and one tire was flat so that the car's appearance would not appeal to many potential customers, if any.

A first-prize-winning "special" Italian sports car, an Italmeccanica, was consigned by me to a dealer. It had a superb paint job that took four men two weeks to put on the car. The dealer left the car outside in the weather. The paint cracked, and the paint that was not cracked became dull. The exhaust manifold developed a crack, and the engine roared out of the crack. The staff of the garage called the car "the bomb." Obviously they had been putting it through its paces on the highway. It cost a good deal of money to get that car back in condition!

The dealer may push his cars and not your car. Very often I will walk into a showroom and express an interest in a car. The dealer will then say, "That's a customer's car," and he will get the idea across that the owner wants to dump a substandard car on a naïve customer. He may then add, "Now here is a really good car." This latter car is, of course, a car that he, the dealer, owns.

Certain cars are "naturals" for consignment. A mint-condition Bugatti Royale is a natural for consignment to a dealer, at least from the dealer's point of view, and probably from the point of view of the owner of the Bugatti. Let's assume that the Royale is a convertible. Its market price is probably $500,000 or more. The owner may take as little as $450,000 or $400,000 for the car. Few dealers have enough working capital to pay $400,000 or $450,000 to any seller for any car.

But—the car is in demand. The right buyer has to be located, and he will be located in time. In this case the car will very likely be treated well, as it is a star for any auto showroom. When it is sold, the dealer may collect $50,000 as his commission, and none of his cash was tied up in the car.

The dealer is able to sell cars better than individual customers. When buyers buy from an individual, they have the feeling that they may be buying "someone else's trouble." Otherwise why would the seller be selling? The buyer does not have this same feeling about buying from a dealer. It is the business of the dealer to sell cars, while it is not the business of the individual car owner to sell cars.

There is also the feeling that if the car is bought from a dealer, the dealer stands behind it and will rectify whatever turns out to be wrong with the car after it is bought. If the car is not repaired by the dealer free of charge, then the dealer may at least do so at a very low cost. This is exactly what the dealer often does: repair the car at out-of-pocket costs to him, not at $40 an hour labor charge plus a big markup on parts he buys for your car.

When the car buyer talks to the dealer about a car, the buyer feels that the dealer is an expert on cars and that he wouldn't have bought the car he is offering in the first place had he not checked it over fully and decided it was a good car in good condition. The buyer also has the feeling that the dealer has gone all over the car and repaired whatever is wrong with it. The buyer also feels that if something is still wrong with the car, the dealer will rectify it before delivery at little or no cost. All dealers take care of certain troubles before delivering cars.

The dealers have the customers. They have long-standing customers in some cases. They can call some on the phone and say, "I have the car you have been looking for for so long, a Bugatti 57SC convertible, and it is in mint condition." Card files are sometimes kept by dealers on customers who want particular types of cars.

In any event, the showroom tends to draw in prospective buyers better than an ad. A fine showroom can be a place to visit regularly as a kind of recreation for car lookers; and lookers often become buyers if they see what they want in a showroom. The showroom may even become a kind of meeting place or "club" for car collectors to pass the time of day.

Be certain that your car is covered by all forms of insurance, including fire, theft and vandalism, plus liability, if the car is to be demonstrated on the road; and be sure the insurance agent knows that the car is consigned for sale. This is an absolute "must."

Retain title to your car until closing. It is too easy for a dealer, in possession of your title, to sell your car and pocket the cash, or at least stall you on payment.

Selling Investment Cars through Auction

If one has a painting with any kind of market in this country or an international market, he immediately thinks of one of the major international auction houses: Christie's, Sotheby's, Phillips. But major auction houses are not necessarily the answer if one has a collectible car for sale. For the most part, the major auctions with the exception of Christie's do not handle antique and classic cars for sale in any volume. In the United States, Phillips is taking on some classic cars for sale with good results. Christie's U.S. handles important and valuable cars from time to time, but not in any great volume. Sotheby's handles only an occasional car or few cars, and to date, at least, it has been their policy not to hold car auctions.

In England and on the Continent, though, Christie's does a very large business in car auctions, ranging all the way from run-of-mine old cars selling for a few hundred pounds sterling to a few in the high five and sometimes six figures. As far as the United States goes, Christie's has had several auctions and in California sold two very high-priced cars in one 1979 auction, one for $400,000 and one for $320,000, both prewar classic supercharged Mercedes-Benz cars.

In the United States, there is a big auction business for all kinds of cars, from postwar classics to antiques to ordinary second-hand cars with some semblance of investment. These car auctions are just that—auctions for cars only—and there is an immense amount of this auction business in cars throughout the United States every year. Possibly as many as several hundred specialist car auctions are held each year (besides the bankruptcy or repossessed car auctions, with which we are not concerned here).

The leading specialist or collector car auction in the United States is probably Kruse Auctioneers, Inc., Kruse Building, Auburn, Indiana. Kruse conducts about two dozen auctions of specialist cars each year, and it conducts these auctions all over the United States.

Kruse will accept a car for auction in almost any condition, from mint to "deplorable," and the car does not even have to be in running condition.

Another major car auction is Hudson and Marshall, Inc., 717 North Avenue, Macon, Georgia. *Hemmings Motor News* and other car publications contain advertisements of literally dozens of other car auctions held throughout the country.

There is an important car auction held once a year: the annual auction of James C. Leake & Antiques, Inc., I.P.E. Building, Expo Square, Tulsa, Oklahoma. This auction presents some fine classics and a few fine antiques, plus a number of lesser cars. Usually almost 50 percent of the cars offered for sale at this auction find buyers, and this is a high percent of cars sold for almost any automobile auction.

The Uses—and Cautions—of Auctioning

Not everything is always on the up-and-up as far as auctioning collector cars goes. There have been examples of an owner selling a car through auction and never receiving payment for the car.

Good-to-excellent lower-priced cars, in general, seem to do the best at auction; the Ford Mustang, in particular, does well, even though any auction seems to bring in these cars in droves. One auction had about two dozen Mustangs for sale, and the market was glutted.

But very rare and high priced cars do not always do well at auction, Duesenbergs included. The buyers may just not be there to bid on the cars. In the Leake sale, a gullwing Mercedes-

Benz coupe, one of the most desirable of all postwar classics, did not find a buyer. Neither did one of the fine Packard 734 boattail roadsters. Also very high priced standard cars often do not sell at auction. A 1979 Ferrari Berlinetta Boxer 512 did not sell, although there are many potential car buyers everywhere who would like to own this car.

If you want to sell at auction, send the car to the best auction that will take the car. As far as the big general auctions go, Christie's, of New York City, can be approached, and this firm conducts auctions in cities other than New York in addition to a few New York auctions.

Once in a while the major auctions, Sotheby's included, will sell one or more cars that are the property of an estate they are selling. The printed catalog will include the car or cars, with illustrations. Many of those attending the auction have the purchase price of the car and may well be interested in the car. Antique furniture dealers seem to like classic cars almost as well as their antiques, and many antique dealers have at least one excellent classic car.

The Classic and Antique Car Owners' Clubs

Last, but not least, there are literally hundreds of car owners' clubs in the United States and abroad. Anyone who owns a classic or antique car can profit tremendously by membership in such a club, not simply to be able to advertise his car for sale in the club journal, but to get much needed and hard-to-obtain parts as well as information on how to rectify troubles that may develop in such cars. "Tip" articles appear regularly in almost every club bulletin or newsletter.

One definite market for, say, a Maserati Ghibli is a Maserati owner. Many, if not most, people in the United States have never heard of a Maserati Ghibli—nor of a Lamborghini Miura. One sports car enthusiast wanted to know whether the Lamborghini Miura was made by Ferrari! Mr. Lamborghini would hardly have been pleased at this question.

Very often ads in the club journal cost nothing. Half of the value in the journal for me, at least, lies in the fact that I can look over the things offered for sale, and maybe just the car I am looking for will come along. As far as effectiveness of the journals is concerned, when the *Sports Car* came out in 1943, the publication then of the Sports Car Club of America, my Mercedes-Benz 500K convertible was advertised for sale with a picture. I doubt whether as many as one hundred copies went out, but I did get an offer on my car.

These are some of the advantages of using car owner clubs to reach potential buyers:

• The seller can reach at least some potential customers directly. The objective of all advertising is to reach potential customers. The clubs consist of people who own the make of car or are interested in the make, and these are potential customers for other cars of the make.

• The cost of such an ad is small in dollars and certainly small per potential customer. Some journals are very happy to place ads in the journal for members at no cost at all since the ads add to the readability of the journal.

• The potential buyer tends to trust the seller he reaches through the car club. If A.B. Motor Sales of Queens Boulevard offers a Lamborghini Miura for sale, the car may be good and it may not be. This car is not a "natural" for these volume dealers, and maybe the dealer won't reveal everything about the car. But if a club member offers a Miura for sale and it turns out to be a poor car, or definitely not as described, there is a possibility of some recourse to the club officers. Club membership says a little something about the sincerity of the car's owner.

• Club membership by the seller of the car may prove the ownership and background of the car. Many cars are stolen and shipped out of the country, and America and Italy are both happy hunting grounds for car thieves, who quickly get the cars on board a ship bound for other countries.

• Little time need be wasted explaining what the car is to a club member. All Maserati club members know what a Ghibli is, and all know its weaknesses, too.

• The geographic area covered by a club publication can be national and international. Thus many potential customers can be reached, no matter where they live. There may be five Maserati owners in Stockholm, but these five probably all would get the club publication.

• There is far less chance of mistrust in the consummation of a sale with a club buyer. There is relatively little chance that a club member will locate the owner of a Rolls-Royce so that he can visit the Rolls-Royce in the middle of the night and steal it. There is little chance that a club member will give the buyer a counterfeit cashier's check in payment of the car.

A good case can be made for any car owner to join the club specializing in the car he owns. If he owns several different makes of collector cars, then he should probably belong to several clubs. The cost of membership is in most cases nominal and will be made up on the first shipment of tires, or parts, or whatever, as these are almost always offered to club members for considerably less money than they can be bought at retail or from dealers in the particular make of car.

CHAPTER 12

Price Trends of Investment Automobiles

AT THIS POINT it is logical to sum up price trends and to pull them together, insofar as possible, into an overall price trend.

We might start out in the order in which the various cars and periods of cars are taken up in the book. The first period is the postwar period. At the same time the first great make to be taken up is the Rolls-Royce, and thus we might summarize the price trend of postwar Rolls-Royces. This is one area that we have studied rather thoroughly, first hand in England and in America, and have bought Rolls-Royces both in America and in England. We have also written several articles, over a period of ten years, on Rolls-Royce as an investment.

Rolls-Royce Silver Cloud III Sedan

1970	$4,000	100%
1973—August	7,500	187
1974—March	11,500	290
1976—End of Year	25,000	625
1981	30,000	750

Prior to 1970 the last Silver Cloud, the III, was not in great demand, nor was the corresponding Bentley. In about the year

1970 I located a Bentley SI in absolutely mint condition, with the rare and desirable Hooper body. The Bentley overhaul firm of Hoffman and Burton had examined the car and pronounced it perfect in every detail. I located the car and arranged to have a friend of mine from America purchase it for 950 pounds sterling, about $2,500. Such was the price level of a fine Bentley or Rolls-Royce in 1970 and earlier.

In 1981 a fine left-hand-drive Rolls-Royce Cloud III sedan could be purchased for about $35,000, possibly as little as $30,000. Prices had risen from a base of 100 percent in 1970 to 750 percent in 1981.

Mercedes-Benz Postwar Cars

	300SL Gullwing		300SL Roadster		300S Roadster	
1970	$6,000	100%	$5,000	100%	$2,000	100%
1975	15,000	250	10,000	200	8,000	400
1977	25,000	416	15,000	300	19,000	950
1979	50,000	833	23,000	460	30,000	1,500
1981	65,000	1,083	35,000	700	40,000	2,000

The price rises in the table are conservative. We appreciate the fact that one gullwing sold for $105,000. This was not the market price for this car. In 1980 a dealer reported selling a 300S cabriolet for $47,000. In 1981 a 300S coupe was advertised for sale for $50,000, and the coupe is the least valuable body style of all of the 300S cars. We believe $40,000 is a conservative market price for the 300S roadster or cabriolet as of 1981. Still, this conservative price represents a gain in value of twenty times in ten years.

Ferrari Cars

	250GT Convertible		Berlinetta Lusso	
1965	$2,500	100%	$8,000	100%
1970	3,700	148	8,000	100
1975	7,000	280	12,000	150
1977	12,000	480	18,000	225
1979	22,000	880	30,000	375
1981	28,000	1,120	35,000	437

The price trend has been started with the year 1965, and for this reason many of the famous Ferraris, such as the great Ferrari Daytona, are not included as they were not in production in 1965. The earlier models (before 1965) are not on the market in any great numbers since they were not made in any great numbers.

The 250GT convertible is a very standard car and is on the market today. So is the Berlinetta Lusso, at least from time to time. The above two cars are a fair sample of Ferrari cars on the collector-investor market.

Other Postwar Classics

Jaguar Open Cars

	XK120		XK140 and XK150	
1970	$1,500	100%	$1,500	100%
1975	6,000	400	5,000	333
1981	16,000	1,067	13,000	866

The XKE (6) has risen far less than the earlier and more classic models. On the other hand, the V-12 of the XKE series has risen more than the 6 because it is a more sophisticated, higher performance car, and the price is at about the level of the XK140 and XK150.

MG T.D. and MG T.C.

	MG T.D.		MG T.C.	
1970	$1,500	100%	$2,500	100%
1975	5,000	333	5,000	200
1981	10,000	666	15,000	600

The T.C. was the car put out in the immediate postwar period, and a number were exported to America. The T.D. was essentially the same car, and it looked the same, but it was an improvement over the T.C., particularly in the brakes. A decade ago the early model was considered to be more classic and rarer, and it brought more than the later T.D. In 1975 both cars sold for about the same thing. In 1981 the T.C. had forged ahead and was selling for 50 percent more than the T.D., which could on occasion be bought for a little under $10,000.

Both cars are good and both are likely to be in demand in the indefinite future.

Early Porsche (1955 to End of 356 Series)

1970	$2,000	100%
1975	7,000	350
1981	12,000	600

This model Porsche, a classic, is very much more classic than the latest cars, which are, in many cases, simply second-hand, very fine, high-performance cars.

Ford Thunderbird—1955–1957

1970	$1,800	100%
1975	7,500	416
1978	16,000	889
1981	12,000	667

The Ford Thunderbird of the mid-fifties is one of the most satisfactory of all American postwar "sporty" cars, if not the most satisfactory. It looks good. It drives well. It has good road holding, and it has the reliability of a simple Ford car.

On the other hand, the Thunderbird is one of the few cars that actually hit a price peak and then declined. Even in the February 1981 Los Angeles sale, the Thunderbird, a model in very good condition, did not get a high bid. In the future, the down price trend may, however, be reversed, as the car is basically good.

Chevrolet Corvette—1955–1962

1970	$1,200	100%
1975	5,000	417
1981	14,000	1,167

The current production Sting Ray is vastly different in body style than the 1955–1962 Corvettes, and the present model has been put out for many years. The 1955–1962 cars were far less streamlined. Over a period of time, however, they have developed a classic look that makes them more or less timeless. A top-notch completely restored 1962 V-8 was recently seen for $15,500, the cost of a good restoration. These early Corvettes still seem to be something of a bargain.

Postwar Classic Cars

1970	100%
1975	308
1979	752
1981	874

The rate of growth in prices of postwar classic cars has been enormous—from 100 percent in 1970 to 874 percent in 1981. The growth rate exceeds that of the prewar foreign classic cars, and these rose from 100 percent in 1970 to 806 percent in 1981. The growth rate from 100 percent in 1970 to 874 percent in 1981 represents a compound interest rate per year of about 24 percent.

As compared with other types of cars, the postwar classics are a natural for a high degree of price rise. In 1970 many of today's collector cars were simply second-hand cars, many of them in simple "second-hand" condition. The Mercedes-Benz cars of the 300 series—the 300SLs and the 300S cars—were not great collector cars. Now they most certainly are.

In 1970 the Ferrari 250GT convertible was worth relatively little, perhaps $3,500 to $4,000. Today one can easily bring $28,000–$30,000 or more.

No postwar classic has experienced a small price rise in our summary of prices, at least none of the thirteen cars in our sample. The 300S Mercedes-Benz convertible rose from $2,000–$2,500 to perhaps $40,000. We know of one that sold for $47,000, and in April 1981 a coupe, the least desirable body style, was advertised for sale at $50,000. This price, of course, probably will not be realized, but the sharp upward price trend for this car is indicated.

Most of the postwar classics in our index of price movement are foreign classics, and many of these come onto the American market, unlike the foreign antique cars. In the period from 1970 to the present, the main American postwar classics were probably the Corvette and the Thunderbird, and their pattern of price increase was similar to that of the foreign postwar classics.

Prewar Classic Cars—American

Duesenberg J and SJ Open Cars

1945	$750	
1962	10,000	100%
1970	60,000	600
1975	150,000	1,500
1979	250,000	2,500
1981	220,000	2,200

In the early 1940s, including the war period, the Duesenberg had almost no value in the market, particularly at the outbreak of the war. As time went on, interest picked up and the cars rose in value. By 1962 many classic cars still were not wanted, but the Duesenberg was, and at high prices for the time.

The year 1970 was the starting year for many postwar classics, but this great prewar classic had arrived, and $60,000 was a huge price for any collector car at the time.

As cars sold they made news, and prices rose to a high of about $250,000 for a tourer or roadster in mint condition in 1979. This was about the peak, and prices slipped a bit. Even in 1981 a fine car, a tourer, was reported to have been auctioned for what the owner, a dealer, considered to be a low price of $200,000. There was, however, a question as to whether this particular car even sold at $200,000. That figure may have simply been the high bid, even though the auction officials reported the car sold.

At the present time a price of about $220,000 does not seem to involve a great deal of financial risk, although perhaps some time will have to pass before the Duesenberg market takes off again. It rose too far and too fast; everyone who wanted to acquire a Duesenberg seemed to have acquired one, with few remaining who wanted to own the car but lacked one!

Auburn Boattail Speedster—851 and 852

1970	$15,000	100%
1975	35,000	233
1980	65,000	433
1981	70,000	467

The Auburn 851 and 852 boattail speedsters of 1935 and 1936 are some of the most spectacular-looking of all collector cars. They are streamlined as of the mid-thirties period, but they have a timeless quality to them. If we go back to the late war years, the car could be picked up for very little; my own 851 speedster cost me $800 in 1945. By 1970, however, the boattail was in demand in the five figure range. Because of the timeless quality of the car it well may never have a setback in price level.

Cord 810 and 812 Convertibles

1965	$3,700	100%
1970	9,000	243
1975	25,000	676
1979	50,000	1,351
1981	55,000	1,486

The new model Cords were put out in the mid-thirties. They are a distinctive-looking car with a boxlike hood and flat lines. They are reasonably good mechanically, and they are in demand. In 1970 they were right behind the Auburn boattails in demand, and since that time they have risen steadily with the boattails, in fairly equal steps. Once in a while, a very fine example will go over the figures in the table. The trend probably will not be reversed.

Chrysler Imperial Eight Late Model Prewar Touring Cars

1955	$750	
1970	18,000	100%
1975	60,000	333
1981	175,000	972

The prewar Chrysler Imperial is one of the most universally approved cars of all investment cars. It is one of the cars in the greatest demand, and at huge prices. The primary reason is probably the beauty of the bodies on these big touring cars with huge hoods. The appearance of the cars outdoes Packard, and prices are often at the Duesenberg level. Such cars probably still have an upward price trend, even though in the 1982 market they are at astronomical levels. In 1970 they already were selling at what were then huge prices.

Chrysler 70 Roadster—Mid-Twenties

1970	$3,500	100%
1975	7,500	214
1981	15,000	429

This price pattern pretty well holds for the later Chrysler 72 of 1928, the Chrysler 75 of 1929, and the three cars—66, 70, and 77—of 1930. The cars were way ahead of their time in both appearance and performance, but they were not too high in price for the semi–mass market.

Lincoln V-8 Touring Car—Early 1930s

1970	$15,000	100%
1975	25,000	167
1981	30,000	200

In some ways the V-8 Lincoln of the 1920s to 1932 was as good a car as the V-12, and less cumbersome. The 1930 model was particularly good mechanically as well as in appearance. Some models in very fine condition can sell for as much as $50,000–$60,000, and as of 1982 there does not seem to be any price weakness. Even in 1970 the Lincoln V-8 was a much-wanted car bid up to very high levels.

Ford Model A Deluxe Roadster or Convertible

1970	$4,500	100%
1973	6,000	133
1974	9,000	200
1981	14,000	311

The table about represents the price of a roadster or convertible from the introductory year of 1928 until the last year, 1931.

The later cars tend to bring the most, but early cars in fine condition are not far behind, not at all behind in many cases. The rise has taken place since 1970 for the most part. For what the car is, and for the number of Model As produced, the price rise has been substantial.

Lincoln Zephyr Convertible

1970	$3,000	100%
1975	6,000	200
1981	20,000	667

The Lincoln Zephyr was more or less an important innovation when it came out in the mid-thirties. It drew a good deal of critical attention. The car was continued until the war. It is a V-12, and the engine was a fair success. In the last half decade the demand for the car has burgeoned and prices have risen substantially.

Lincoln V-12 Convertible

1970	$10,000	100%
1975	40,000	400
1981	95,000	950

The Lincoln V-12 is quite a different car from the Lincoln Zephyr. The Zephyr was a lower priced car. The V-12 was a very high priced, top quality car on a level with Packard and Cadillac, at least. It is also very much of a connoisseurs' and collectors' car on today's market, and prices for this model rarely are low. As indicated, even in the low year 1970, the V-12 was in the five-figure range.

Cadillac V-16 Early Open Cars—1930–1931

1970	$35,000	100%
1975	80,000	228
1979	150,000	428
1981	200,000	571

Here we lump the roadsters and the touring cars, although the roadsters are in greater demand and at higher prices than the tourers. If we had to pick the three highest-priced, prewar American collector cars they would probably be Chrysler Imperial, Duesenberg, and Cadillac, with the Cadillac V-16 roadster possibly at the top. Even as early as 1970 the Cadillac V-16s, the early open cars, were high in price. They will probably remain so.

La Salle—Early Convertibles

1970	$10,000	100%
1975	25,000	250
1981	70,000	700

The 1927 to 1932 convertibles are the ones in demand. The later models are not in the same demand, and a decade ago the later models brought very little. The early cars, both five passenger and two passenger, are in demand and have been in demand for some time. While some sold for less than $70,000 in 1981, an early convertible in mint condition would bring in the neighborhood of $70,000.

Prewar Classic Cars—American

1970	100%
1973	133
1974	200
1975	256
1979	464
1981	566

The important years, the years in which we have prices for a fairly large number of makes of prewar American classics, are 1970, 1975, and 1979. The other years do not have a large number of samples in the price index. These in-between years, however, fit into the price curve pretty well, and so we have included them.

In the decade, prices rose over five times for these American cars. We have included eleven makes and models of cars in the index. This curve represents a compound interest rate of about 18.5 percent per year—a very high rate of return. The rate of increase would have been greater had we eliminated some of the great collector cars, including the Duesenberg J and SJ and the early 1930s Lincoln V-8, both of which were in demand at high prices by 1970. In fact, the Duesenberg was in the five-figure range in the early 1960s.

At the other extreme, the Ford Model A was at a relatively high level by the year 1970, and its rise in the following decade was not outstanding.

To overbalance these slow risers in the decade from 1970 to 1980, we have the Chrysler Imperial which rose tremendously and stands at about ten times its price in 1970. The same degree of rise holds for the Lincoln V-12, a great favorite in the market as of 1982.

Prewar Classic Cars—Foreign

In the prewar classics, we have considered Rolls-Royce and Mercedes-Benz separately. In Europe many, many prewar cars come up for sale fairly regularly. Some of these cars are definitely classics, some are borderline. Some are doubtfully classics—such as, say, the Austin Seven or the Humber Super Snipe.

In the United States there are fewer of these less important old cars—at least, few of them seem to come up at the automobile auctions. The emphasis in this country is on the finer—and finest—prewar classics. For that reason we have traced the price history of these finer prewar classics, or at least a sample of them.

Isotta Fraschini Tipo A Convertibles

1970	$18,000	100%
1975	40,000	222
1981	110,000	611

If an Isotta Fraschini Tipo A convertible is included in a car auction, that inclusion goes a long way toward making the auction a success. The Tipo A is a drawing card; people want to see it sold and expect the final price to be high—as it almost always is. The car is unique and rare, and people sometimes come to the auction just to see the car. Big and impressive looking, it can be used to "top" a collection of collector cars. The price rise in ten years has been very great. At times, these cars do not find buyers, but all the owner has to do is wait for the next auction when the right price will very likely be achieved. The cars are rare and much wanted.

Hispano-Suiza V-12 Convertible

1970	$35,000	100%
1975	50,000	143
1979	95,000	271
1981	125,000	357

From the point of view of the collector who wants the very best mechanically that the prewar classic period had to offer, Hispano-Suiza may stand at the top. The V-12 is a very sophisticated car, and some of the bodies were the last word in conservative elegance. Even in 1970 these cars brought well into five figures—about the annual salary of a fairly important business executive at the time! The cars will probably always remain in demand.

Bugatti Type 57 Convertible

1955	$1,500	100%
1970	12,000	800
1975	30,000	2,000
1981	60,000	4,000

The type 57 Bugatti convertible coupe is a very sophisticated and well styled car, and it appears on the market from time to time, as do the 57S, the 57C, the 57T, and the 57SC sometimes. It was one of these type 57 cars that, for me, was the "fish that got away" in 1955—priced then at $1,500.

There are many other types of Bugatti that come up for sale from time to time, the most notable being the type 35. We have chosen the type 57 because the price is not hard to trace and it is a more or less standard, but top rung, prewar classic. It does tend to measure the market for Bugattis.

Bentley Eight-Liter Open Car

1970	$8,000	100%
1974	70,000	875
1981	125,000	1,562

The eight-liter Bentley is the largest of all the "Bentley" Bentleys, and it is probably the most treasured and the most expensive. We could, however, have used the Speed Six to trace prices, or some other model. The Speed Six probably showed a somewhat similar price trend. We followed Bentley prices from 1970 on, particularly in England.

Alfa Romeo Type 1750 Roadster

1970	$8,000	100%
1974	35,000	438
1979	70,000	875
1981	80,000	1,000

We have used the Alfa Romeo type 1750, very much a sports car, to measure the market for Alfa Romeo cars. We could have used the type 2300 which has moved about like the type 1750 in price.

To go back to the immediate prewar period, the Alfa Romeo roadsters were in demand, particularly by the younger group of buyers. In this period, one firm in New York, Whalen and Gilhooly, offered a type 1750 for sale for $3,000. At the same time they were offering many Mercedes-Benz S and SS models for prices up to $550, and they sold an earlier Rolls-Royce Silver Ghost touring car in fair condition for $100. Duesenbergs could be bought for $600–$750 each and Cadillac V-16 coupes for $250 apiece (one lot had two such cars for sale for just this price).

Thus the Alfa roadsters were in demand and at good prices in the prewar period, but since that time many other cars have caught up with the Alfas, particularly the big, elegant cars.

Prewar Classic Cars—Foreign

1970	100%
1975	207
1979	573
1981	806

The prewar classics rose about eight times in a little over a decade. This growth amounts to a compound interest rate of about 23 percent per year—an enormous rate of growth.

The above table is, of course (by definition), an average. Certain cars rose more, others less. Certain moved up more quickly than the average and certain others lagged. The eight-liter Bentley rose rapidly. The touring car was a great favorite of collectors in England, and it was not plentiful. It rose much faster than the other cars in the index and rose much higher by the year 1981.

The Antique Cars

Mercer Raceabout—Early Teens Series

1970	$40,000	100%
1973	45,000	113
1976	50,000	125
1981	150,000	375

In the recession of 1970—the deepest recession since the Great Depression of 1932—the Mercer Raceabout commanded a princely sum of money. The percentage rise has not been as great as for many other classic cars simply because the base that we used, 1970, represented a high price. The Raceabout comes onto the market from time to time priced by sellers at about $150,000. Perhaps a lower price might be negotiated, but we are using $150,000 as of 1981. The Raceabout is one of the two great American antique cars.

Stutz Bearcat—Early Teens

1970	$22,500	100%
1973	29,000	129
1975	45,000	200
1980	85,000	378
1981	150,000	666

The other American antique great is the Stutz Bearcat of the same period as the Mercer Raceabout. The Stutz was a little less popular than the Raceabout in 1970 as well as in the World War II years. Now, however, prices of the two cars are comparable, and they are both offered from time to time at about $150,000.

These two cars epitomize the fine antique car market in the United States.

The One- and Two-Cylinder Antiques

1958	$1,000	100%
1960	2,500	250
1970	6,000	600
1974	7,500	750
1979	8,500	850
1980	12,000	1,200
1981	12,000	1,200

In the "oldies" of one- and two-cylinders, we have lumped the cars for sale. Prices do not seem to vary by make as much as the classics. We would like to have traced, say, the Curved Dash Olds or the Brush, but the market for these cars is very thin, and if two dozen of both makes combined were sold in the course of one year I would be surprised. Thus we would be measuring the market for these simple old cars by a limited total of dollar sales per year.

In addition, we do not, as we have implied, see a great deal of difference in the price of one mint-condition, one-cylinder car and another—or in the price of two such cars in poor condition. A very rare car such as an early Mercedes or an early Benz will certainly bring a very high price, but since these cars rarely appear on the market, they do not measure the market for antiques.

The simple cars have gone up in value, but not nearly so steeply as many of the classics.

Ford Model T Touring Cars

	1925–1927 Cars		1915–1916 Cars	
1959	$500	100%	$1,200	100%
1970	2,000	400	3,500	292

1974	4,000	800	6,000	500
1980	4,800	960	7,000	582
1981	5,000	1,000	7,500	625

At the end of the decade of the 1950s, the only people who seemed willing to pay anything much for Model T Fords were Model T Ford collectors. The appeal of the Model T Ford as a collectible was not widespread. The early Fords, the brass radiator Fords, did not sell for much more than the last Model Ts of 1927, although far fewer brass radiator Fords were produced and far fewer remain in existence.

The earlier Model T cars command a premium, but when we get back to the fairly rare cars made prior to 1910 the price goes way up to double the level of the cars of the teens. The disparity in price between old and latest Model Ts will probably increase markedly in the future. In any event, the Model T is now an investment collectible with a broadening group of collectors. Collectors still want the big luxury cars, but more and more collectors want the Model T.

In antique cars we have concentrated on American cars for two primary reasons. The first is that relatively few European antiques are sold in America, and this fact is indicated by reviewing the car auction sales as well as good price summaries such as the *Old Car Value Guides*. The second reason is that we have covered certain important cars in the chapters on Rolls-Royce and Mercedes-Benz.

In England and on the Continent the market is far different. There European antique cars are plentiful and come up at auction regularly—but so do American antique cars.

Lord Montagu of Beaulieu is writing a book on investment in automobiles. He has access to all of the sales data from his numerous auctions as well as the records and photos of cars sold in conjunction with Christie's. We hope and believe he will cover European antique car sales thoroughly.

Antique Cars

| 1970 | 100% |
| 1973 | 121 |

1975	200
1980	255
1981	297

The rise in price of antique cars here in the U.S. has not been outstanding; this is so for several reasons. In the first place, in the United States there are few great *European* antique cars sold, and some of these rose tremendously in the decade of the 1970s. Had we created a price index of antique cars sold in England and in Switzerland we would have shown a considerable rise in the decade.

In the second place, a number of antique cars rose greatly in the period *before* 1970, which we have made our base period equal to 100 percent. The small one- and two-cylinder American cars rose six times from 1958 to 1970, so that 1970 really should not have been the base of reference, if we are trying to indicate high degree of price rise. We have made all price bases equal to 100 in 1970 so as to combine them into an antique car index—a correct statistical procedure.

The Model T Ford of 1925–1927 (the last of the Model Ts) quadrupled in price from 1959 to 1970. In 1959 the price of such cars was essentially nothing. The 1915–1916 Model Ts about tripled in price from 1959 to 1970. They were worth a little more in the late 1950s than the later model, but not a great deal more.

A third reason for the modest rise in the price trend of antique cars from 1970 to 1980 is that the two great American antiques, the early Mercer Raceabout and the Stutz Bearcat, were already high in 1970 when other investment cars such as the Mercedes-Benz 300S, the Ferrari 250GT convertible, and many other cars now at peak prices, could be bought for $2,500 easily.

Very often the impressiveness of the rising price curve depends on the year chosen as the base period equal to 100 percent. It does in the case of American antique cars, although these old cars have not been quite at the top of investor-collector interest.

Price Trend of Investment Automobiles

	All Cars	Cars without Antiques
1970	100%	100%
1975	242	257
1979	503	596
1981	636	748

The above figures combine all the classifications of cars we have used. All cars in the sample have been included in the above figures. These cars break down, by model, to:

Postwar Classic Cars	13
Prewar Classics—American	11
Prewar Classics—Foreign	5
Antiques	5

In addition we made special studies covering the entire history of Rolls-Royce, Mercedes-Benz, and Ferrari (Ferrari being nonexistent, of course, in the prewar period).

All cars in our sample, taken together, went up two and one-half times from 1970 to 1975. They better than doubled from 1975 to 1979. In 1981 they were at a level of almost six and one-half times the 1970 level.

The rise in the antiques was not of this magnitude, and when the antique cars are eliminated from the price index, the index rose seven and a half times from 1970 to 1981.

The entire rise, antiques included, represents a compound interest rate of a little over 20 percent per year. With the antique cars *not* included in the index of price rise, the annual compound interest rate is slightly over 22 percent.

This is a combination of prewar and postwar classic cars. These are not simply the high flyers that I have owned. They are a good sample of classic cars. Other cars could have been added without changing the degree of price appreciation much. Certain other cars in the collection didn't appreciate as much as this combination did (see following page); still, the degree of price rise is not a contrived one.

Price History of a Selection of Investment Automobiles Owned in the Past, or Presently Owned, by the Author—Richard H. Rush

	1965	1970	1975	1981
Mercedes-Benz SS touring, 1928	$7,500	$15,000	$35,000	$125,000
Mercedes-Benz 500K convertible, 1935	7,500	13,500	37,500	125,000
Mercedes-Benz 300S convertible, 1955	1,500	2,000	15,000	40,000
Ferrari 250GT convertible, 1960	2,500	3,000	10,000	30,000
Rolls-Royce Cloud I James Young	3,500	5,000	9,500	30,000
Bentley Graber coupe, 1951	2,800	4,500	10,000	40,000
Auburn boattail speedster, 851	7,000	12,500	37,500	70,000
Ford Model A sports coupe, 1928	1,000	2,500	4,000	7,000
	33,300	58,000	158,500	467,000
1965 as Base	100%	174%	476%	1,400%

There was a fair degree of price appreciation between 1965 and 1970. The rate of appreciation accelerated between 1970 and 1975, and prices tripled between 1975 and early 1981, about half a decade. The table obviously combines prewar and postwar classics, the main areas of investment automobiles.

I know the exact condition of these cars. Some of them I worked on extensively myself. I know that the Ferrari 250GT was mint, with new Italian leather and new Pirelli tires, among other new things. The paint was new and excellent, as was the chrome. The car had 35,000 kilometers on the odometer.

The Model A Ford was certainly not mint—not in upholstery, paint, or even mechanically. Still, on today's market it would be worth $7,000. The other cars are priced by time periods according to the market at the time and according to the condition of each car.

For this selection of cars, using the year 1965 as the base equal to 100 percent, prices in the next five years rose to a level of 174 percent. They did not double.

As we have indicated, the year 1970 is the Year One. Everything seemed to take off in investment automobiles after 1970. From a level of 174 percent in 1970, prices rose 476 percent in the five-year period. They about tripled. In the next six years, they tripled again, increasing to 1,400 percent over 1965.

In this investment period of about fifteen years, the compound interest rate on this group of cars would be about 20 percent per year. This is a very high rate; money market funds and the stock market hardly compare with this rate, particularly in the past decade.

Classic Cars Owned by Richard H. Rush—Year by Year

Make and Model	Year Car	Year Purchased	Price Paid	Value in 1981
Mercedes-Benz S convertible	1927	1938	$350	$35,000
Mercedes-Benz SS tourer	1928	1938	550	125,000
Mercedes-Benz 500K convertible	1935	1944	1,550	125,000
Mercedes-Benz 540K coupe	1940	1941	1,500	45,000
Mercedes-Benz 170S convertible	1950	1952	1,500	18,000
Mercedes-Benz 300S cabriolet	1951	1955	4,500	40,000
Mercedes-Benz 300S roadster	1953	1958	4,000	40,000
Mercedes-Benz 300S cabriolet	1953	1960	2,800	40,000
Mercedes-Benz 300S roadster	1955	1966	800	35,000

Classic Cars Owned by Richard H. Rush—Year by Year

Make and Model	Year Car	Year Pur- chased	Price Paid	Value in 1981
Porsche 1300 coupe	1951	1955	1,700	6,000
Ferrari 250GT coupe	1957	1964	2,700	10,000
Ferrari 250GT convertible	1960	1967	2,500	28,000
Maserati Ghibli coupe	1967	1973	6,800	12,000
Maserati Ghibli coupe	1967	1980	10,900	15,000
Lamborghini Miura coupe	1967	1980	20,500	28,000
Offenhauser Cisitalia coupe	1950	1952	3,150	40,000
Fiat 8V Ghia coupe	1955	1956	4,500	25,000
Italmeccanica coupe	1950	1951	3,750	10,000
Mercury Ghia coupe	1953	1953	5,200	7,500
Rolls-Royce Phantom I town car	1928	1939	550	75,000
Rolls-Royce Cloud I James Young	1960	1974	9,500	30,000
Rolls-Royce Cloud II sedan	1960	1977	7,000	25,000
Bentley Graber coupe	1951	1960	2,800	40,000
Jaguar XK120 roadster	1950	1950	3,750	15,000
Auburn sports coupe	1932	1936	195	15,000
Auburn 851 boattail speedster	1935	1945	800	70,000
Phantom Corsair	1939	1947	5,000	100,000 plus
Stutz DV32 sedan	1932	1946	175	35,000
Marmon 16 sedan	1931	1951	500	40,000
Lincoln touring car	1930	1939	32	45,000
Packard Eight sedan	1930	1936	225	20,000
Packard Caribbean convertible	1954	1956	250	8,000
Chrysler 70 roadster	1925	1930	125	8,500
Chrysler 70 coupe	1930	1935	65	7,000

Classic Cars Owned by Richard H. Rush—Year by Year

Make and Model	Year Car	Year Pur- chased	Price Paid	Value in 1981
Studebaker special six touring car	1921	1928	15	10,000
Studebaker special six touring car	1923	1929	25	15,000
Studebaker big six touring car	1926	1929	25	15,000
Buick six touring	1923	1930	35	12,500
Buick special six convertible	1940	1951	550	11,000
Buick super convertible	1947	1955	750	7,000
Buick special convertible	1955	1956	1,900	4,000
Ford Model T touring car	1927	1929	35	5,000
Ford Model A convertible coupe	1931	1934	35	12,000
Ford Model A coupe	1928	1932	65	8,000
Ford V-8 two door	1934	1943	50	7,000
Ford Mustang convertible	1966	1978	1,600	5,000
Stearns-Knight coach	1924	1931	120	8,000
Essex four coach	1921	1931	35	3,500
Willys Jeepster	1947	1949	650	3,000
Cadillac V-8 touring car	1918	1929	25	18,000
Cadillac 75 sedan	1938	1955	195	12,000
Cadillac 60 special sedan	1941	1944	2,400	15,000
Cadillac convertible	1947	1948	2,700	15,000
Cadillac convertible	1947	1949	1,900	15,000
Cadillac convertible	1947	1950	1,900	15,000
Cadillac convertible	1947	1951	1,800	15,000

Classic Cars Owned by Richard H. Rush—Year by Year

Make and Model	Year Car	Year Pur- chased	Price Paid	Value in 1981
Cadillac convertible	1954	1956	1,995	7,500
TOTAL			$129,022	$1,456,500
With late cars (Miura, Ghibli, Rolls-Royce Cloud) out			$80,632	$1,388,500

Of the eighty-eight automobiles I have owned in my lifetime, fifty-four can be considered classic cars. This inclusion of fifty-four cars is stretching the classic car definition. I have included my 1921 Essex coach—hardly a classic when I bought it for everyday transportation for $35 in 1931. It isn't a better car today, although it is considered at least "a special interest car" and has appreciated. Some of my eighty-eight cars have not been included at all, such as my Ford Anglia two-door and my Vauxhall Wyvern two-door. These cars are hardly classics or even special interest cars, at least in my judgment.

In these cars I originally put $129,022. In 1981 the value of all fifty-four would have been, conservatively, $1,456,500.

Three of these cars I bought recently, and they have not been held long enough to realize much appreciation: the Lamborghini Miura, bought in 1980 for $20,500, the Maserati Ghibli, bought in the same year for $10,900, and the Rolls-Royce Silver Cloud II sedan bought in 1977 for $7,000. For the rest of the cars, restoration costs were very small. For these latter cars, restoration was much more substantial, and we would really have to add this restoration in to determine the actual appreciation of the cars over the years. The Rolls-Royce required by far the most restoration.

With these three cars omitted from the table, the investment actually made was $80,632 and the present value would be $1,388,500. The average holding period for the cars would have worked out to thirty-three years. In these thirty-three years since the average cars were bought, they rose 17 times in value. This works out to be a fair appreciation as far as growth goes. It is, however, fairly unrealistic. I don't know any investor who would buy an Essex 1921 two-door coach and hold it from 1931 to 1981, even though he paid only $35 for it. One would have had literally to wait decades for any appreciation in his investment at all—and insure, store, and maintain this automobile all those years.

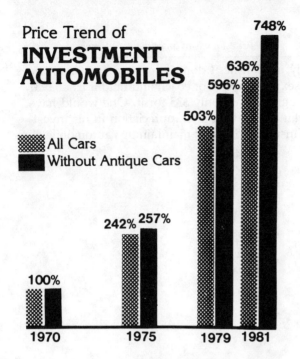

Price Trend of
INVESTMENT AUTOMOBILES

All Cars
Without Antique Cars

748%
636%
596%
503%
257%
242%
100%

1970   1975   1979 1981

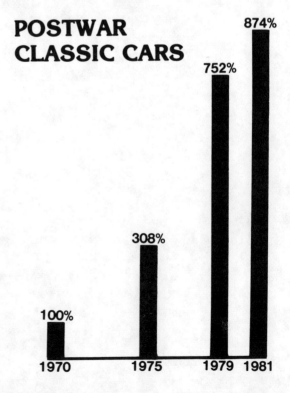

POSTWAR CLASSIC CARS

874%
752%
308%
100%

1970   1975   1979 1981

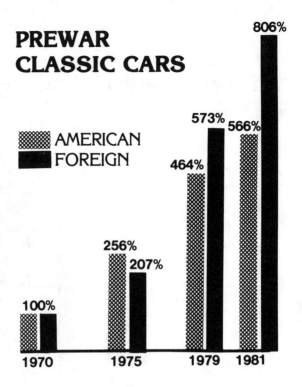

PREWAR CLASSIC CARS

AMERICAN
FOREIGN

806%

573% 566%

464%

256%
207%

100%

1970 1975 1979 1981

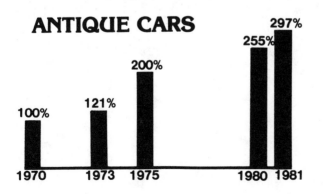

ANTIQUE CARS

297%
255%

200%

121%

100%

1970 1973 1975 1980 1981

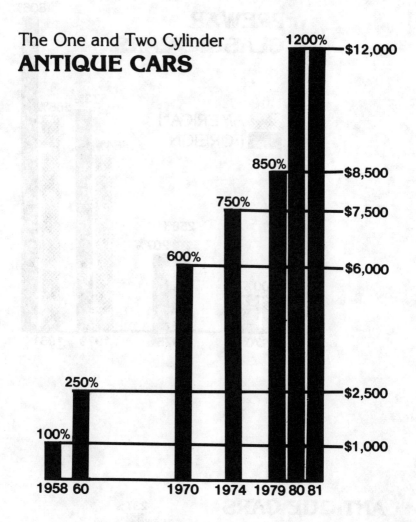

The One and Two Cylinder
ANTIQUE CARS

1200% — $12,000

850% — $8,500

750% — $7,500

600% — $6,000

250% — $2,500

100% — $1,000

1958 60   1970   1974 1979 80 81

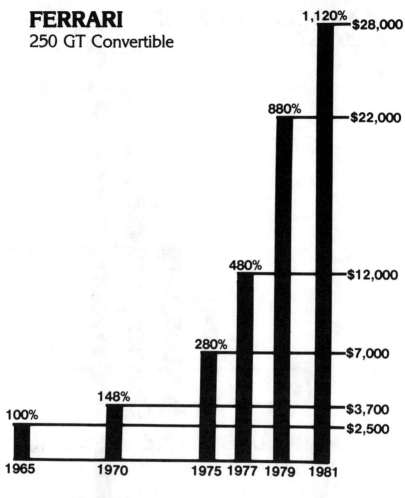

FERRARI
250 GT Convertible

1,120% $28,000
880% $22,000
480% $12,000
280% $7,000
148% $3,700
$2,500
100%

1965　1970　1975 1977 1979　1981

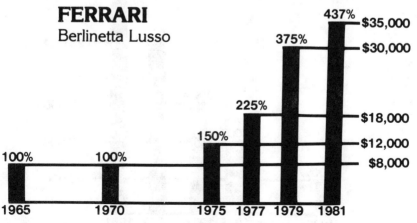

FERRARI
Berlinetta Lusso

437% $35,000
375% $30,000
225% $18,000
150% $12,000
$8,000
100%　100%

1965　1970　1975 1977 1979　1981

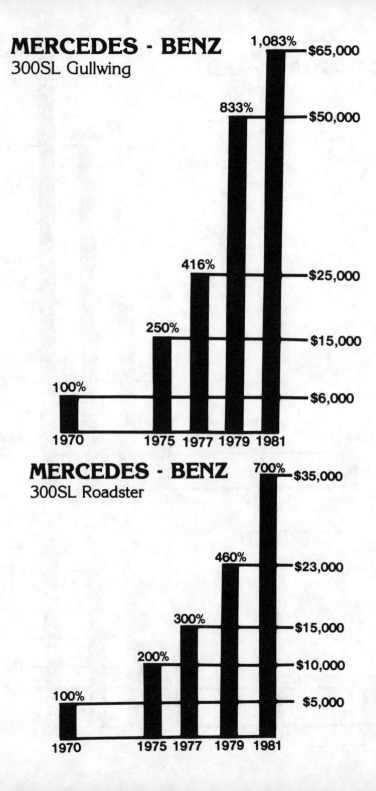

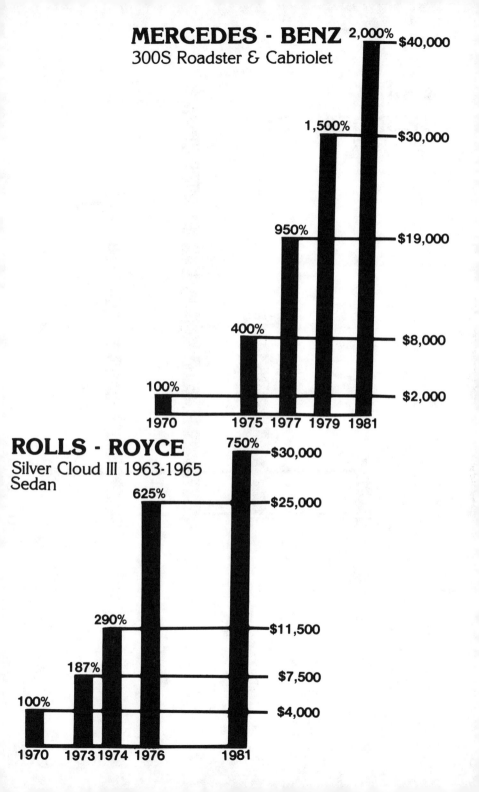

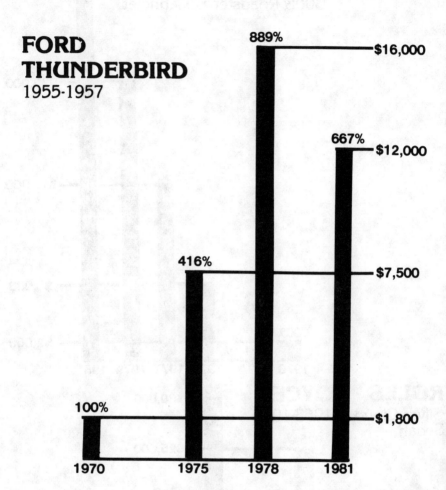

FORD THUNDERBIRD
1955-1957

CHEVROLET CORVETTE
1955-1962

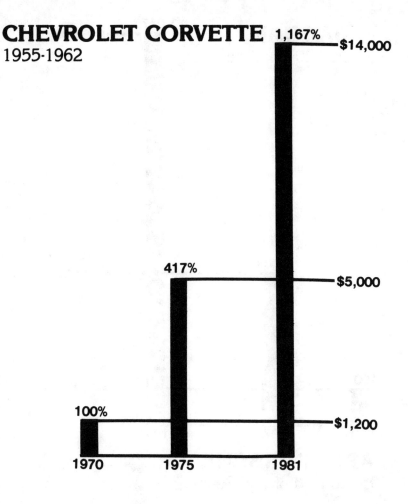

1,167% — $14,000

417% — $5,000

100% — $1,200

1970   1975   1981

MERCER RACEABOUT
Early Teens Series

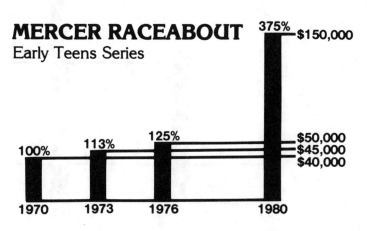

375% — $150,000

100%   113%   125% — $50,000
— $45,000
— $40,000

1970   1973   1976   1980

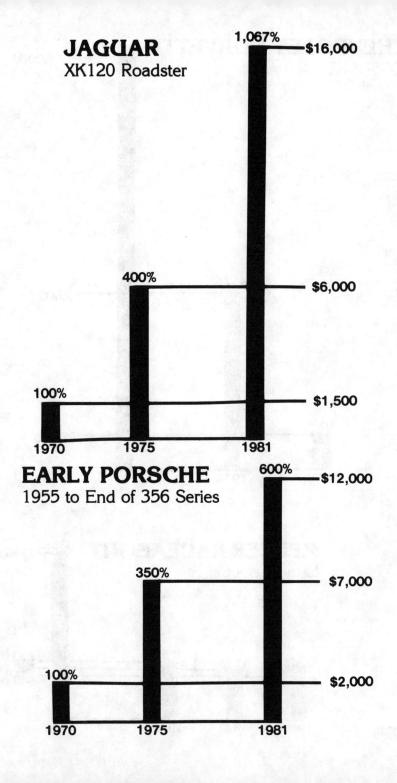

JAGUAR
XK120 Roadster

1,067% — $16,000

400% — $6,000

100% — $1,500

1970   1975   1981

EARLY PORSCHE
1955 to End of 356 Series

600% — $12,000

350% — $7,000

100% — $2,000

1970   1975   1981

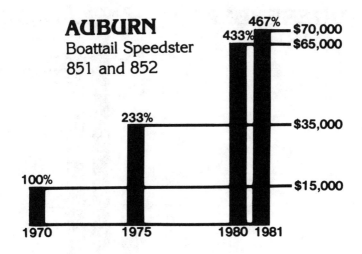

AUBURN
Boattail Speedster
851 and 852

- 100% — 1970
- 233% — 1975
- 433% — 1980
- 467% — 1981

$70,000
$65,000
$35,000
$15,000

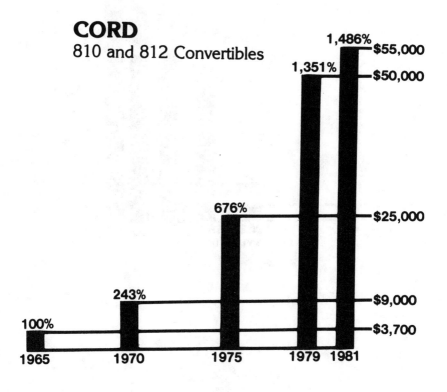

CORD
810 and 812 Convertibles

- 100% — 1965
- 243% — 1970
- 676% — 1975
- 1,351% — 1979
- 1,486% — 1981

$55,000
$50,000
$25,000
$9,000
$3,700

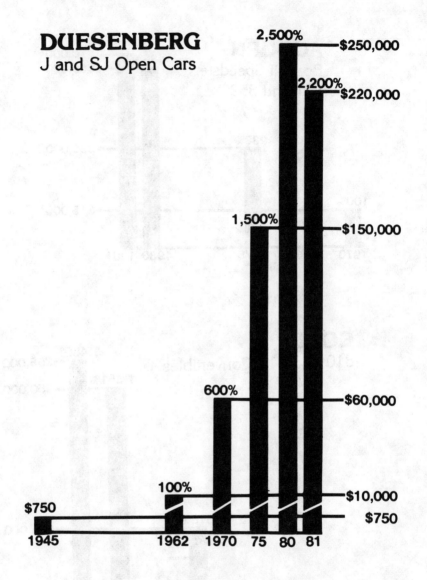

DUESENBERG
J and SJ Open Cars

2,500% — $250,000
2,200% — $220,000
1,500% — $150,000
600% — $60,000
100% — $10,000
$750 — $750

1945   1962   1970   75   80   81

CADILLAC V-16
Early Open Cars 1930-1931

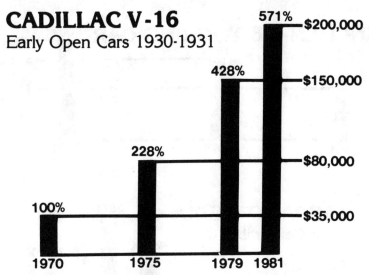

571% — $200,000
428% — $150,000
228% — $80,000
100% — $35,000
1970 1975 1979 1981

CHRYSLER EIGHT
Late Model Prewar Imperial Tourers

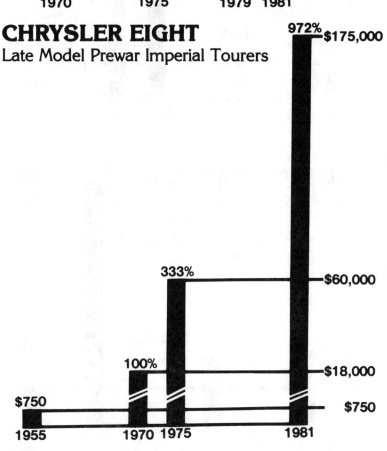

972% $175,000
333% — $60,000
100% — $18,000
$750 — $750
1955 1970 1975 1981

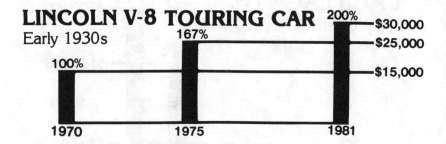

LINCOLN V-8 TOURING CAR
Early 1930s

200% — $30,000
167% — $25,000
— $15,000
100%

1970   1975   1981

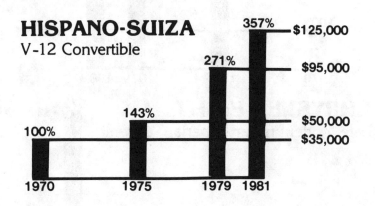

HISPANO-SUIZA
V-12 Convertible

357% — $125,000
271% — $95,000
143% — $50,000
100% — $35,000

1970   1975   1979   1981

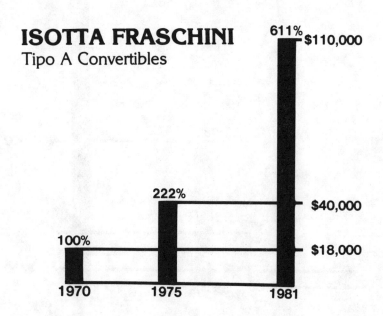

ISOTTA FRASCHINI
Tipo A Convertibles

611% — $110,000
222% — $40,000
100% — $18,000

1970   1975   1981

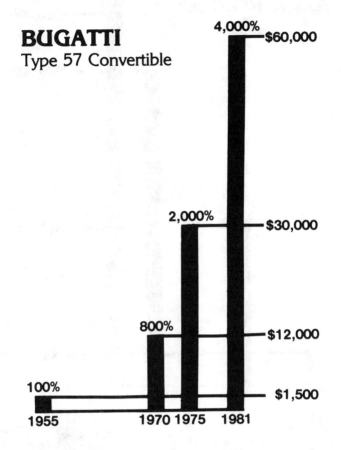

BUGATTI
Type 57 Convertible

4,000% — $60,000

2,000% — $30,000

800% — $12,000

100% — $1,500

1955   1970 1975   1981

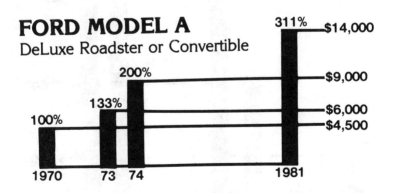

FORD MODEL A
DeLuxe Roadster or Convertible

311% — $14,000

200% — $9,000

133% — $6,000
— $4,500

100%

1970   73   74   1981

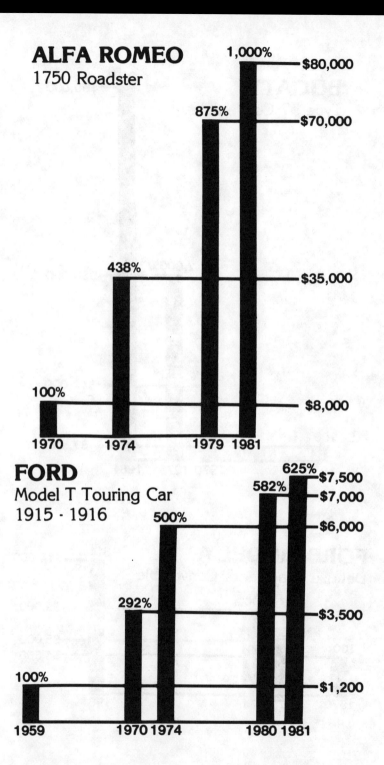

CHAPTER **13**

The Outlook—Investing for the Future

FUTURE TRENDS ARE difficult to forecast. It is even more difficult to say, "Invest in a Duesenberg. It is bound to go up—maybe 100 percent in five years!"

It is difficult to forecast in any area of collectibles—or *any* area at all, even the stock market! In our book *Art as an Investment* (Prentice-Hall, Englewood Cliffs, N.J., 1961, page 1), we said:

The stage was well set for the sale at the Parke-Bernet Galleries in New York, of the Georges Lurcy collection on November 7 of the same year, 1957.

Then the bidding started. After the first few minutes the whole atmosphere became electrified. It was obvious that history was being made. New high prices were not simply being established, but a boom in art works throughout the world was being signaled.

Prices rose to heights that at the time became more and more difficult to grasp the higher they rose. One had a feeling, "This is it! This is the high point. Nothing can ever go higher in the Impressionist category. This is the time people have finally taken leave of their senses *en masse.*"

A Renoir sold for $200,000, a staggering sum. It was bought by the Henry Ford IIs who were there in person to do their bidding.

[261]

This same painting sold in the Henry Ford II sale, held by Christie's in New York in 1980, for $1,200,000—$1,000,000 more than it cost the Fords in 1957!

In the famous Goldschmidt sale of seven paintings, Impressionists and Post Impressionists, in October 1958, a van Gogh brought what I considered to be the staggering sum of $369,600. In Christie's Henry Ford II sale of 1980, this same van Gogh brought $5,200,000.

Where are we in the price curve of investment automobiles? Are we at the high point in 1982 (and there is weakness in 1982)? Have Duesenbergs topped out at about a quarter of a million dollars—topped out for good? Or will the $200,000 Duesenberg perform like the $200,000 Renoir that Henry Ford II resold thirteen years later for $1,200,000? We don't know. All we can do is to make a somewhat informed guess about the future price trend of investment cars. It is even safer to point out certain cars that appear to be candidates for a price rise in the future—maybe!

In *Art as an Investment* we went so far as to make up lists of paintings by various artists in the major schools of art, together with their then (1961) prices. If anyone reading the book in 1961 took these lists seriously, he might have invested in these paintings at somewhere near our "target prices."

When I look back at these target prices, they look so low as to be ridiculous. It is difficult to believe that a good Monet could ever be bought for $30,000, or a good Picasso for $30,000 or a fine Homer for $20,000 or a Kandinsky for $3,000 or an Inness landscape for $1,500.

Is a 500K Mercedes-Benz roadster at $400,000 a fluke? Can such a figure ever again be approximated? On the other hand, maybe this was a "price breakthrough," and we will see many six-figure prices for such cars in the future, if and when they come onto the market. A price of $1,000,000 seeems hard to visualize for a 500K in the future—at any time in the future.

Maybe we need historical perspective. Maybe we should learn some lesson from the price trend of paintings, or from the price trend of Tiffany lamps that rose to the seemingly impossible height of $350,000—the auction price of one such lamp sold by Christie's in 1980.

Certain investment automobiles seem like good selections for a future rise in price. It is difficult, however, to select candidates for a price rise solely on the basis of which cars look as though they may go up in value in the future. It is very hard to divorce investment value from one's own opinion of a car as a fine object to own. In the February 1981 Los Angeles automobile sale, lot seven was a 1923 Nash touring car. It was far from mint condition. The catalog stated, "Paint and tires are fair." The car had large disc wheels and very small hubcaps, and the body was not smooth. The lines of the car were far from beautiful. I didn't much care for this model car when it was new and perfect, and I like this particular car far less, especially in its poor condition. It was estimated to bring $12,000–$14,000. It didn't sell. I would far rather have the 1923 Buick six touring car that I once owned than this Nash; and for the estimated price of $12,000–$14,000, I would far rather have a Maserati Ghibli in excellent condition.

Obviously I don't like the Nash, and I admit that my opinion is to an extent subjective. It is very hard for anyone interested in antique and classic cars to consider strict investment and ignore how he personally feels about a car—whether he likes the car or not.

In any event these are some selections which I would make today, automobiles as investments and as candidates for a price rise in the future:

A Selection of Prime Postwar Classic Cars

Mercedes-Benz 300SL gullwing	$60,000
Mercedes-Benz 300S cabriolet or convertible	50,000
Ferrari 275GTB-4 coupe	60,000
Ferrari Daytona coupe	50,000
Lamborghini Miura P-400	30,000
Shelby Cobra 427	60,000
Maserati Ghibli Spyder	35,000
Rolls-Royce Silver Cloud III convertible	75,000
Bentley Continental Flying Spur—SIII	35,000
	$455,000

One could hardly get a finer collection of postwar classic cars than the above list. The price estimates may be a little on the low side, particularly as the year 1982 wears on.

All cars should be in excellent condition but not necessarily mint. The Ferrari Daytona was put out as early as 1969, and the earlier the Daytona the less its value, so the $50,000 target price is only an approximation. We did not include the tremendously popular Daytona Spyder because its price is at least $125,000, a very high figure.

The Ferrari 275GTB-4 coupe is a top connoisseur's car and a great performance car. Still, the two-cam 275GTB is an excellent comparable car and much less expensive—perhaps $30,000. There is also the desirable 275GT convertible that may be purchased for about $35,000. The 250GT convertible is a splendid car, for about $28,000–$30,000. The coupe might be purchased for $17,000–$18,000, perhaps less.

The Lamborghini Miura is a true "great," and in 1979 it rose tremendously in value. The early cars—1967–1969—might be purchased for $30,000, but the later cars cost much more. A late model 1972 SV with separate crank case and transmission might cost as much as $60,000.

While the Cobra 427 is no doubt more in demand, and at a higher price, than the 289, the latter is still a tremendously impressive and wanted car, for at least $10,000 less than the 427.

The Maserati Ghibli Spyder is a rather rare and superb-looking convertible, possibly the finest looking sports convertible ever designed. The price of $35,000 should secure the latest model car in top condition.

The Rolls-Royce and Bentleys are the finest examples of the Cloud III and SIII series that ended in 1965. The cars are fine, impressive, and classic—as well as hard to find.

We have made our own personal selection of the cars on each list, with what we consider the best at the top. The Ford Mustang is hardly in the class of a Maserati Ghibli or a Bentley in quality; it is, however, a car in tremendous demand and at prices that in 1981 and 1982 seem to be increasing every month. One such Mustang sold at auction for $21,500, and others sold for from $7,000 to $9,000. On the other hand, many good Mus-

A Selection of Lower Price Postwar Classic Cars

Ford Mustang convertible—1965–1966	$5,000
Chevrolet Corvette roadster—1956–1957	12,000
Jaguar XK120 roadster	17,000
Maserati Ghibli coupe	15,000
Jaguar XKE (six) convertible	6,000
MG T.D.	9,000
Bentley sedan—SI or SIII	12,000
Chevrolet Corvair Spyder—1964	4,500
	$80,500

tangs are offered for sale. For $5,000 one should be able to buy one in good condition. The 289 V-8 is preferred, but the six has a superb engine and seems to run without trouble literally forever. In any event, this is my transportation car that I use to go anywhere and everywhere—short distance and long distance.

The 1956–1957 Corvette is only a suggestion. Recently we saw a superb 1962 roadster with a restoration from the ground up—for $15,500. I would have picked this car without bothering to look at any other models had I been in the market for a Corvette.

The Jaguar XK120 roadster is the most popular car of all of the XK series (XK140 and XK150). It is the most classic and the most sought after, and still not too expensive on any basis.

The Maserati Ghibli coupe is almost certainly the most beautiful sports coupe ever built. It was designed by the incomparable Giorgetto Giugiaro, and it is his masterpiece. It is a car of splendid mechanical design but temperamental. For a little more than $15,000 you might get the slightly larger-engined 1972 car, an improved version. For a little less you might get a very good 1967–1969 car. If and when this car takes off in the market, it should *really* take off pricewise.

The Jaguar XKE (six cylinder) is a very good and very reliable car, and inexpensive compared with the V-12, a complicated and temperamental car that costs more than twice as much as the six but has the same body. The XKE (six) seems to be underpriced and is a good sports car by anyone's standards.

The MG T.D. is very much in demand. It is an early postwar

classic but with the bugs of the MG T.C. worked out. It is a simple, classic automobile that will probably always be in demand.

The Bentley is essentially the same car as the Rolls-Royce, but very much less expensive. The SI is the six and the SIII, the eight, is the last of the S series that ended in 1965. The car should be a left-hand-drive model in very good condition. The target should be $12,000, but the target is getting a little hard to hit.

The 1964 Chevrolet Corvair Spyder is a very inexpensive semi-sports car, a quality machine that seems to be increasing in demand. There is a large number of strict Corvair collectors. The price is still low, and there are all kinds of Corvairs to fit almost everyone's taste, including those who are used to the great sports cars, but some of the rare Corvairs run into five figures.

One might possibly add the last of the great convertibles: the Cadillac Eldorado series that ended in 1976. If these cars appear on the market with no miles on them (and they do appear this way from time to time) they may be bought for somewhere in the region of $20,000, possibly more. The used 1976 car, in average condition, may be bought for as little as $7,500–$8,000.

The 1975 and 1976 models use unleaded gas. The earlier models use regular gas. One of the earlier models—1971–1974 —might be bought, in good condition, for $5,000. These cars have probably hit a low point in value. They are big, impressive cars, beautifully designed from the point of view of a big, luxury convertible. The cars in mint condition should go up in value in the future, but not so for the average or poor condition cars, at least for many years.

In early 1979 a Mercedes-Benz SS roadster sold in California at auction for $320,000. The same model car has been offered since that time for far less money. It is possible that one can be secured for around $150,000. If one prefers, he might get the touring car for about the same price. He could get a Mercedes-Benz S for a little less than the SS, but not very much less.

Of course the person interested in the SS and S would probably be vastly more interested in the SSK, and these cars do

A Selection of Prime Prewar Classic Cars

Mercedes-Benz SS roadster	$150,000
Mercedes-Benz 540K convertible	125,000
Duesenberg SJ tourer	200,000
Packard 734 roadster	125,000
Cadillac V-16 roadster, 1931	225,000
Alfa Romeo 2.9 supercharged roadster	100,000
Hispano-Suiza (1934) V-12 convertible	100,000
Bugatti type 57 convertible	55,000
Horch V-12 convertible	30,000
Auburn 851 (852) boattail speedster	70,000
Rolls-Royce Phantom I Ascot phaeton	75,000
	$1,255,000

come up for sale from time to time. The price would, however, hardly be under $500,000.

The next choice might be the Mercedes-Benz 540K convertible of the mid-thirties. One could not buy the roadster for $125,000, and the last figure for a roadster in mint condition ($400,000) might easily be the price today. One could also get the 500K (and the Christie's car for $400,000 was a 500K rather than a 540K, although there is little difference between the two cars or their values). A 500K or 540K with a less desirable body than the type on the beautiful Christie's car, but still a roadster or two-seater convertible, could possibly be purchased for $125,000. The 380K is a car of about the same size as the 500K and 540K but with a slightly smaller engine. It came equipped with the same desirable bodies (made in Sindelfingen) and the 380K sells for slightly less. The 380K is a fairly hard car to find.

The Duesenberg may have risen too fast and too far, and prices had to be consolidated before rising again. In any event, Duesenberg seems to be *the* car for the ultimate car collector here in America. It is also getting a reputation for being the greatest car ever made in America—if it didn't already have that reputation before the investment car boom started. The SJ speedster is the most desirable car of all, but these cars hardly ever appear on the market. The SJ is the most desirable car, followed by the J (close behind), and the roadsters and tourers are the most wanted body styles.

The Packard 734 roadster with boattail is a splendid car and a rarity. It is a strict connoisseurs' car, and it does not seem to be priced on today's market as high as it might be. It is certainly a show car when in mint condition. Right behind the roadster, and at about the same price, is the 734 tourer.

The Cadillac V-16 of 1930 and 1931 is one of the most desirable of all classic cars from any country, if a roadster and in mint condition. It is a great-looking car by any standards, and it was a well developed piece of machinery, not simply a fancied-up, mass-produced automobile.

The Alfa Romeo 2.9 twin supercharged roadster always has been one of my favorite cars ever since I saw my first one in 1938. There is one roadster body that surpasses all other bodies—that of the former Huguely Alfa. The rest of the bodies, while good, are less attractive.

For a dignified but beautiful car, you might well seek out a mid-thirties Hispano-Suiza convertible coupe—if you can find one. Mechanically the Hispano-Suiza is at least the equivalent of any prewar classic car made in the world. *Possibly* such a car could be located for $100,000 or a little more.

One of the prewar greats is the Bugatti type 57 convertible coupe, a fine pioneering piece of machinery and a well designed car. These cars are still inexpensive for what they are, and $55,000 *might* purchase one of them.

The Horch V-12 convertible is a big, impressive car and well designed. It is not in as great demand as many other classics and is not as well known in the market. Once in a while one comes up, and judging from past auction prices $30,000 might purchase one in very good condition.

The Auburn boattail speedster of 1935–1936 (the 851 and 852) is about as striking today as when it first came out. It is the most copied car in the world, and over a dozen replica car companies turn out "modern" boattail speedsters.

The car is not up to the other cars on this list mechanically, but in appearance it is, and in demand it certainly is.

The Rolls-Royce Ascot touring car (phaeton), the PI, is one of the all-time classic cars. If you want an idea of the appearance of this car in action, you might look at a rerun of the movie of *The Great Gatsby* by F. Scott Fitzgerald. We have put down a target price of $75,000. On the other hand, the buyer might have to go as high as $125,000.

A Selection of Lower-Priced Prewar Classic Cars

Ford Model A convertible	1931	$14,000
Ford V-8 convertible	1932	17,500
Buick Super convertible	1940	12,000
Lincoln Continental convertible	1940	20,000
Lagonda six-cylinder convertible	1939	20,000
		$83,5000

Probably the most popular prewar classic car in the United States is the Model A Ford put out from 1928 to 1931. There is always a market for Model A Fords, especially the convertible coupes. However, the earlier models do not bring quite the prices of the later cars, which are a good deal more elegant. For $14,000 you should be able to get a Model A restored from the ground-up, and certainly a mint car of the vintages prior to 1931.

Of all of the V-8s, perhaps the early ones of 1932 are the most desirable. The later the car, the more nondescript it became. Still the later V-8s are in demand too and at high prices.

The 1940 Buick Super is an excellent-running car, and the convertible is a very good looking car. It is not the 1940 Cadillac convertible, but the price of the Buick is very much less than the Cadillac. If you cannot get a 1940 then look at a 1941, which has more or less the same appearance, has about the same mechanical design, and runs equally well. One collector was fortunate enough to buy a 1941 Buick Special convertible in very good condition for $3,500. He bought it privately, as might be expected.

The prewar Lincoln Continental was a standout with its low, long look and its horizontal planes. It is reasonably good mechanically, although not great. It is most certainly a collectors' car and should not decline in value in the future. The early postwar Continental is more or less the same car, and it sells for about the same price.

One of the most desirable of all prewar convertibles is the Lagonda V-12 Rapide. This car, is, however, very costly on the present market. The six can be bought for around $20,000, whereas the V-12, with essentially the same fine lines, would cost about $35,000. The six is not inferior mechanically to the V-12.

A Selection of Antique Cars

Mercer Raceabout, 1913	$150,000
Stutz Bearcat, 1914	150,000
Rolls-Royce Silver Ghost touring car, 1915	75,000
Packard twin-six touring car, 1915	40,000
Curved Dash Olds, 1903	10,000
Ford Model T, 1909	15,000
	$440,000

The Mercer Raceabout is a tradition in the United States, and it was in the high four-figure level even as early as the World War II period. Still, for this car, with its design in advance of its time and its glamour, $150,000 does not seem to be an excessive price. Its only drawback is the fact that it is a stark machine, and you don't quite see what you get for your money. If you collect antique cars, at least in America, the Mercer Raceabout is almost a must, provided you have the money to acquire one.

The Stutz Bearcat of the same period is about the same as the Mercer Raceabout, a stark four-cylinder machine and a great tradition. This would be the number two (or possibly number one) selection of an antique car collector with plenty of investment funds. These two cars were not put out only in the years 1913 and 1914; we are simply citing the general period of the car, not the later Stutz cars or Mercer cars which are far less desirable as antiques.

The early Rolls-Royce Silver Ghost—like the 1915 model—is a fine-looking, but somewhat stark, automobile and a little hard to shift. The same model was put out for several years, and we are talking about the cars with less refined bodies than those put out in the 1920s.

The Packard twin six touring car of the year 1915 is a good deal more attractive in many ways than the later twin sixes. For what you get—a refined, big car—the price seems reasonable in the present market.

In the category of Oldies (one- and two-cylinder cars) the 1903 Curved Dash Olds typifies all of the cars and is the best known and possibly the most revered car. Ten years ago a good Curved Dash Olds could have been bought for $3,000. In 1981 the price was about $10,000—still not a high price for this unique automobile. It must be remembered, however, that the old one- and two-cylinder cars are not in tremendous demand by investor-collectors in today's market.

The last selection is the old Model T Ford. The earlier the car the higher the price, but the earlier the car the fewer were produced. The 1909 is about the earliest one you can get for any reasonable sum of money. One day, the Model T may be traded on the market like American coins: standard investments at more or less standard prices, considering condition of individual cars.

Index

[273]